Reading the Book of Revelation

Society of Biblical Literature

Resources for Biblical Study

W. Ross Wagner, Editor

Number 44

READING THE BOOK OF REVELATION
A Resource for Students

Volume Editor
David L. Barr

Reading the Book of Revelation

A RESOURCE FOR STUDENTS

David L. Barr, editor

Society of Biblical Literature
Atlanta

READING THE BOOK OF REVELATION
A Resource for Students

Copyright © 2003 by the Society of Biblical Literature.

All rights reserved.

Library of Congress Cataloging-in-Publication Data

Reading the book of Revelation : a resource for students / edited by David L. Barr.

    p.   cm. — (Resources for biblical study ; no. 44)
    Includes bibliographical references and index.
    ISBN 1-58983-056-3 (pbk. : alk. paper)
    1. Bible. N.T. Revelation—Criticism, interpretation, etc. 2. Bible. N.T. Revelation—Textbooks. I. Barr, David L., 1942– II. Series.
BS2825.52.R43 2003
228'.06—dc21   2003004535

03 04 05 06 07 08 09 10   5 4 3 2 1

The book is printed in the United States of America
on acid-free paper.

Contents

List of Abbreviations   *vii*

Introduction
Reading Revelation Today: Consensus and Innovations
David L. Barr   1

1. The Story John Told:
Reading Revelation for Its Plot
David L. Barr   11

2. Ordinary Lives:
John and His First Readers
Leonard L. Thompson   25

3. The Beast from the Land:
Revelation 13:11–18 and Social Setting
Steven J. Friesen   49

4. Wolves in Sheep's Clothing:
Literary Opposition and Social Tension in the Revelation of John
Paul B. Duff   65

5. A Tale of Two Cities and (At Least) Three Women:
Transformation, Continuity, and Contrast in the Apocalypse
Edith M. Humphrey   81

6. Doing Violence:
Moral Issues in Reading John's Apocalypse
David L. Barr   97

7. Undercurrents and Paradoxes:
The Apocalypse to John in Process Hermeneutic
Ronald L. Farmer   *109*

8. Taking a Stand on the Sand of the Seashore:
A Postcolonial Exploration of Revelation 13
Jean-Pierre Ruiz   *119*

9. Spirit Possession:
Revelation in Religious Studies
Leonard L. Thompson   *137*

10. The Lion/Lamb King:
Reading the Apocalypse from Popular Culture
Jon Paulien   *151*

Conclusion
Choosing between Readings: Questions and Criteria
David L. Barr   *163*

Bibliography   *173*
Contributors   *181*
Index of Ancient Sources   *183*
Index of Modern Authors   *191*
Subject Index   *195*

Abbreviations

Bibliographical (see the bibliography for further details)

ACNT	Augsburg Commentaries on the New Testament
ANF	*Ante-Nicene Fathers*
AUSS	*Andrews University Seminary Studies*
BDAG	Bauer, W., F. W. Danker, W. F. Arndt, and F. W. Gingrich. *Greek-English Lexicon of the New Testament and Other Early Christian Literature.* 3d ed. Chicago, 1999
BR	*Biblical Research*
CBQ	*Catholic Biblical Quarterly*
CC	Continental Commentaries
CNT	Commentaire du Nouveau Testament
GRBS	*Greek, Roman, and Byzantine Studies*
HNT	Handbuch zum Neuen Testament
HTR	*Harvard Theological Review*
HTS	Harvard Theological Studies
IBC	Interpretation: A Bible Commentary for Teaching and Preaching
ICC	International Critical Commentary
IGR	*Inscriptiones graecae.* Editio minor. Berlin, 1924–
Int	*Interpretation*
IvE	*Die Inschriften von Ephesos*
JBL	*Journal of Biblical Literature*
JSNTSup	Journal for the Study of the New Testament: Supplement Series
KEK	Kritisch-exegetischer Kommentar über das Neue Testament (Meyer-Kommentar)
NCB	New Century Bible
NHL	*Nag Hammadi Library in English.* Edited by J. M. Robinson. 4th rev. ed. Leiden, 1996

NICNT	New International Commentary on the New Testament
NTS	*New Testament Studies*
OTP	*Old Testament Pseudepigrapha.* Edited by J. H. Charlesworth. 2 vols. New York, 1983
PGM	*Papyri graecae magicae: Die griechischen Zauberpapyri.* Edited by K. Preisendanz. Berlin, 1928
QR	*Quarterly Review*
RB	*Revue biblique*
SBLDS	Society of Biblical Literature Dissertation Series
SIG	*Sylloge inscriptionum graecarum.* Edited by W. Dittenberger. 4 vols. 3d ed. Leipzig, 1915–1924
TJ	*Trinity Journal*
WBC	Word Biblical Commentary

For a comprehensive listing of abbreviations to journals, reference works, and series, see Patrick H. Alexander, *The SBL Handbook of Style for Ancient Near Eastern, Biblical, and Early Christian Studies* (Peabody, Mass.: Hendrickson, 1999), 89–152.

Ancient Writings

The following abbreviations are used in the notes. See also the index to ancient authors.

1QS	*Rule of the Community,* Dead Sea Scrolls
4Q403	*Song of the Sabbath Sacrifice,* Dead Sea Scrolls
2 Bar.	2 Baruch
Adv. Haer.	*Against Heresies*
Agr.	*Agricola*
Ann.	*Annals*
Ant.	*Antiquities of the Jews*
Apoc. Ab.	*Apocalypse of Abraham*
Apol.	*Apology*
Ascen. Isa	*Ascension of Isaiah*
Barn.	*Barnabas*
Contempl	*On the Contemplative Life*
Dial.	*Dialogue with Trypho*
Did	*Didache*
Ep.	*Epistle*
Gos. Pet.	*Gospel of Peter*
Hist.	*History*
Hist. Eccl	*Ecclesiastical History*
Ign *Phld.*	Ignatius *Philadelphians*
Ign *Rom.*	Ignatius *Romans*

Ign. *Magn.*	Ignatius *Magnesians*
Jub.	*Jubilees*
Mand	*Mandate*
Mor.	*Moralia*
Nat.	*Natural History*
Peregr	*Peregrinus*
Praescr	*Prescription against Heretics*
Pyth. Orac.	*De Pythiae Oraculis*
Quis div.	Salvation of the Rich
Sib. Or.	*Sibylline Oracles*
Sim.	*Similitude*
Tob.	Tobit

General

B.C.E.	Before the Common Era (same dates as BC)
C.E.	Common Era (same dates as AD)
c.	about, approximately
cf.	compare
d.	died
e.g.	for example
f.	following verse
ff.	following verses (to end of paragraph)
fl.	flourished

Introduction
READING REVELATION TODAY:
CONSENSUS AND INNOVATIONS

David L. Barr

The main purpose of this book is to introduce the reader to some of the variety of methods (or ways of reading) the Book of Revelation today and to show how these methods elicit a variety of meaningful interpretations. Our goal is always to probe the various ways Revelation can be understood, while being self-conscious about the tools we use. Still, we are not interested in the tools so much as in the results they produce. Among the approaches gathered are historical, literary, social, philosophical, ethical, political, and cultural ways of reading. Before I explore these approaches, however, it will be useful to review briefly the history of the reading of Revelation. It is a work with a complex and conflicted history.[1]

The Book of Revelation was written late in the first century (95 is the commonly accepted date, though a few argue for a date as early as 65), but the earliest comment on its interpretation comes from the next generation. Even then Revelation generated controversy; here is how Eusebius described the views of a second-century interpreter named Papias (fl. c. 125):

> He says that after the resurrection of the dead there will be a period of a thousand years, when Christ's kingdom will be set up on this earth in material form. I suppose he got these notions by misinterpreting the apostolic accounts and failing to grasp what they had said in mystic and symbolic language. For he seems to have been a man of very small intelligence, to judge from his books.[2]

This contrast between a "material" interpretation (imagining that the events

---

[1] For a good summary of the history of the interpretation see Arthur Wainwright, *Mysterious Apocalypse: Interpreting the Book of Revelation* (Nashville: Abingdon Press, 1993).

[2] Eusebius *Ecclesiastical History* 3.39.11–13; Eusebius's views will be discussed further in chapter 2, "Ordinary Lives: John and His First Readers."

described in Revelation will happen in the material world) and a "mystic and symbolic" interpretation (imagining that the events described refer to spiritual realities) has marked much of the history of reading the Apocalypse and continues to divide interpreters even today.

The material interpretation was very popular in the second century, when it was often associated with an intense expectation of the end of the world. The second century saw an outbreak of several "prophetic" movements predicting the near-end of the world, and it is hard to say whether Revelation was influencing these movements or whether their views were influencing the interpretation of Revelation. Melito of Sardis (fl. c. 175), for example, wrote a commentary on Revelation and probably also wrote a book of his own prophecy, both of which took a material view.[3] Justin Martyr (fl. c. 150 and lived at Ephesus about 130) wrote that "those who believed in our Christ would spend a thousand years in Jerusalem" (*Dialogue* 81.15). Irenaeus (fl. c. 180) was born in Asia Minor, probably at Smyrna—one of the cities mentioned in Revelation. He frequently quoted from Revelation and clearly understood it in a material way.

Most of these writers seem to have understood Revelation as predicting the events that would occur between the "first coming" of the Christ and the "second coming." But as time stretched on, this interpretation became more difficult to hold. One way out of this bind was to read Revelation as a non-linear story. Thus a third-century writer named Victorinus (fl. c. 280) advanced the view that Revelation should not be read in chronological order but that later scenes recapitulated the same events as earlier scenes, retelling them with new perspectives and new information. Thus Revelation was not a blueprint of the future but an image of the end times.

And there were other voices. Some rejected the Apocalypse altogether; others advanced a symbolic interpretation (the most famous being Origen of Alexandria, fl. 240). In the symbolic reading, Revelation was not predicting the future at all; rather, it was presenting images of the struggle between good and evil in the world. A version of this symbolist view would soon dominate.

One of the reasons that the symbolist reading became so attractive was that the historical situation of Christians changed dramatically in the fourth century. When Constantine converted to Christianity and the Christians began to exercise worldly power, the material interpretation—which saw worldly power as demonic—waned. Some symbolists then worked a complete reversal of meaning, interpreting the new situation in which Christians exercised worldly power as the beginning of the thousand-year reign of Christ promised in Revelation.

By the fifth century the dominant view was symbolic. The most influential thinker of the time, Augustine of Hippo (fl. 410), saw Revelation as

---

[3] See Eusebius *Ecclesiastical History* 4.26.2

a kind of allegory of the Christian life: Satan was bound whenever one turned to God; the New Jerusalem came down from heaven whenever one received God's grace.[4] More pointedly, the City of God already existed on earth in the form of the church. With variations, this view persisted for more than seven hundred years as the dominant interpretation of the Apocalypse.

Augustine, however, maintained a vestige of the material reading: he saw the millennium as an actual period of a thousand years between the first and second coming of Christ. Thus the end should come around the year 1000. When it did not, the established reading of Revelation lost some of its power, and other readings came forward.

Among these other readings, one proved particularly influential. The great Christian mystic Joachim of Flora (fl. c. 1200) adapted Augustine's view in a way that revived millennial expectations. Joachim (pronounced Wa'-a-keem) lived in a time of great social unrest, the time of the Crusades and of conflicts between the pope and the Holy Roman Emperor. He agreed with Augustine that the millennium could be seen as the time of the church's rule and that it lasted for the thousand years after Christ, but he went further in suggesting that it was then coming to an end. He then posited two other epochs, one before and one after the time of the church:

The age of the Father	=	period of the Old Testament
The age of the Son	=	the age of the church (it lasted one thousand years, a millennium after Christ)
The age of the Spirit	=	the new age just beginning

He saw this third age as a time of purity and inwardness: an age of perfect monasticism.

Even more important, he saw Revelation predicting the actual events of history from the time of Jesus to his own day. Thus the various heads of the beast were identified with specific rulers. For example, the fifth head was the emperor Henry IV, who fought the pope over the right to appoint bishops. The sixth head was the Muslim conqueror of Jerusalem, Saladin. The seventh head, yet to appear, would be a false pope. Although Joachim remained loyal to the church, his interpretation opened the door to dissent, and his followers soon developed anti-Roman interpretations: identifying the present pope with the antichrist and papal Rome with the prostitute astride the beast. This view was very useful to the Protestants in their break with Rome in the sixteenth century.

While the details changed with each new generation and each new crisis, this predictive view of Revelation dominated into the nineteenth century. It remains the view of most fundamentalists today, and it is most likely the view you will hear on the radio or television or read in popular

---

[4] See Augustine *City of God*, especially book 20.

books like Hal Lindsey's *The Late Great Planet Earth*.[5] The utter failure of all such predictive views[6] has turned most academic interpreters in other directions. With the birth of historical criticism in the seventeenth century, interpreters began to explore what the book might have meant to its original readers in the first century. Clearly it would have been of no use to them to hear that the world would end some two thousand years after their time. What information would have been of use to them?

Historical criticism is the attempt to see the past in its own terms, to understand that it is different from the present. Applied to literature, it is the attempt to read literature through the eyes of the people of the time in which the text was written. This became the standard way scholars approached all literature and soon dominated the way scholars read the Bible. The Gospels and Paul's letters were read in their first-century context, and there was no reason why Revelation should not be read the same way. The vast majority of nineteenth- and twentieth-century scholarship on Revelation has attempted to reconstruct its historical setting and to read it within that setting.

Thus important preliminary questions include: Who wrote Revelation? When? Where? And why was it written in this form? While individual scholars may disagree on one or another detail, most today are convinced that the Book of Revelation was written in the form of an apocalypse (more in a moment) by an otherwise unknown prophet named John, who traveled through the cities of Asia Minor in the late first century. Although tradition identified this John with John the apostle, the disciple of Jesus, this is unlikely. The way the author refers to the apostles as the foundations of the divine city (21:14) assumes that the time of the apostles is in the past. Nor does the author imply that he belongs to this select group. Rather than having authority based on the office of apostle, our author's authority comes from his prophetic call by the risen Jesus (described in Rev 1), and that authority is challenged by others who claim to be prophets (for example, 2:20). The details of the social and historical context of the Apocalypse are explored in chapters 2, 3, and 4.

Historical criticism has led to another insight about the Apocalypse: namely, that it was one of many such works. There existed in the ancient world a kind of literature that revolved around the revelation given to some prophet. These writings are very different from the Prophetic Books in the Hebrew Scriptures, and modern scholars have coined a name for them, drawn in fact from the opening word of this story: apocalypse (meaning revelation). The standard short definition is:

---

[5] New York: Bantam Books, 1970. For further discussion see chapter 10, "The Lion/Lamb King: Reading the Apocalypse from Popular Culture."

[6] Lindsey, for example, originally predicted the world would end in 1988, forty years after the founding of the state of Israel (*Planet Earth*, 43).

"Apocalypse" is a genre of revelatory literature with a narrative frame-work, in which a revelation is mediated by an otherworldly being to a human recipient, disclosing a transcendent reality which is both tempo-ral, insofar as it envisages eschatological salvation, and spatial insofar as it involves another, supernatural world.[7]

Thus an apocalypse envisions some goal or end toward which the world is moving—which is what is meant by "eschatological salvation" in the definition—and it manifests this vision by looking into the world above. In fact, it is common to list the traits of an apocalypse as follows (the ref-erences in brackets indicate where the traits can be seen in Revelation):

1. The claim that a secret revelation has been given to some seer or prophet. [1:1–2]
2. This revelation is imparted either in a dream, vision, or transporta-tion of the seer to heaven—though often the three means are com-bined. [1:10–11; 4:1–2]
3. The revelation is usually mediated by some figure, such as an angel, who acts as guide and interpreter to the seer. [17:1–2]
4. The revelation is usually not self-explanatory, but consists in a variety of arcane symbols involving animals (often composites of different animals, with multiple heads), mythological figures, and numbers. [13:1–2; 12:1–2; 13:18]
5. The reception of the revelation is often attributed to some figure from the past: Isaiah, Zephaniah, Enoch, Daniel, Ezra, Adam, Peter, Moses. [not found in Revelation]

Not all apocalypses have all these traits, though they all feature a hero who receives a secret revelation in highly symbolic form. These symbols can be simple and widely used, as are the numbers: for example, 7 is al-ways perfection; 12 is always the people of God; 10 is always a complete unit. But even here there are many nuances; 144,000, for example, is built on the base numbers 10 (all) and 12 (God's people) and thus signifies "all God's people." Other symbols are highly charged emotionally and unique to John (such as the mark of the beast in Rev 13). Any standard commentary will help the reader decode these numbers.[8] The point is that the reader of an apocalypse must always remember that these are highly symbolic accounts. Do not take the symbols at face value.

While scholars today do not agree on all the details, they all agree on the necessity of locating the author and audience in a real time and place in order to understand the writing. Nearly all academic work on the Apocalypse today recognizes the need to read it historically, to discover what it may have meant and how it may have functioned in first-century Roman Asia Minor. Most of the authors in this volume assume that this is

[7] John J. Collins, *Semeia* (Chico, Calif.: Scholars Press) 14 (1979): 9. The issue theme is "Apocalypse: The Morphology of a Genre."

[8] One of the best at probing the symbols is J. P. M. Sweet, *Revelation* (Philadel-phia: Westminster Press, 1979; reprint, Trinity Press International, 1990).

the first and vital reference point of their work, even if they are primarily focused on literary studies (Barr), social analysis (Friesen), social conflict theory (Duff), philosophy (Farmer), women's studies (Humphrey), ethics (Barr), history of religions (Thompson), liberation theology (Ruiz), or popular culture (Paulien). All paint their scenarios against the backdrop of Asia Minor, for history is the essential beginning point of all analysis.

Still, American scholarship on the Apocalypse of John has undergone a sea change over the last few years as new approaches, new issues, and new methodologies have been applied.[9] There is far less concern with a purely historical reading and far more concern with literary and social readings. That is, we ask not just *what* happened but *how* the event is portrayed in the Apocalypse and *why* it is portrayed in such a manner. Thus we ask not simply what the city of Ephesus was like, but how it is portrayed in the Apocalypse. How does that portrayal relate to historical reality? Why is the city portrayed this way? We want to know not only the economic data from Smyrna and Laodicea, but why John chose to portray the former as living in poverty and the latter as wealthy. And how does such portrayal relate to the political and social force of this story?

The essays that follow illustrate some of these new approaches, showing in each case how a particular approach shapes the way one interprets the work. The essays attempt neither to summarize the work of others nor to present an overview of methodologies. They are the working papers of working scholars, each doing a particular reading. These scholars have worked together over the past ten years, listening to each others' papers and offering alternatives. Each has been a member of the "Seminar on Reading the Apocalypse: The Intersection of Literary and Social Methods" within the Society of Biblical Literature (SBL).[10] This book attempts to make some of what we have learned from each other available to the public.

We have struggled hard to make this a book, not just a collection of essays. Thus we open with a literary study of the Apocalypse, which should be accompanied by an actual reading of the Apocalypse itself. You will find these essays much more accessible once you become familiar with the actions, characters, symbols, and themes of the story. This first chapter, "The Plot of the Story: Reading Revelation as Literature," examines the organization of the Apocalypse. Plot, as opposed to the idea of an outline or a structure, rests on the reader discovering (or inventing) relationships between incidents: how does one incident lead to the next? This essay reconstructs the plot of the Apocalypse as a series of three individ-

[9] For a convenient summary see Arthur Wainwright, *Mysterious Apocalypse: Interpreting the Book of Revelation* (Nashville: Abingdon Press, 1993), 141–58.

[10] The SBL is the national professional organization of biblical scholars For more information, go to http://www.sbl-site.org.

ual stories within a common frame. The first story shows John encountering a majestic human figure while in the spirit on the island of Patmos. The second story shows John ascending into heaven, where he witnesses a celebration around God's throne. The third story shows a cosmic war, waged on earth, between the forces of good and evil. Each story is independent and built on separate mythological traditions. The stories appear to have something in common because the storyteller has set up a series of echoes (characters and scenes) between them and has placed them in a common set of frames. Meaning emerges both from the individual stories and from their implicit interaction, which the reader must piece together.

After becoming familiar with the story of the Apocalypse, the reader needs to see that story in historical context. Chapter 2, "Ordinary Lives: John and His First Readers," demonstrates how a historian approaches the difficult task of determining where, when, and by whom the Apocalypse was written. The first task is to set the rhetoric of the Apocalypse in the context of what is known of the time, showing the ambiguities that arise when we do not privilege one source over another. In this reconstruction we must pay attention not only to John but also to the voices of others whom John resisted. Arguing that in real life one position is seldom all good or all bad, the author helps us understand the views of both the Roman authorities and the Christian factions that John opposed.

These twin contexts of empire and church are pursued more fully in the next two essays. Chapter 3, "The Beast from the Earth: Revelation 13:11–18 and Social Setting," explores the significance of the fact that all the churches John addressed were located in important cities with close political ties to Rome, three with temples to the emperor. The idea of "emperor worship" is widely misunderstood, and this essay uses archaeological data and current social theory to discuss the meaning of Revelation in a setting in which the dominant culture included the worship of the emperors. We are able to see John's world more clearly when we see it both through his eyes and through the eyes of the dominant culture in which he lived. Of course, not everyone in the churches saw things the same way John did.

Chapter 4, "Wolves in Sheep's Clothing: Literary Opposition and Social Tension in the Revelation of John," explores the church context more fully. This essay examines John's use of irony to vindicate his point of view against that of his opponents, focusing especially on the analogies between Jezebel (a symbolic name for a historical person)[11] and Babylon, the great whore (a symbolic name for the ultimate evil of Rome). In various places throughout his narrative, the author of the Apocalypse juxtaposes his imagery in a rather startling manner. Negative figures at times seem to "parody" positive characters, providing a kind of ironic subtext.

[11] For the source of the symbolism see 1 Kgs 19 and 2 Kgs 9.

We see that John's ironies reinforce the fundamental dualisms within the world that are basic to his story. This literary juxtaposition is interpreted in the light of a social situation that finds John vigorously rejecting other prophetic voices in the community. John's language of irony sounds a warning to the Christians in his community. Evil forces and evil individuals can look surprisingly like their beneficent opposites. One should be vigilant.

Chapter 5, "A Tale of Two Cities and (At Least) Three Women: Transformation, Continuity, and Contrast in the Apocalypse," takes another look at the female characters. Beginning with a narrative reading of the Apocalypse as a work of literature, this chapter explores the roles of the mother queen (the harlot Babylon) and the bride (the new Jerusalem) both in terms of their critical importance within the structure of the book and their intricate interrelationships. These images and other explicit and implicit female imagery (including the mysterious figures of Jezebel and mother earth) are explored, not so much to read for gender as to observe and analyze the function and potency of feminine imagery within the Apocalypse as a whole.

Chapter 6, "Doing Violence: Moral Issues in Reading John's Apocalypse," explores the apparent irony that this story condemns the violence and domination of a coercive state yet seems to endorse a similar tyranny—with Jesus acting with all the oppressive power of the emperor. Does violence ever lead to justice? Further, is justice delayed justice denied? Reading for ethics leads to a story that involves neither coercion nor delay. Still, the violence of the story—and especially the violence against women characters—requires some critique. The essay explores the types of violence portrayed and sets such violence in the historical, social, and intellectual milieu of John's community.

Chapter 7, "Undercurrents and Paradoxes: The Apocalypse to John in Process Hermeneutic," develops a reading strategy that allows the reader to be honest with the ethical tensions and contradictions within the story. The essay employs two reading strategies drawn from process philosophy to explore John's views of power and coercion. Process hermeneutic seeks to discover "undercurrents" within a text and to hold paradoxes in "the unity of a contrast." This chapter seeks to embrace the paradox between the dominant current (of power and coercion) and the undercurrent (of suffering love) to produce a reading of Revelation relevant for modern readers. The author attempts to give full force both to the surface story of power and coercion and to the more subtle theme of suffering for the sake of others—with the paradox between the two creating space for a more imaginative reading of the text.

Chapter 8, "Taking a Stand on the Sand of the Seashore: A Postcolonial Exploration of Revelation 13," continues the analysis of the Apocalypse as an anticolonial message, introducing ideas from liberationist and postcolonial perspectives—two movements with their bases in the so-called third world. The Apocalypse's unrelenting critique of first-century Roman imperial power has found deep resonance with readers in Africa, Asia, and Latin America who experience the powers of this world from the underside. Like the residents of Asia Minor in John's time, these readers find their lives pervaded by a dominant colonial power. The vision of Revelation, with its promise of life wrested from the grasp of oppression unto death, grounds the hopes of readers who struggle for survival from day to day. For such readers, liberationist philosopher and theologian Enrique Dussel suggests, the mystery revealed in the Book of Revelation is actually more current today than ever, and merits our close attention.

Chapter 9, "'In the Spirit': The Book of Revelation in Religious Studies," continues the examination of the Apocalypse from the perspective of a modern academic discipline. Taken at face value, Revelation is a record of what John saw and heard when spirit-possessed (Rev 1:10; 4:1–2). Since spirit possession is a fairly widespread phenomenon in apocalyptic and millenarian movements, research from the history of religions can help interpret aspects of John's record: for example, its visual imagery, the presence of throne scenes and hymnic liturgies, the occasional blurring of lines between John and Jesus, and John's compulsion to write.

The last article not only demonstrates a particular way to read Revelation, it also shows why such reading is important in modern America, in which apocalyptic themes and ideas permeate popular culture. Chapter 10, "The Lion/Lamb King: Reading the Apocalypse from Popular Culture," explores contemporary apocalyptic tendencies in popular movies, popular music, and popular science. After reviewing the appearances of the Apocalypse in popular culture—from action movies like *Terminator*, *The Road Warrior*, and *Waterworld* to family films like *Lion King*—this essay explores the ways the Apocalypse offers a critique of culture.

All these perspectives raise central questions of how one ought to read a book like Revelation and how we should deal with competing, even conflicting, readings. Are all readings valid? Are some better than others? How does one use multiple interpretations? How does one choose among interpretations? These are significant issues, but they will be best addressed in the conclusion to this book, after you have experienced the various possible interpretations.

1

The Story John Told

READING REVELATION FOR ITS PLOT

David L. Barr

We are all familiar with the distinction between *form* and *content*, the latter referring to what is said and the former to how it is said. This distinction is helpful for understanding the variety of opinions about how the Book of Revelation is organized, about which there is no agreement.[1] Those who look primarily at the form of the writing generally divide the work into two parts: the letters to the seven churches (chs. 1–3) and visions of the future (chs. 4–22).[2] Those who look primarily at the content of the writing often focus on the several numbered series of seven things,[3] some even going so far as to create other sets of seven things that John did not number.[4] Others who focus on content divide the work by the three

---

This chapter is a revision and expansion of David L. Barr, "Using Plot to Discern Structure in John's Apocalypse," *Proceedings of the Eastern Great Lakes and Midwest Biblical Societies* 15 (1995): 23–33.

[1] Many commentaries will include a brief survey in their introductions; see, for example, the list in J. Ramsey Michaels, *Interpreting the Book of Revelation* (Grand Rapids: Baker Book House, 1992), 69, n. 9. For a chart of eight representative outlines, see Edith M. Humphrey, *The Ladies and the Cities: Transformation and Apocalyptic Identity in Joseph and Aseneth, 4 Ezra, The Apocalypse, and the Shepherd of Hermas* (Sheffield, England: Sheffield Academic Press, 1995), 82–83.

[2] For example, Mitchell Reddish, *Revelation* (Macon, Ga.: Smyth & Helwyns, 2001), 23, and David E. Aune, *Revelation* (3 vols.; WBC; Dallas: Word Books, 1997), c–ci.

[3] For example, Austin Farrer, *A Rebirth of Images: The Making of St. John's Apocalypse* (1949; reprint, Gloucester, Mass.: Peter Smith, 1970), 55–56.

[4] See chapter 1 of Adela Yarbro Collins, *The Combat Myth in the Book of Revelation* (Chico, Calif.: Scholars Press, 1976); Austin Farrer, *The Revelation of St. John the Divine* (Oxford: Oxford University Press, 1964).

mentions of John being "in the spirit."[5] These are all useful observations and point to real aspects of the Book of Revelation. And there are many other suggestions.[6] But there is a third way of considering the material that promises to be even more useful.

Some scholars have begun to analyze the parts of the Apocalypse not just by their form or content but also by the relationship between the parts. How do the various segments relate to one another? Thus M. Eugene Boring has suggested three scenes: the address to the church in the city; the judgment of the great city; and the redemption of the holy city.[7] I wish to pursue this type of analysis, focused more particularly by the notion of plot.

Reflecting on Plot

At the heart of the notion of plot is the idea of a cause-and-effect connection between events in a sequence, so that event B happens not only after event A but in some sense because of event A. This understanding of plot goes back to Aristotle, who defined plot as the relationship between the incidents (*Poetics* 1450a51), the cause-and-effect logic that binds the incidents together and mandates that one follow the other. If a story consists of a series of events, plot consists of the logic that binds them together.

E. M. Forster illustrates this difference between mere sequence and plot with the little story:

> The king died and then the queen died.

This is a story, but it lacks a plot, for there is no cause-and-effect logic between the incidents. He suggests another story, one with a plot:

> The king died and then the queen died of grief.[8]

Now a causal relationship exists—or can be imagined—between the incidents; the king's death is the logical cause of the queen's death. Forster's point is a useful one, helping us see more clearly what is meant

---

[5] For example, J. Ramsey Michaels, *Revelation* (IVP New Testament Commentary Series; Downers Grove, Ill.: InterVarsity Press, 1997), 30–32.

[6] For example, Elisabeth Schüssler Fiorenza has posited a concentric pattern in *Revelation: Vision of a Just World* (Minneapolis: Fortress Press, 1991), 35–36. See also her more extended discussion in "Composition and Structure of the Book of Revelation," *CBQ* 39 (1977): 344–66. Jan Lambrecht has sketched a similar pattern in "A Structuration of Revelation 4:1–22:5," in *L'Apocalypse Johannique et l'apocalyptique dans le Nouveau Testament* (Louvain, Belgium: Louvain University Press, 1980). For an elaborate proposal, see Nils Wilhelm Lund, *Studies in the Book of Revelation* ([Chicago]: Covenant Press, 1955).

[7] M. Eugene Boring, *Revelation* (IBC; Atlanta: John Knox, 1989), 30–31. Although Boring calls his organization an outline, it is clearly a more literary scheme, based on narrative principles of action, characters, and place.

[8] E. M. Foster, *Aspects of the Novel* (New York: Penguin Books, 1962), 87.

by causal connection. But I wonder if he gives the reader enough credit, for even in the first sequence one tries to imagine a connection between the events and may well have made a plotted story of them even before the writer supplied the explicit connection. Plotting—creating causal connections between events in a sequence—is a cooperative venture involving both author and audience. Sometimes authors make plots explicit, but at other times the relationship between incidents is left open and the reader must fill in the gap. One should not assume that there is only one possible plot, except in the simplest of stories.

In fact, stories range over a spectrum from simple, unilinear, tightly plotted sequences (such as a joke) to complex, multilinear sequences wherein any number of possible connections between events may be inferred (as in an epic). The Apocalypse is a complex story, and no reader will ever imagine all the possible connections between incidents. What follows is one reading of one set of interconnections.

One way critics simplify complex stories is by classifying incidents into two separate categories: *kernels* (incidents that are directly linked and determinative of the future course of the action) and *satellites* (incidents that orbit around these kernels adding nuance and complexity).[9] This is a useful tool, as long as we recognize that the selection of kernels is an interpretive act; different readers may see different relationships. Nor should we think that kernel incidents are more important than satellite incidents. They are more significant for plot, but plot is only one aspect of story. Other incidents may be more important for other aspects (such as characterization or point of view). In fact, the satellites carry experiences and information crucial to the reading experience.

One final caveat is that one person's satellite might be another person's kernel. And if it is, a different story will be imagined. Wolfgang Iser has suggested an interesting analogy in the way different viewers look at the night sky. Some see one kind of constellation, others see something different:

> Two people gazing at the night sky may both be looking at the same collection of stars, but one will see the image of a plough, and the other will make out a dipper. The "stars" in a literary text are fixed; the lines that join them are variable.[10]

The incidents depicted in a text are like the fixed stars of the heavens, objectively available to all. But the constellations (the way the incidents

---

[9] The terms are from Seymour Chatman, *Story and Discourse: Narrative Structure in Fiction and Film* (New York: Cornell University Press, 1978), 53–54. According to Chatman, "Kernels are narrative moments that give rise to cruxes in the direction taken by events. . . . Kernels cannot be deleted without destroying the narrative logic."

[10] Wolfgang Iser, *The Implied Reader: Patterns of Communication in Prose Fiction from Bunyan to Beckett* (Baltimore: Johns Hopkins University Press, 1974), 282.

are imagined to fit together) depend on our observations. One observer draws lines between these two, another between those.

The metaphor would be more compelling if one believed that the stars were placed with purpose by some grand artist who was trying to tell us something. But even so, the metaphor reminds us that the construction of meaning is neither an objective nor a subjective process; it is both. All reading involves a dynamic interaction between the words objectively available on a page and the subjective meanings attached to those words in the mind of the reader. But this subjective element does not make agreement impossible, for we can talk. There is thus a third way between objectivity and subjectivity, which philosophers call intersubjectivity. We can share our subjective understanding of the objective phenomenon and try to show each other the constellations we have found.

My own reading, elaborated below, of the dominant line of action in the Apocalypse sees it as a series of three interrelated stories set in a common frame.

Constructing a Plot

Since a plot is a logical sequence, much can be learned by examining the beginning and ending. Many have observed the strong correlation between the beginning and the ending of Revelation. There are at least eleven points of correspondence.

Opening	Point of Correspondence	Closing
1:1, 4, 9	John names himself	22:8
1:1	An angel sent	22:6
1:1	Will soon take place	22:6
1:1	The servants	22:6
1:3	Reader blessed	22:7
1:3	The time is near	22:10
1:4	Grace to you	22:21
1:8	The Alpha and Omega	22:13
1:10	The Spirit	22:17
1:16, 20	Stars and angels	22:16
1:17	John falls at feet	22:8

But the parallels are more than just verbal and thematic; there are also parallels of form and action. The overall form is that of a letter that begins

"John to the seven churches" (1:4) and ends with the letter formula so familiar from Paul's letters, "the grace of the Lord Jesus Christ be with all" (22:21). The letter provides the setting for the action, which starts with John directly addressing the audience and describing his sojourn on Patmos, where he has a vision (1:9–10), and ends with John directly addressing the audience, saying this *is* what he heard and saw (22:8). It is the classic technique of the storyteller: I was off alone one day and I saw something very interesting. . . . This action provides a second frame around the larger story; I will call it the *vision-report frame*. Thus the actual story of the Apocalypse is two stages removed from the audience, placed within this double container of letter and vision-report, which frame all the action of the story.

If we now try to trace logical sequences of events, we discover that within these frames, John tells three stories. The first story concerns what happened to him on Patmos (John sees a vision of a majestic human being who appears to him, comforts him, explains things to him, and then dictates seven messages to the angels of seven churches). The second story concerns what John saw when he ascended into heaven through an open door in the sky (4:1). John finds himself in the throne room of God, where he observes a scene at the divine court. This second story concerns the process by which a slaughtered-yet-standing lamb opens a divine scroll and reveals its contents. John's attention now shifts from God's throne to God's temple. Peering into the heavenly temple, John sees strange new signs. In this third story a cosmic dragon pursues a cosmic woman but is eventually defeated by a cosmic warrior, resulting in the establishment of a wholly new cosmic order.[11]

Notice first how these three stories are ever more fantastic. We begin with a somewhat realistic scene set on a Greek island—easy to imagine. Then we observe the events at the divine court, which correspond in some ways to the worship of the earthly church—harder to imagine. Finally, we are shown the ultimate battle between good and evil, a cosmic war of such dimensions that it is nearly impossible to imagine. But then we are brought back down to earth, so to speak, with John's closing address, spoken directly to the audience: this is what I saw. It is like we have gone on a journey, and the farther we get from home the more strange

---

[11] Perhaps closest to my own view of the structure of Revelation is that of Jürgen Roloff, who sees four thematic sections to Revelation in chapters 1–3; 4–11; 12–19:10; and 19:11–22:21, with the last three growing out of the throne vision in 4:1–5:14, "the theological fulcrum of the entire book" (*The Revelation of John: A Continental Commentary* [Minneapolis: Fortress Press, 1993], 15–17). Whereas Roloff sees two actions in the last half of the book (demonic attack and divine conquest), I see them as two parts of the one action of holy war. See also the divisions proposed by Robert W. Wall in *New International Biblical Commentary: Revelation* (Peabody, Mass.: Hendrickson, 1991), 41–42, who presents similar divisions but with quite different significance.

the territory becomes, until finally we return home again. It is a fantastic journey—rather like a shaman's journey.[12]

Second, notice how each of these stories represents a different literary type. The first story type is common in the Hebrew Scriptures and in many religious traditions; it is the story of an encounter with a divine being, technically known as a theophany (from *theos*, god; and *phainein*, to show, to make appear; thus the appearance or revealing of a god). The second story type, wherein the mystic ascends to heaven and sees the throne of God, is rare in the Hebrew Scriptures but common in ancient mystical literature (see Isa 6 and Ezek 1–3).[13] While both the theophany and the throne vision involve a revelation of the divine, the former has the divine appearing on earth while, in the latter, the human ascends into the divine realm. The third story is of yet another kind; it is a story of holy war.[14] These three fantastic stories of theophany, throne vision, and holy war are sandwiched between realistic narratives of John on the island of Patmos. These stories may be set forth schematically as follows:

	Story One	Story Two	Story Three
Place	Patmos	heaven	Earth
Characters	Jesus as Majestic Human John churches	Jesus as Lamb-Slain elders and heavenly beings	Jesus as Heavenly Warrior dragon and beasts woman and her children
Action	letter writing	worship	war
John presented as	secretary	heavenly traveler	seer/prophet
Mythic paradigm	theophany	throne vision	holy war
Chapters	1–3	4–11	12–22[15]

Before considering whether these three stories have any logical connections to each other, let me sketch what I take to be the kernel incidents of each.

[12] See the vivid story of the shaman's descent into the womb/underworld in Claude Lévi-Strauss, "The Effectiveness of Symbols," in *Structural Anthropology* (New York: Anchor/Doubleday, 1967), 181–202.

[13] See the seminal study of Ithamar Gruenwald, *Apocalyptic and Merkavah Mysticism* (Leiden: E. J. Brill, 1980), and the extensive review in Aune, *Revelation*, 276–79.

[14] See the excellent review by Collins, *Combat Myth*.

[15] More precisely, the new action begins with the opening of the heavenly temple in 11:19; I use the round chapter numbers for convenience. See Aune, *Revelation*, 661.

Story one: A majestic human being appears to John on Patmos and commands him to write a scroll and to send it to the seven churches of Asia. After a detailed description of this divine figure, the figure comforts John, explains particular symbols to him, and then dictates seven messages to the angels of the seven churches.

Story two: John hears a voice out of heaven, inviting John to come up. He ascends to heaven, sees God on the throne surrounded by the heavenly court, and hears the heavenly hymns. A scroll is presented, but it is sealed and no one can open it, causing John to weep. Then a character, announced as a lion but revealed as a slain-yet-standing lamb, proceeds to open the scroll in seven stages. At each stage various visions are seen. The seventh seal produces a time of silence, then seven trumpets sound, each also accompanied by various visions. When the last trumpet has sounded, we hear the announcement: God's kingdom has come.

Story three: A majestic heavenly woman who is about to give birth is pursued by a heavenly dragon who seeks to consume her child. The woman is saved and the child preserved, but the dragon turns to make war on her other children. Two armies are gathered; the dragon conjures two great beasts, one from the sea and one from the earth; the lamb gathers 144,000 on Mount Zion. Scenes of heavenly harvest predict earthly judgment, which is then enacted in seven plague events, leading to the great announcement: it is done. Just what is done is now related in two sets of scenes involving two women: one a prostitute (war against heaven, heavenly warrior, destruction, a thousand years of peace, final battle, final judgment, new creation) and the other the bride of the lamb (restoration of Eden as the new Jerusalem).

Thus each of these three units can be viewed as a unified action, though it would take more detailed analysis to show the logical connections between each action in each story.[16] But this raises a larger issue, for there seems to be little connection between these three stories. The action of the first story (letter writing) does not lead to that of the second (the throne scene) or the third (holy war). They do not form a causal sequence, yet within each movement there is a reasonably clear causal sequence. How should we understand the stories' relationship? Is Revelation one story or three?

Stated differently, how can we understand that Revelation consists of three different stories within one narrative framework? Perhaps an analogy will help. An O. Henry short story called "Roads of Destiny" offers some analogy to John's narrative strategy. In O. Henry's story a young man leaves his native village to explore the world and write poetry. But when he comes to a fork in the road, he cannot decide which way to proceed. So the story is told showing him take all three options: first he takes

---

[16] David L. Barr, *Tales of the End: A Narrative Commentary on the Book of Revelation* (The Storytellers Bible 1; Santa Rosa, Calif.: Polebridge Press, 1998).

one branch; then the second; and finally he returns to his village. For each path taken a different series of events ensues, but each leads inexorably to the same end: the young man is shot and killed—each time with the very same pistol. Now clearly all three events belong in the same narrative, for the narrative could not make its point without all of them. Yet just as clearly the actions within each event can have no causal connection with actions in the other two, for the initial act of choosing one road excludes what might happen down another path. It would be to miss the point were we to ask whether our young man went down path two *before* or *after* going down path one. The connection is not one of before and after. What then are the connections among the three?

These connections have to do with theme (destiny) and characters rather than with sequential actions. Yet the actions gain their meaning only by being seen in comparison within the same narrative.[17] When one finishes O. Henry's story one understands the seductive/destructive allure of poetry in a new way, and one is challenged to understand destiny as more than just the accidental encounters of a chosen path. In this story the decision to leave the village entailed consequences that no later choice could ever eliminate. One also understands that action within a story is not necessarily sequential.

In a similar way, John's three dramatic actions do not constitute a sequential, unified action. One action does not happen before or after the other. They represent alternative tellings of the story of Jesus with a common theme and overlapping characters. The dragon does not attack the woman's children (ch. 12) after Jesus dictates the letters (chs. 2–3) or after the triumphant consummation of heavenly worship (ch. 11); in John's story that attack is contemporaneous with the life of the church and is as old as Eve.[18] The third action is a retelling of the story of the coming of God's rule with a new focus. It is as if the narrator had finished the triumphant heavenly announcement that the kingdoms of this world had become the kingdom of God and of the Christ (11:15) and then turned to the audience and said, "Do you wonder how that came about? Well, let me tell you . . ." The focus now is on the attack of the dragon and the ensuing cosmic war, with Jesus being presented (rather ironically) in the guise of the Divine Warrior.

Rather than one unfolding event, Revelation presents three interrelated tellings of the story of Jesus. The first tells the story from the perspective of Jesus active in the communities of John's time, as their judge

---

[17] I first encountered the O. Henry story in Thomas M. Leitch's *What Stories Are* (State College: Pennsylvania State University Press, 1986), 47–48. Leitch makes the point that what changes in such a story is the audience's, not the hero's, understanding of the world.

[18] For, at one level, the woman in chapter 12 is Eve. See J. P. M. Sweet, *Revelation* (Philadelphia: Westminster Press, 1979; reprint, Trinity Press International, 1990), 203, and Barr, *Tales of the End*, 112–13.

and support. The second tells the story from the perspective of Jesus enthroned in heaven, already ruling the world. The third tells the story of Jesus the suffering savior who defeated evil in the past and future war. One story does not lead to the other, yet they gain their meaning by appearing together within the common frame of John's vision and letter. As we might say, these seven messages to the churches (story one) could only be written by one who has himself fought evil (story three) and been vindicated (story two). Rather than pursue the details of the stories further, I now turn to what I see as the significance of this narrative strategy.

Interpreting the Plot

The author of the Apocalypse obscures the distance between these three stories by setting up a remarkable number of echoes: events and characters are echoed between stories, and the stories themselves echo the foundational stories of Western culture. A closer look at these echoes will help us formulate a sense of the whole.

Carried-Over Characters

One of the primary ways that John gives the illusion of unity to the larger story is by the use of characters and characterization. John is the only character who persists by name through all three stories, and even his characterization varies from scene to scene. Jesus appears in all three stories, but under radically different images: majestic human, lamb, divine warrior. But here something interesting happens, for the lamb wanders.

While the lamb belongs logically only to the second story, a story of liturgy, he also shows up in the third. Often this is a mere reference, having the effect of referring back to the second story.[19] But in three places in the third story the lamb actually usurps the action of the divine warrior. At the beginning of chapter 14, it is the lamb who gathers the 144,000 sacred warriors on Mount Zion; at 17:14, it is the lamb who will conquer ten kings; and, at 19:7, it is the lamb who will marry in the postwar victory celebration.

This is strikingly inappropriate, of course, and is probably motivated largely by ideological concerns.[20] John is never far from his conviction that the divine will prevails through faithful witness rather than through the exercise of power. Even the heavenly warrior slays his enemies by "the sword of his mouth" (19:21). Carrying over the character of the lamb allows John to undermine much of the ideology of holy war, deconstructing the basic framework of his own third story.

But more than ideology is at work. For by carrying over the character

---

[19] This referential effect can be seen at 12:11; 13:8; 14:10; 15:3; 21:14; and 21:22–23.

[20] On subverted images, see David L. Barr, "The Apocalypse as a Symbolic Transformation of the World: A Literary Analysis," *Interpretation* 38 (1984): 39–50.

of the lamb John ties these two stories together and sets up echoes between them. John's portrayal of Jesus-as-victim and Jesus-as-victor are both inadequate until the two images permeate each other.

Most of the other characters stay "home," with modest exceptions. The 144,000 sacred warriors first emerge in the throne vision (7:1ff.); the beasts make an unannounced appearance in the throne vision (11:7); the elders make a cameo return appearance in the war sequence (14:3; 19:4). At one point the voice that dictated the seven messages seems to appear out of nowhere in the war sequence (22:7), and the heavenly warrior is given some of the descriptive traits of the majestic human of the theophany story (19:12–16). All in all, these overlapping characters give one the illusion that these actions are related. This illusion is furthered by John's creative use of repetition.

Redundant Actions

> And there came flashes of lightning, rumblings, peals of thunder, and a violent earthquake, such as had not occurred since people were upon the earth, so violent was that earthquake. (16:18)

Maybe so, but this is at least the *fifth* such quake in Revelation (6:12; 8:5; 11:13; 11:19). Even the most naive and preliminary reading of Revelation must notice the repetitiveness of some of the actions in the story. Often the repetition is not so formulaic as John's earthquake language, and serves more than summary and transitional needs.

Genette's classic study of temporal sequence in story distinguishes frequency of occurrence (repetition) as one of the three crucial aspects of narrative action.[21] In addition to straight repetitions, wherein the same action is repeatedly told, Genette notes actions that are repeated in differing contexts so as to constitute different actions. It is this second type of repetition that I am calling echoed actions.

Every commentator, for example, notices that the actions of the seven bowls (in story three) echo the actions of the seven trumpets (in story two). This redundancy causes the audience to sense that these two stories are connected even though there is no connection between the logic of the actions of the two narrative sequences. That is, the narrative sequence of the throne vision now seems to be connected to the narrative sequence of the holy war by means of this echoed action, even though there is no

---

[21] The three elements of time relations in narrative are order, duration, and frequency. See Gerard Genette, *Narrative Discourse: An Essay in Method* (Ithaca, N.Y.: Cornell University Press, 1980), 33–160. Genette sought to call attention to the impact of the ways stories are told by examining the congruences and incongruences between story and discourse (event and narrative; signified and signifier). In regard to frequency he noted the *singulative* (one event, one narration), the *repetitive* (one event, multiple narrations), the *repetitious* (similar events, multiple narrations), and the *iterative* (many events, one narration).

causal connection posited in the narrative. Even more, this echo reinforces the correspondence between the heavenly liturgy and the earthly war: as in heaven so on earth. The myth of sacrifice and the myth of conquest are blended.

Most of the echoed actions of Revelation occur within a single story. The angel with the censer of prayers (8:3ff.) echoes the actions of the fifth and sixth seals (6:9ff.). The open temple of 11:19 is repeated in 15:5, when judgment is enacted. The final battle never seems to be quite final, for it recurs four times (16:16; 19:19; 20:8ff.). The fall of Babylon gets three enactments (17:16; 18:2ff.; 18:21ff.). The echoes between the revelation of the two women are of quite a different sort; with their antithetical themes we might call them negative echoes (17:1ff.; 21:9ff.). One incident—the worship of the angel by John (19:10; 22:8)—is repeated in such close detail that one wonders if one incident is narrated twice.

Such repetition serves a variety of purposes, requiring more careful analysis than I can pursue here.[22] But one purpose of repetition is to create a sense of unity in the story by creating a sense that we have heard this before. Before concluding I want to consider briefly another kind of echo, in which John's stories echo other cultural stories.

Echoed Stories and Ancient Myths

I observed above that each of these stories in Revelation is built on a different literary type or model (theophany, throne scene, and holy war). I now want to take that idea a bit further and suggest that these models are deep and pervasive paradigms properly called myths. It is unfortunate that the term *myth* in popular speech has come to mean a misconception or an untrue story, whereas in scholarly discourse it means that which is most true. It is even more unfortunate that we do not have another English word with the same power and meaning. I sometimes speak of myths as *charter stories*, and that captures some of the meaning. They are the stories that charter, undergird, and give warrant to what a society believes and does. Myths are not tested by whether they correspond to the real world; myths create the world we take as real. So here I use the term *myth* to mean those foundational stories and paradigms that shape and support a culture.

Long before John's day, the ancient hope of the Hebrew prophets for the renewal of history had been combined with the religious rituals celebrating the renewal of nature, producing a new myth of renewal: the renewal of the cosmos. Thus the old idea that God would intervene in Israel's history to purify the people and establish justice was combined with creation myths, producing the notion of the end of history and the

---

[22] A useful study could be done using the insights developed by Robert Alter, *The Art of Biblical Narrative* (New York: Basic Books, 1981) on repetition and variety in biblical stories.

birth of a new creation.[23] Other mythic traditions were also incorporated; in fact, John employs a great variety of such myths and archetypes.[24] Among the more prominent I would include the traditions of the Danielic Son of Man (1:13ff.); the myth of correspondence, with a heavenly world corresponding to the earthly world (1:20, for example); the myth of the heavenly throne (4:2ff.); myths connected to Jewish festivals (7:1–17); the myth of Israel reconstituted (7:5ff.); the myth of the eschatological prophet (11:3ff.); the myth of the great mother (12:1ff.); war in heaven (12:7ff.); the two primal beasts (13:1ff.); myths from the wilderness, exodus, and temptation (17:3ff.); myths about Rome (17:3ff.); and a whole sequence connected with the archaic creation myths of the ancient Near East—chaos, war, order, marriage, and rule (chs. 19–21). In addition, John uses important archetypes, including the temple, the plagues, Egypt, Babylon, the dragon, righteous violence, virginity, and wilderness.

I am not at the moment interested in the source of these traditions or in whether John is using them consciously, or even in what they mean in the story being told. Rather, I want to raise the question of their larger significance in the structure of the Apocalypse. For it seems to me that these traditions function in a way analogous to the echoed incidents discussed above. Just as the echoed incidents allowed John's audience to feel a connection between discordant story elements, so these echoes of the mythic traditions allowed the audience to feel not only that the stories hang together but also that they are true.

This suggestion is based on my own experience of stories as well as on observations of how stories are used today. I was impressed, for example, with the skill with which policy makers swayed public opinion during the Gulf War of 1991. Skillfully blending elements of two mythic traditions (a myth of evil and a myth of redemption), they taught us to see the Gulf War as a contest between the forces of untold evil and the forces

---

[23] I find Paul D. Hanson's tracing (*The Dawn of Apocalyptic: The Historical and Sociological Roots of Jewish Apocalyptic Eschatology* [Philadelphia: Fortress Press, 1979]) to be persuasive.

[24] For a recent summary of the treatment of myth in Revelation, see Steven J. Friesen, *Imperial Cults and the Apocalypse of John: Reading Revelation in the Ruins* (Oxford: Oxford University Press, 2001), 167–79. See also John M. Court, *Myth and History in the Book of Revelation* (Atlanta: John Knox, 1979). Special studies of the conflict myth include Collins, *Combat Myth* (see n. 4 above), and John Day, *God's Conflict with the Dragon and the Sea in the Old Testament* (Cambridge: Cambridge University Press, 1985). See also James E. Altenbaumer, "The Apocalyptic Drama of Salvation in Revelation: Myth and Cult in the Hymnic Strophes" (Ph.D. diss., Emory University, 1988), and S. W. Sykes, "Story and Eucharist," *Interpretation* 37, no. 4 (1983): 365–76. Haken Ulfgard provides a good study of the use of Jewish festival tradition in *Feast and Future: Revelation 7:9–17 and the Feast of Tabernacles* (Stockholm: Almqvist & Wiksell, 1989).

of justice.[25] For shorthand let me refer to the one as the Hitler myth and the other as the Lone Ranger myth (though in fact these names are only instances of the myths).

The Hitler myth imagines a scenario in which the actor is in the service of some great evil, an evil that pushes the perpetrator beyond all humanity. Any action that would stop this evil is permitted, perhaps required. The Lone Ranger myth imagines some innocent victim (preferably a female) being abused by someone in power; all seems lost. Then the mysterious stranger appears and, through an act of sudden and righteous violence, establishes justice before riding off into the sunset—taking nothing for his troubles. Following these myths, the rape of Kuwait by demonic Saddam Hussein had to be stopped by the virtue of American power.

Let me then offer a hypothesis: stories told so as to echo our mythic expectations are felt to be true and consistent. This is the reason, I think, why parts of John's story remain so potent today, for the myth of holy war remains strong. It is no accident that this part of the story is what most people know of the Book of Revelation. The other myths have lost their power, but not this one.

In John's time, I imagine, the mythic tradition was richer and more felt. To be able to echo the stories of Eve and of Leto in his story of the Great Mother would have a powerful literary effect—whether or not John's audience believed in either. One does not, after all, have to believe in the Lone Ranger to feel the power of the story. By reaching back to the theophanic traditions associated with Israel's past, by incorporating temple traditions elaborated in mystical experiences of God's throne, and by portraying his hostility to Greco-Roman culture as the cosmic struggle of the heavenly warrior with the beasts of evil, John is able to suggest a unity to his story that goes beyond the surface. For, ultimately, all myths cohere.

It is such coherence that I have sought to explore in this essay. For in spite of the incredible diversity of John's Apocalypse, when one reads it through, aloud, one senses (feels, experiences) an overwhelming unity. I have presented one way of reading of Revelation that sees the book as three interrelated, inter-acting stories, tied together by a common storytelling framework. While these three stories are independent stories with virtually no connections in terms of the actions portrayed in each, the audience imagines connections between them because they are presented together. The author encourages this imagination by setting up a series of echoes between the stories. These echoes exist on the level of characters, actions, and mythic paradigms. These echoes allow the author to guide our reading of each story so that it is read in the light of the others.

[25] See George Lakoff, "Metaphor, Morality, and Politics: Or, Why Conservatives Have Left Liberals in the Dust," in *The Workings of Language: From Prescriptions to Perspectives* (ed. Rebecca S. Wheeler; Westport, Conn.: Praeger, 1999).

2

Ordinary Lives

John and His First Readers

Leonard L. Thompson

Some might think the title above should be "Extraordinary Lives." What, after all, could be ordinary about Revelation? It tells of fabulous events and fantastic beings. It predicts a cataclysmic end to the world when pure good conquers thoroughgoing evil. And didn't John write in extraordinary times? We hear stories about good Christians being hunted down and thrown to the lions by evil, mad emperors and about God being with the good Christians so that they eventually won the battle against evil Rome—not, however, until many of the faithful were martyred, burned alive, torn open by dogs, and nailed to crosses. How can these be called ordinary lives?

In this chapter, I want to tell a different story, one more ambiguous and less clear-cut: a story in which none of the actors is two-dimensional and none of the events is a stock situation. It is a story filled with an abundance of the history of real people who, like all real people, sometimes act in unexpected ways, leaving events unfinished or giving them a surprising turn. If I tell the story truthfully, you will not be able to sort out the actors as good guys and bad guys. You may even feel "a sense of spontaneous tolerance" toward all the actors: Roman emperors, Christians, John, and Jezebel.[1] At the end, you will still have to make moral judgments and take a position on how to read Revelation in relation to that abundance. But, if I have told the story in its fullness, those judgments will not be so easily made.

In order to tell the story fully, I shall have to take you into what may

---

[1] The phrase "a sense of spontaneous tolerance" belongs to Grazia Borrine-Feyerabend in Paul Feyerabend, *Conquest of Abundance*, edited by Bert Terpstra (Chicago: University of Chicago Press, 1999), xi. I borrow the notion of abundance from that book.

at times appear to be byways and alleys, far off the main highway of the one hundred or so miles between John at Patmos and his first readers. Moreover, I shall have to draw on Roman as well as Christian sources. For Christian sources often present Roman officials as stereotypical evil rulers, and Roman sources dub Christianity as just another new, disgusting superstition. In the abundance of history, however, all the actors are more complex in temperament and motivation, a mixture of good and bad impulses.

Pinpointing the Historical Situation

Historians of early Christianity try to pinpoint exactly the situation in which the Book of Revelation was written. They do that by reading Revelation for clues, and then correlating what they find in Revelation with the reigns of certain emperors as described by Roman historians from the early second century. Once a correlation is made, information from those Roman historians and what John wrote in Revelation are mixed together, with each informing the other. One early Christian author in particular has decisively influenced later writers, including those today who write about Revelation; he lived in the early fourth century, and his name was Eusebius. For that reason, I shall give special attention to what Eusebius says and how he went about establishing the historical conditions in which John wrote.

Let us begin by asking two simple questions: Where did John write Revelation? When did he write it? John gives the following information:

> I, John, your brother and partner, sharing with Jesus tribulation, royalty, and perseverance, was on the isle called Patmos because of the word of God and the witness of Jesus. On the Lord's Day, becoming spirit-possessed, I heard behind me a voice, loud like the blast of a trumpet: "What you see, write in a scroll, and send to the seven churches—to Ephesus, Smyrna, Pergamum, Thyatira, Sardis, Philadelphia, and Laodicea." (Rev 1:9–11, my translation)

John answers the first question about where Revelation was written. He was on the isle of Patmos, one of the Sporades Islands in the Aegean Sea about thirty-five miles off the western coast of modern-day Turkey in the direction of Greece. John also gives the names of the seven cities where his first readers lived. Earlier, he mentioned that those seven cities were in Asia (Rev 1:4). Today, the term "Asia" may evoke the lands of India and east, but in Revelation it refers to a province in the Roman Empire located in the western part of what we now call Turkey.

John does not answer the second question about when he wrote, at least not in a way that is helpful for dating Revelation. He states that he had his visions "on the Lord's Day." The Lord's Day was the time when Mary Magdalene found an empty tomb when she and others went to weep and lament over Jesus' death (*Gos. Pet.* 12.50), and it was the day that Christians came together to hold Eucharist and to worship (*Did.* 14). For John, setting his visions in ritual time was more important than in calendar time.

Since John did not include the date when he wrote Revelation, we must try to establish it indirectly either from historical allusions in Revelation or from references to Revelation by other Christian writers. The first reference to Revelation occurs in the writings of Justin Martyr, a convert to Christianity who died in 165 of the Christian era. In *Dialogue with Trypho,* Justin supports his argument for the resurrection of the dead and the rebuilding of Jerusalem by referring to Revelation.[2] This dialogue or debate with Trypho, a Jew, probably took place not long after 135 of the Christian era when Justin was in Ephesus.[3] Let us assume, somewhat arbitrarily, that it took a couple of decades for Revelation to become available to Justin as an authoritative Christian work. If so, Revelation would have been in existence *no later than* around 120 of the Christian era. How much earlier could it have been written? If, as most likely, Rev 17:8 and 17:11 refer to legends in which Nero returns to Rome to rule again, then John was written after Nero's death (or disappearance) in 68.[4] Revelation was, thus, written sometime in the roughly fifty-year period between 70 and 120 of the Christian era.[5]

In sum, Revelation was written to Christians living in the Roman province of Asia at the eastern end of the Roman Empire sometime during that period technically called the Roman Principate. The following emperors ruled from 68 to 180; Revelation was written sometime between the end of Nero's reign and the beginning of Hadrian's:

54–68	Nero
69	Year of four (Galba, Otho, Vitellius, Vespasian)
69–96	Flavian dynasty (69–79 Vespasian; 79–81 Titus; 81–96 Domitian)
96–98	Nerva
98–117	Trajan

[2] *Dial. Trypho* 81: "And further, there was a certain man with us, whose name was John, one of the apostles of Christ, who prophesied, by a revelation that was made to him, that those who believed in our Christ would dwell a thousand years in Jerusalem" (*ANF*).

[3] Eusebius places the debate in Ephesus (*Eccl. Hist.* 4.18). In *Dial.* 1, Trypho identifies himself as having recently escaped from the Bar Kokhba war in and around Jerusalem. Simon bar Kokhba (or sometimes Kosiba), regarded as the Messiah by Rabbi Akiba, in 132 declared Israel liberated from Rome. Justin says in *1 Apology* 31 that during the revolt Christians suffered cruel punishments.

[4] For those stories about Nero, see, for example, Suetonius, *Nero* 57; Tacitus, *Hist* 2.8–9; *Sib. Or.* 3.63–70; 4.119–20, 130–39.

[5] Within Revelation there is no other evidence conclusive for dating the book. For a discussion of the internal evidence, see David E. Aune, *Revelation 1–5,* (WBC; Dallas: Word Books, 1997), lx–lxix.

117–38   Hadrian
138–61   Antoninus Pius
161–80   Marcus Aurelius

Clues from Revelation

John did not write history. He recorded visions that he had while spirit-possessed. It is possible, however, to read those visions in such a way as to provide information about the situation of Christians in the Roman Empire. In Revelation, chapters 2 and 3, John recorded exhortations to each of the seven churches to persevere in the face of adversity. In those exhortations, the speaker describes the situation of Christians in mythic symbols drawn from earlier Jewish writings: Those at Pergamum dwell under the shadow of Satan's throne; the devil is soon to cast some at Smyrna into prison where there will be ten days of tribulation; those at Philadelphia will be kept from the hour of testing soon to come upon the world. The source of this adversity is not stated explicitly, but it is clearly bound up with threats from the non-Christian world (Roman and Jewish) and from John's expectation of the imminent coming of Christ. If Antipas, "my witness, my faithful one, who was killed among you," was a historical person, then that intensifies the sense of persecution (Rev 2:13).[6]

In scenes of heaven, John saw the souls of those slaughtered because of their Christian witness. Those souls were told that in a little while, more of their comrades would be killed (Rev 6:9–11). In another scene, a great crowd in heaven stood before the throne and the lamb. They came through the great tribulation, and now praised God day and night before the heavenly throne (Rev 7:9–17). Later, John saw the souls of those beheaded on account of their witness to Jesus. They reigned for one thousand years (20:4). Throughout, the visions are punctuated with phrases such as "blessed are the dead, those who die united with the Lord" (Rev 14:13). In those heavenly scenes, faithful Christians are portrayed as having been under siege, persecuted and martyred.

Historians have also grafted many of the mythic images of evil and terror in the second half of the book (chs. 12–22) onto the ruling powers. When this is done, the seven hills upon which the whore is seated (Rev 17:9) are the seven hills of Rome; therefore, the whore called Babylon is Rome. The seven kings are Roman emperors (17:9–11). The ten kings are native rulers of Rome's client kingdoms (17:12). Fornication and idolatry, images drawn from prophetic sayings in the Old Testament, describe Rome's commercial, economic activity. Participating in the Roman economy is a corrupt business for it requires the stamp of the beast or the number of its name (13:17). The good, heavenly beings in John's visions

---

[6] For more details, see Leonard L. Thompson, *Revelation* (Nashville: Abingdon, 1998), 62–88.

rejoice as they watch Rome burning, for in her was found the blood of prophets and saints (Rev 18:24).

From those visions, historians have concluded that Revelation was written at a time when the emperor and other imperial officials were a threat to faithful Christians. It was a time of radical social disruption and political unrest.[7] About twenty-five years ago, J. A. T. Robinson went so far as to write that if there was no disruption and unrest in the social sphere, then Revelation would have to be "the product of a perfervid and psychotic imagination."[8]

With this assumption that Revelation was written during a time of social conflict, Revelation became a literary tool for Christians to wield during times of crisis. When Avars from the Caucasus attacked Constantinople in the medieval period, they were identified as the antichrist. In the sixteenth century, Luther and Bullinger took to Revelation when faced with Catholic persecution of Protestants. In more recent times various crises and catastrophes have been taken as the context for reading Revelation: nuclear warfare, the Arab-Israeli conflict, the Persian Gulf War, and, after September 11, 2001, Islamic fundamentalism (an ancient theme).

Domitian (according to Eusebius)

If clues from Revelation point to a time of social conflict between Christians and the Roman Empire, then the next step is to identify a time in Roman history when such conflict occurred. Eusebius, who completed his history of the early church around 325 (at least two hundred years after Revelation was written), took that step: John wrote Revelation in the last, tumultuous years of the reign of Emperor Domitian (81–96).[9] Eusebius writes the following:

> Many were the victims of Domitian's appalling cruelty. At Rome great numbers of men distinguished by birth and attainments were executed without a fair trial, and countless other eminent men were for no reason at all banished from the country and their property confiscated. Finally, he showed himself the successor of Nero in enmity and hostility to God [i.e., Christianity]. He was, in fact, the second to organize persecution against us [Christians, second to Nero], though his father Vespasian had

---

[7] The mythic, symbolic nature of John's language leaves open more ambiguity than most historians consider. For more on that language, see the section "The Role of the Spirit and Spirit-Language" in chapter 9, "Spirit Possession: Revelation in Religious Studies," in this volume.

[8] J. A. T. Robinson, *Redating the New Testament* (Philadelphia: Westminster, 1976), 231.

[9] On Eusebius's history, see Robert M. Grant, *Eusebius as Church Historian* (Oxford: Clarendon Press, 1980), 14, 163; also Timothy D. Barnes, *Constantine and Eusebius* (Cambridge: Harvard University Press, 1981), 126–47. Eusebius's final draft of the *History* celebrated the union of church and state under Constantine.

had no mischievous designs against us. Meanwhile, [Christian] tradition relates, the apostle and evangelist John was still alive, and was condemned to dwell on the island of Patmos because of his witness to the divine word. At least Irenaeus, writing about the number of the name . . . [says that John's revelation] was seen not long ago . . . toward the end of the reign of Domitian. (*Hist. Eccl.* 3.17–18, my translation)[10]

Eusebius then goes on to mention that even the Roman historians noted that Flavia Domitilla, a niece of Flavius Clemens, along with many others were sent to the island of Pontia as punishment for their testimony to Christ (*Hist. Eccl.* 3.18).[11]

Although Eusebius's statement, quoted above, appears to be simple and straightforward, it is a complex statement, in which three separate items have been pieced together. All three items were needed before Eusebius could argue that Revelation was written during social upheaval at the end of Domitian's reign.

1. First of all, Eusebius describes Domitian's appalling cruelty toward distinguished, eminent Romans. Here, Eusebius followed the standard portrait of Domitian painted by Pliny the Younger, Pliny's slightly older hunting buddy Cornelius Tacitus (*Ep.* 1.6), and his protégé Gaius Suetonius Tranquillus, all of whom wrote early in the second century after the death of Domitian. Here it is relevant only to note that those historians had their own axes to grind: They hoped for an emperor who would share more power with the senate, another governing body at Rome, than either Domitian or other emperors before him had been willing to share. Pliny and Tacitus, writing at the beginning of Trajan's reign, had hopes that Trajan would be that emperor, and Trajan encouraged them in their hopes. Domitian was not the megalomaniacal tyrant that those historians made him out to be nor were the final years of his reign tumultuous and chaotic. He especially supported the provinces, by opening up senatorial ranks to provincials and protecting provincials from provincial elites and Roman entrepreneurs. One provincial source—recall that John and his first readers lived in an eastern province—described Domitian's reign as "a great kingdom whom all mortals will love" (*Sib. Or.* 12.125–132). In short, Domitian's character and reign were far more abundant, with a mixture of good and bad, than Tacitus, Pliny, and Suetonius portrayed. They strained out that abundance and pre-

---

[10] For the number of the name, see Rev 13:18.

[11] The island parallel between John and Flavia Domitilla is a nice one, but Eusebius incorrectly identifies her as a Christian. Cassius Dio mentions a Flavia Domitilla whose husband was Flavius Clemens, but he identifies her as Jewish, not Christian (67.14.2). As E. M. Smallwood points out, Dio, writing in the early part of the third century, would have known the difference between Jews and Christians; see *The Jews under Roman Rule* (Studies in Judaism in Late Antiquity; Leiden: E. J. Brill, 1981), 382. There she gives a succinct summary of the Domitilla issue.

sented him in the stereotype of a lustful, tyrannical emperor who claimed to be divine.[12]

2. Eusebius linked that description of Domitian's appalling cruelty toward eminent Romans to Domitian's persecution of Christians ("Finally, he showed himself . . ."). Roman historians made no mention of Christian persecution under Domitian, so Eusebius had to turn to Christian writings to establish that point. Toward the end of the second century, Melito of Sardis had written to the emperor Marcus Aurelius, "The only emperors who were ever persuaded by malicious men to slander our teaching were Nero and Domitian, and from them arose the lie, and the unreasonable custom of falsely accusing Christians" (preserved in Eusebius, *Hist. Eccl.* 4.26.9).[13] Then, a few years later, Tertullian wrote an appeal to the magistrates of the Roman Empire: "Consult your histories. There you will find that Nero was the first to rage with imperial sword against this school [Christianity] in the very hour of its rise in Rome. . . . One who knows Nero can understand that, unless a thing were good—and very good—it was not condemned by Nero. Domitian too, who was a good deal of a Nero in cruelty, attempted it" (*Apol.* 5).

Melito and Tertullian traded on the portraits of Nero and Domitian in Roman histories (principally Tacitus and Suetonius) in order to strengthen their defense of Christianity (hence they are called apologists). Neither Marcus Aurelius nor the magistrates should persecute Christians, for the only emperors in the past who did so were the same ones whom your historians condemned. So, says Tertullian, "Consult your histories." He makes his case primarily from Nero, but mentions Domitian at the end. Melito went so far as to argue that Christianity and the empire sprang up and flowered together, so Marcus Aurelius should protect Christians so that both could continue to flourish.[14]

From records such as those of the apologists Tertullian and Melito, Eusebius made his second point, that Domitian persecuted Christians. Later, Eusebius had to grant that Domitian's persecution was not as extensive as Nero's. For Tertullian, one of Eusebius's primary sources, goes on to make the point that Domitian fairly quickly stopped his persecution of

[12] For more details about the historiography surrounding Domitian's reign, see Leonard L. Thompson, *The Book of Revelation: Apocalypse and Empire* (New York: Oxford University Press, 1990), 95–115.

[13] A connection between the reigns of Domitian and Nero had been made previously by Tacitus and Pliny, for their friends who belonged to the "Stoic opposition" to autocratic rule had been either executed or banished by those two emperors (see Tacitus, *Agr.* 45; Pliny, *Ep.* 1). For the lineage of this Stoic opposition, see Betty Radice's introduction in *The Letters of the Younger Pliny,* translated and edited by Betty Radice (Harmondsworth, England: Penguin Books, 1969), 21–23.

[14] Eusebius, *Hist. Eccl.* 4.26. Actually, Jesus' ministry took place under Tiberius, and the Christian church did not spread beyond Syria until the time of Claudius.

Christians. In Tertullian's words, "[B]ut, I believe, inasmuch as he [Domitian] had some intelligence, he quickly stopped it and recalled those whom he had banished" (*Hist. Eccl.* 3.20.7, quoting Tert. *Apol.* 5).[15] According to Eusebius, however, John did not return to Ephesus from banishment on Patmos until the reign of Trajan (*Hist. Eccl.* 3.23). Why didn't John return when Domitian recalled those whom he banished? Eusebius was apparently not troubled by the inconsistencies in his sources.

3. By referring to Roman historians and Christian apologists respectively, Eusebius made two critical points: Domitian was a bad emperor, and he persecuted Christians. Eusebius then added that John was among those persecuted. He does that somewhat awkwardly with a weak connecting word, "meanwhile" (*en toutō*), which functions like the segue in TV westerns, "Meanwhile, back at the ranch": "Meanwhile, [Christian] tradition relates, the apostle and evangelist John was still alive, and was condemned to dwell on the island of Patmos because of his witness to the divine word. At least Irenaeus, writing about the number of the name . . . [says that John's revelation] was seen not long ago . . . towards the end of the reign of Domitian." Irenaeus says nothing about John being persecuted by Domitian; he simply states that John saw his revelation toward the end of Domitian's reign (*Haer.* 5.30.3). Eusebius's first two pieces are essential to establish that John was condemned to dwell on Patmos.

So far as I know, no other writer before Eusebius referred to John's being banished to Patmos by Domitian.[16] In Revelation, John refers to his presence on Patmos as follows: "I, John, your brother and partner, sharing with Jesus tribulation, royalty, and perseverance, was on the isle called Patmos because of the word of God and the witness of Jesus. On the Lord's day, becoming spirit-possessed, I heard behind me a voice . . ." (Rev 1:9–10).[17] Eusebius paraphrases the causal phrase, "because of the word of God and the witness of Jesus," as "because of his witness to the

---

[15] Eusebius records an anecdote from Hegesippus's memoirs (d. 180) that makes the same point (3.19–20).

[16] It is possible that Clement of Alexandria (c. 200) draws on this tradition in a tale (*mythos*) or story (*logos*) about John reclaiming and rebaptizing a young lad who had fallen into a sinful life. Clement says that John did that "after the tyrant's death," when he returned to Ephesus from Patmos (*Quis div.* 42). The tyrant is not named, but Eusebius, who quotes this tale, assumes that it is Domitian (*Hist. Eccl.* 3.23).

[17] For "tribulation" (*thlipsis*), the NRSV translates idiosyncratically "persecution," presumably because the translator thought John and others were being persecuted. Compare other translations that correctly translate the Greek word as "tribulation" (RSV, KJV, ASV); "Trübsal" (Luther); *tribulātio* (Vulgate); "suffering" (Goodspeed, NEB); "sufferings" (JB); "distress" (NAB). Elsewhere in Revelation, *thlipsis* is associated with poverty (2:9–10), the suffering of Jezebel (2:22), and the ordeal undergone by those before the throne (7:13–14). Elsewhere in the NT it is connected to childbirth (John 16:21), marriage (1 Cor 7:28), being an orphan

divine word [that is, his preaching]." An equivalent of Eusebius's paraphrase can be found in most modern handbooks and commentaries.[18]

There are, however, difficulties with that interpretation, given what
we know about Roman law.[19] Being banished to an island was punishment given to the upper classes in lieu of being sent to work in quarries
or mines, or being killed.[20] John did not belong to that group. The
penalty for being a Christian was execution, unless the Christian was a
Roman citizen (see the discussion of Pliny below). Further, Patmos is
never mentioned as an island for exile and was probably not suitable for
such a purpose, for it was not an uninhabited, barren island. It had an active, lively community with a gymnasium and various religious temples.[21]

John simply says that he was in residence there.[22] The causal phrase
can mean that he was there on behalf of "the word of God and the testimony of Jesus," that is, to proclaim it or even to receive it (Rev 1:2).[23] If we
read the rest of the sentence without the baggage of banishment, then we
will assume that John was meeting with a congregation "on the Lord's
Day," the day of Christian worship, for spirit possession occurred in a

---

(James 1:27). At Matt 24:9 it is a sign of the end of the age. At Acts 11:19 it could be
translated as "persecution," though the more generic "trouble" is preferable.

[18] That paraphrase is often justified by appealing to Rev 20:4 and 6:9, where
the causal phrase is connected to the execution of Christians.

[19] For a legal discussion of various forms of exile, see Alan Watson, ed. and
trans., *The Digest of Justinian* (Philadelphia: University of Pennsylvania Press,
1998), 48.22, and John A. Crook, *Law and Life of Rome* (Ithaca, N.Y.: Cornell University Press, 1967), 272–73.

[20] See, for example, Tacitus, *Ann.* 4.30; Crook, *Law and Life*, 273: "Exile in its various forms was on the whole for the upper class, hard labour for the lower. Beyond this came the death penalty. . . ."

[21] Regarding Patmos, see H. D. Saffrey, "Relire L'Apocalypse a Patmos," *RB* 82
(1975): 393–407. When old Serenus was exiled during the reign of Tiberius,
Tiberius rejected the notion of sending him to either Gyaros or Donusa (see Pliny,
Nat. 4.70), for both those islands were waterless, "and if a man were granted his
life he must be allowed the means to live" (Tac. *Ann.* 4.30). So he was returned to
Amorgos, a mountainous island among the Cyclades that at least had a few
towns. For a complete (I think) list of places of exile including islands, see John
Percy Vyvian Dacre Balsdon, *Romans and Aliens* (Chapel Hill: University of North
Carolina Press, 1979), 113–15. H. D. Saffrey refers also to Kinaros as an island of
exile ("Relire").

[22] The Greek phrase translated "was on" (*egenomēn en*) simply indicates that
John resided at Patmos; cf. Matt 26:6; Mark 9:33; Acts 7:38.

[23] Our understanding of the historical situation in which Revelation was written will thus be partially determined by the meaning of a preposition, "because
of" (*dia* + accusative). See Rom 4:25, where "for our trespasses" is retrospective,
while "for our justification" is prospective. At Rev 1:2, John refers to the revelation
that he received as "the word of God and the testimony of Jesus."

congregational setting of worship.[24] While in that setting, John was possessed by the spirit. John was on the island, either visiting a congregation as an itinerant prophet or living there with Christians as a settled, community prophet.[25]

Summary of Eusebius's view. For the reasons given under each of the points above, Eusebius's view is untenable. Domitian was not a mad tyrant. There is little evidence that he persecuted Christians. And the notion that he banished John to the island of Patmos has no credibility. Yet his view persists. Even if historians today reject the notion that Domitian persecuted Christians, the Eusebian influence hovers in the background, as historians continue to place the writing of Revelation toward the end of Domitian's reign because that was a period of crisis and distress for Christians.[26]

Nero

A few historians, recently J. Christian Wilson, place the writing of Revelation around the time of Nero, who, according to early Christian writers, was Domitian's only predecessor in having "enmity and hostility to God."[27] In contrast to Domitian, there can be no doubt about Nero having killed Christians. Not only do Eusebius and Tertullian describe graphically the martyrdoms of Paul and Peter, but Suetonius and Tacitus also describe Nero's persecution of Christians.[28] In a list of novel enactments by Nero, such as restricting food sold in wine shops, Suetonius mentions "punishing Christians, a sect professing a new and mischievous religious

[24] See the section "The Setting of Spirit Possession" in chapter 9, "Spirit Possession," in this volume. Also cf. Acts 11:27; 13:1; 15:32; 21:9–12; 1 Cor 14:26–32; *NHL* VI.6–7; Plut. *Pyth. orac.* 21.

[25] For further discussion of itinerant and community prophets, see below. An intriguing comment toward the end of Revelation suggests that John was there with a circle of prophets and that Jesus sent his angel to them. The comment reads, "I [Jesus is speaking] . . . sent my angel to *you* [plural, not singular] with this testimony for the churches" (Rev 22:16). Such circles of prophets were known in early Christianity. See David E. Aune, *Prophecy in Early Christianity and the Ancient Mediterranean World* (Grand Rapids: Eerdmans, 1983), 197–98. Aune, however, imagines that the other prophets are John's runners to the churches.

[26] Some place Revelation in that period simply because Irenaeus said so, but most do so because they assume some kind of disruption, if not persecution, at that time. See J. Christian Wilson, "The Problem of the Domitianic Date of Revelation," *NTS* 39 (1993): 588–89. See also the review in Thompson, *Book of Revelation*, 202–10.

[27] Wilson, "Problem." In that article Wilson gives a succinct review of scholars who placed John in either Nero's or Domitian's reign.

[28] According to Eusebius, Paul was beheaded and Peter was crucified, upside down, in Rome during Nero's reign (*Hist. Eccl.* 2.25.5; 3.1.2). Cf. Tertullian, *Praescr.* 36.

belief" (*Nero* 16). Tacitus is ghoulish in his detail about how Nero dressed Christians in animal skins and then had them torn to pieces by dogs or crucified them or made them into torches to be ignited after dark (*Ann.* 15.44). Both Roman historians were concerned to portray the brutishness and barbarity of Nero (not the plight of Christians), so as to make him, like Domitian, a stock figure in their histories of the empire. So Wilken comments about Tacitus: "Tacitus's account tells us more about Roman attitudes in his own time, the early second century, than it does about the misfortunes of Christians during Nero's reign."[29]

In addition, there can be no doubt that during the years 68–69, Rome was in turmoil. With rebellion in both the senate and the army, Nero committed suicide midyear in 68 C.E. and ended the Julio-Claudian dynasty. For a few months, Galba was emperor, having come from his governorship in northern Spain. After being lynched by his household troops, Galba was replaced by Otho, who had been governor in another part of Spain. Otho lasted four months before committing suicide in July 69, as his rival, Vitellius, marched into Italy from his post in Germania, east of the Rhine River. Troops in the eastern end of the empire, however, supported Vespasian. By December, the army supporting Vespasian attacked Rome, overcame all resistance, and dragged Vitellius through the streets to his death.

Persecution of a few Christians at Rome and turmoil in the capital and some of the western provinces did not, however, affect John and other Christians in Asia. Nero's last years had little impact on the eastern provinces, nor did the successive reigns of emperors in 69. Mucianus probably passed through Asia, as he collected troops in support of Vespasian, on his way to Rome, but, otherwise, the contenders to the throne did not come from the east nor did they do battle in that geographical area. Tacitus says that Asia was "upset by a false alarm. It was rumoured that Nero was on his way to them" (*Hist.* 2.8). Perhaps that is how John knew of the story of the return of Nero. In any case, I do not find Bell's statement convincing that John would have seen 68–69 as a time of universal chaos in which the Roman Empire would come to an end and God's kingdom would be inaugurated.[30]

Summary

John's portrait of Christian persecution in Revelation cannot be satisfactorily correlated with the reign of either Domitian or Nero. That Nero and Domitian are still the historians' reigns of choice reflects the shadow of Eusebius and the Christian apologists who emphasized that *only* those two emperors treated Christians badly—that, in spite of the fact that

---

[29] Robert L. Wilken, *The Christians as the Romans Saw Them* (New Haven: Yale University Press, 1984), 49.

[30] See Albert A. Bell, Jr., "The Date of John's Apocalypse: The Evidence of Some Roman Historians Reconsidered," *NTS* 25 (1978): 102.

Christians were killed under Trajan (see below). In fact, those two reigns differed little from the reigns of other Roman emperors in the first 120 years of Christianity. Only subtle differences distinguished emperors and dynasties in their shifting mix of liberty and stability, of republican forms and imperial control. Nor did Domitian and Nero differ from other emperors in their attitude toward Christianity. All of them considered Christianity a fanatical superstition whose members were hated for their abominations and perversity. *The solution to John's portrait of Rome in Revelation must be found within normal, not abnormal times, in established policies of the empire toward Christianity, not in eccentricities of a particular emperor.*

Rome's Double-Edged Policy toward Christians

The earliest evidence for an established, official Roman policy on Christianity comes from correspondence between Pliny the Younger and the emperor Trajan. Pliny was on special envoy in the area of Bithynia and Pontus, provinces in Asia Minor just north of Asia. (Young Suetonius was probably with him.) Pliny was very cautious about doing anything without checking first with Trajan, so book 10 of *The Letters* contains approximately sixty queries to the emperor and sixty replies on a whole range of topics.

Around 112 at either Amisus or Amastris on the Black Sea in Bithynia, Pliny writes to Trajan about Christians: "I have never been present at an examination of Christians. Consequently, I do not know the nature or the extent of the punishments usually meted out to them" (*Ep.* 10.96.1). Pliny explains that he has had several people brought before him accused of being a Christian. Should he treat them all alike? Some had renounced their faith, having ceased being Christians two or more years previously. What should be done with them? Is the name "Christian" itself punishable or must the person also be associated with some crime? Pliny then explains to Trajan that for the moment he has killed those who would not deny their faith, unless they were Roman citizens. They were being sent to Rome for trial. In Pliny's judgment, the "stubbornness and unshakeable obstinacy" of Christians should not go unpunished. Finally, Pliny indicates that he has received an anonymous pamphlet containing the names of accused persons. What should he do with that?

In letter 97 of book 10, Trajan responded: Pliny, you were right in handling separately persons charged with being Christians. There is no uniform rule. Further, Christians should not be hunted down. But if charges are made properly and proven before you, then Christians must be punished simply for being Christians. (Trajan does not indicate what the punishment should be, nor does he comment on Pliny's actions.) Those who deny being Christians and prove it by worshiping "our gods" should be pardoned, however suspect their past conduct. Finally, Pliny, do not take into account evidence submitted anonymously in pamphlets. "They create the worst sort of precedent and are quite out of keeping with the spirit of our age" (10.97). Trajan's official response (rescript), not Pliny's actions, established Roman policy.[31] It is the first imperial statement regarding Christians that we know of, though he does not seem to be instituting a new policy. Much the same policy was probably in effect during Domitian's reign, perhaps earlier.

That policy had a double edge. On the one hand, Christians were not hunted down. They were tried only if accusations from local provincials were brought against them. But if accused and convicted, then Christians who were not Roman citizens were killed simply for being Christians. That was more or less the policy of Rome through the second century. Tertullian, the ex-lawyer and defender of Christianity, writing at the end of the second century, seized upon the contradiction in Trajan's rescript: "He [Trajan] says they must not be sought out, implying they are innocent; and he orders them to be punished, implying they are guilty. . . . If you condemn them, why not hunt them down? If you do not hunt them down, why not also acquit them?" (*Apol.* 2.8).

This policy had a double effect for Christians. On the one hand, a Christian could live a normal, ordinary life in the empire for years, sometimes all of his life. She could buy and sell as a merchant of wares. He could work at a craft alongside non-Christians. Christians could live quietly and cordially among neighbors in apartment complexes without harassment. On the other hand, if someone chose to bring charges against them, they most likely would be tried and executed. Some could travel throughout the empire, taking advantage of its peace and prosperity, visiting and founding Christian congregations. Others might immediately be viewed with suspicion and killed by officials of that same empire. Thus, some could view the Roman Empire as a source of divine blessing, while others could see it as an evil power destroying the godly. Every Christian, however, would be more or less aware of the contingency of life.

Consider Ignatius of Antioch. At the beginning of the second century,

---

[31] Both *rescripta* and *decreta* had the status of pronouncements of the emperor (*constitutiones principis*) and the force of law; see Barry Nicholas, *An Introduction to Roman Law* (Oxford: Clarendon Press, 1962), 17–18; John A. Crook, *Law and Life of Rome* (Ithaca, N.Y.: Cornell University Press, 1967), 20–22. Note that Trajan's rescript makes no mention of offering wine and incense to his statue, which Pliny had required (10.96.5). The issue was worship of "our gods," not of the emperor. The importance of emperor worship for early Christianity has been overstated in many commentaries and handbooks. R. M. Grant suggests that Pliny's use of the emperor's statue may have been Pliny's own "ad hoc procedure" (*Greek Apologists of the Second Century* [Philadelphia: Westminster, 1988], 30). Grant also notes parallels between Pliny's procedures and treatment of Bacchanalia (29, 203–5). John of Revelation deliberately opposes the sovereignty of Christian divinities to that of the empire in order to make his case that Christians must choose one or the other.

he traveled through Asia in chains on his way to Rome and presumably martyrdom. He stayed at Smyrna, from there writing to churches at Ephesus, Magnesia, Tralles, as well as Rome. Later, at Troas, he wrote back to churches at Philadelphia and Smyrna. He engaged in all this Christian activity while under arrest. The guards were apparently indifferent to the Christians that they met.

Or consider Polycarp, who was executed around 150 in Smyrna. He had been living there for eighty-six years as a Christian (presumably all his life). Moreover, he was well-known in the area, a leader of the church, and probably a man of some wealth. He would have been about four years old at the end of Nero's reign, six years old when the temple was destroyed in Jerusalem, thirty-one years old at the end of Domitian's reign, forty-eight years old when Pliny under Trajan was killing Christians in Bithynia. Thirty-eight more years passed before he was tried and executed for his Christian faith during the reign of Antoninus Pius (138–61).

The Benign Edge of Rome's Knife: Ordinary Life in Asian Cities

The cities of Asia were good places for Christians to live. They were large, diverse cultural centers in the Roman Empire. Ephesus had a population of more than two hundred thousand people, while Smyrna, Pergamum, and Sardis were roughly half that size. Located strategically on roadways and shipping lanes that extended eastward into Syria, Palestine, Armenia, and the Parthian Empire and westward into Thrace, Macedonia, Greece, and Italy, the cities attracted an ethnically diverse population from all those areas as well as constant movement of traders, merchants, and shipmasters. The cities were also rich in religious diversity. Indigenous gods combined with Greek or Roman deities. Temples to Asclepius, the god of healing, present in virtually every city, also housed shrines to Isis and Serapis from Egypt. The Greek goddess Artemis joined with the Persian Anaitis. In most of the cities there was a large Jewish community.

Asia was also a wealthy area, rich in natural resources, commerce, and manufacturing.[32] The textile industry flourished in most of the cities. Crafts were practiced by free men, not slaves. The cities offered opportunities for leather workers, tanners, shoemakers, linen weavers, dyers, and wool workers, as well as potters, bakers, and coppersmiths.[33] The cities also supported architects, physicians, teachers, lawyers, actors, and performers. Wealth is never equally divided, but the wealthy in the cities were obliged to support civic well-being through grants, foundations, and city governance. Shop owners, retail traders, money changers, crafts-

---

[32] River valleys provided rich land for agricultural crops; forests were harvested for wood; there were rich veins of copper, iron, salt, and marble. See T. R. S. Broughton, "Roman Asia," in *An Economic Survey of Ancient Rome* (ed. Tenney Frank; Baltimore: Johns Hopkins University Press, 1938), 607–26.

[33] Ibid., 817–30.

men, along with teachers and doctors, were able to ply their trades successfully. And free laborers could go on strike or slowdowns when they were not fairly compensated.[34] Relatively speaking, there was a minimum amount of conflict between the wealthy and the poor.

The cities also had good relations with Rome and imperial authorities. No Roman legions were ever posted there. Rome benefited from Asia's wealth, and in times of calamities, such as earthquakes, imperial authorities helped the cities rebuild. The governor of Asia, as well occasional envoys sent out by an emperor, protected all residents of a city from local aristocratic oppression or irresponsibility on the part of the wealthy. The government of the empire was, thus, popular among the lower classes, and it was the avenue for greater prestige among wealthy provincials.[35]

In that economically and politically stable province—especially in the cities diverse in ethnicity, wealth, and religion—Christianity flourished. Traveling craftsmen who were followers of this new way infiltrated the area during the middle of the first Christian century; the most important such traveler was Paul, who spent a few years in Ephesus and wrote at least some of the Corinthian correspondence from there. The apostle John came to be associated with Ephesus as well.[36] And Peter (or someone writing in his name) addressed Christians in "Pontus, Galatia, Cappadocia, Asia, and Bithynia" (1 Pet 1:1). In a real sense, Asia became the second cradle of Christianity.

Christianity was, thus, well established in Asia before John wrote to the seven churches. Christians in those churches reflected the diversity present in the cities. Slaves, those freed from slavery, and those born free, with or without spouses, joined men and women more and less financially successful in trades and possibly professions. In a rare instance, there even may have been a wealthy city magistrate. Ethnic diversity reflected the demographics of the cities, with a higher proportion of Jews in the churches than in the cities.[37] In the Letter to the Colossians (near Laodicea), there is reference to "Greek and Jew, circumcised and uncircumcised, barbarian, Scythian, slave and free" (Col 3:11). J. Nelson Kraybill has shown that Christian provincials engaging in commerce included Lydia of Thyatira; Paul of Tarsus, tent maker and leather worker; Phoebe, a deacon of the church at Cenchreae (Rom 16:1); Hermas, a freedman

---

[34] Ibid., 841.

[35] See Thompson, *Book of Revelation*, 154–58.

[36] The three epistles under the name of John were probably written from Ephesus at the end of the first or the beginning of the second century. For John at Ephesus, see Helmut Koester, "Gnomai Diaphoroi: The Origin and Nature of Diversification in the History of Early Christianity," in *Trajectories through Early Christianity*, ed. James M. Robinson and Helmut Koester (Philadelphia: Fortress, 1971), 154–55.

[37] See Carolyn Osiek, "House Churches and the Demographics of Diversity," *Religious Studies Review* 27 (July 2001): 228–29.

possibly of some wealth (*Herm. Sim.* 1.1); and Marcion, a wealthy ship-master.[38]

In their diversity, Christian churches were, thus, similar to a private religious association in Philadelphia in which, according to an inscription from the first pre-Christian century, Zeus commanded a householder to grant access "to his own house both to free men and women, and to household slaves" to worship at "the altars of Zeus," if they were "conscious of no guile toward man or woman" nor given "any philter or any abortive or contraceptive drug."[39]

Christians also met together in houses.[40] There they listened to Revelation being read (Rev 1:3). Sometimes, perhaps often, the householder served as a kind of patron of the church. Among those coming to the house church were members of the family and—for a wealthy householder—slaves, servants, laborers, freedmen, other tenants, and even business associates. Others would join that nucleus.[41] So at the church in Colossae (near Laodicea), Paul addressed one of his letters to Philemon, Apphia, and Archippus (those of Philemon's family) and "the church in your house" (Phlm 2). If the householder was wealthy, then the house was freestanding. If not so wealthy, Christians met in apartment complexes.[42]

In large cities, more than one house church could exist. Paul's greeting to the Christians at Laodicea suggests more than one house church there: "Give my greetings to the brothers and sisters in Laodicea, and to Nympha and the church in her house" (Col 4:15). Members of separate house churches were linked by their common Christian beliefs, but some conflicts among Christians in a particular city, reflected possibly in Rev 2–3, could arise among house churches.

With much the same demographics as the population in the cities, members of the seven churches also carried on a style of life similar to that of non-Christians. They did not live in small, divine enclaves, separate from the rest of the world. As in urban Corinth, non-Christians came to Christian meetings, and Christians ate dinner with non-Christians in, for example, guild meetings of their trade.

[38] J. Nelson Kraybill, *Imperial Cult and Commerce in John's Apocalypse* (JSNTSup; Sheffield: JSOT, 1996), 94–101.

[39] *SIG* 985. Translation in Frederick C. Grant, ed. and trans., *Hellenistic Religions: The Age of Syncretism* (Indianapolis: Bobbs-Merrill, 1953), 28–30.

[40] Christians also sometimes rented halls or warehouses to meet in. See Acts 19:9.

[41] See Abraham J. Malherbe, *Social Aspects of Early Christianity* (Philadelphia: Fortress, 1983), 69.

[42] At Ephesus there were multiple dwellings constructed in the first Christian century. Some of them were above shops that faced the street. Perhaps some Christians met in that apartment building (*insula*). See David C. Verner, *The Household of God: The Social World of the Pastoral Epistles* (SBLDS; Chico, Calif.: Scholars Press, 1983), 58–59.

So the anonymous writer of the Epistle to Diognetus, writing in defense of Christians sometime in the second century, says: "They do not dwell in cities in some place of their own . . . nor do they live lives out of the ordinary. . . . [They follow] local customs, both in clothing and food and in the rest of life" (*Diogn.* 5).[43] There were important differences: Christians were intolerant in their worship of only one god, and some of their moral codes were different from others, but, as R. M. Grant notes, "the differences must not blind us to the general coincidence between the life-styles and attitudes of non-Christians and Christians alike."[44]

The Threatening Edge of Rome's Policy: John's Position

Although the cities of Asia were some of the best places for Christians to live, they did not all experience the same freedom from fear and danger or from accusations of being Christians. Moreover, not all viewed Roman authorities with the same level of tolerance. If Antipas was executed at Pergamum for being a Christian, those present at his death viewed the Roman Empire differently from a Lydia from Thyatira who enjoyed the peace of the empire as she traveled around selling purple dyes (Acts 16:14, 40).

Other factors than social experience entered in.[45] The theology of some Christians, such as John, emphasized imitating Christ's suffering and death more than that of other theologies. Ignatius also seemed especially eager to follow Jesus in being killed.[46] Those factors fed on each other: Theological understanding shaped social experience, just as social experience shaped theological understanding. From Revelation it seems likely that John saw Rome as an evil, satanic empire opposed to the divine forces of the church, eager to destroy those who followed Jesus. In response, Christians were urged to avoid participating in the economy and society of Rome. In fact, John condemned such participation (Rev 18:4). Christ's crucifixion and resurrection gave Christians the pattern: Victory would come through suffering and death. Christians should willingly die at the hands of Roman authorities, though John does not suggest that Christians seek death out.

Probably John's social experience, as well as his theology, contributed to his attitude toward Rome. If John was in Palestine during the Jewish

[43] See also Tertullian, *Apol.* 2.

[44] Robert M. Grant, "The Social Setting of Second-Century Christianity," in *Jewish and Christian Self-Definition* (vol. 1, ed. E. P. Sanders; Philadelphia: Fortress, 1980), 29.

[45] Psychological makeup no doubt also varied from person to person. About that we have no information.

[46] See Ign. *Rom.* 4.1–2: "Suffer me to be eaten by the beasts, through whom I can attain to God. I am God's wheat, and I am ground by the teeth of wild beasts that I may be found pure bread of Christ. Rather entice the wild beasts that they may become my tomb."

uprising against Rome in 66–70, as Eusebius and more recent historians have assumed, his experience of the Roman authorities there could have shaped his attitude toward them after he migrated to Asia.[47] In response to that uprising, the Roman army under Vespasian, and later under his son, Titus, destroyed Jerusalem and razed the sacred Jewish temple. Although Christians tended to see that destruction as divine judgment on the Jews for not accepting Jesus as the Christ, John—especially if he were a convert from Judaism—could well have been profoundly disturbed by Rome's apparent insensitivity to the sacred city and its temple.

John's role as a Christian itinerant prophet may also have shaped his negative attitude toward Rome.[48] It placed him socially on the periphery, outside the civic order.[49] John, like other prophets, had voluntarily relinquished "property, work, and income" and depended upon the hospitality of Christian communities that he visited.[50] Those communities buffered John from direct engagement in the economy and society of a city (in either Palestine or Asia). An itinerant prophet stayed long enough in a congregation to know something about the leadership, factions, if any, and the social makeup of the congregation. That is the type of knowl-

---

[47] So Eusebius (*Hist. Eccl.* 3.1). See also R. H. Charles, *A Critical and Exegetical Commentary on the Revelation of St. John* (ICC; Edinburgh: T. & T. Clark, 1920), 1:xliv, and Elisabeth Schüssler Fiorenza, "Apokalypsis and Propheteia: Revelation in the Context of Early Christian Prophecy," in *The Book of Revelation: Justice and Judgment* (ed. Elisabeth Schüssler Fiorenza; Philadelphia: Fortress, 1985), 140–42.

[48] Though John never explicitly states that he is a Christian prophet, he writes words of prophecy (1:3; 10:11) and the prophets are his brothers (22:9). It is unlikely that he was one of the twelve apostles, even though Justin Martyr (*Dial.* 81), Irenaeus (*Adv. Haer.* 4.20.11), and Eusebius (*Hist. Eccl.* 3.18.1) assumed that he was. Bishop Dionysius of Alexandria (d. 264/5), however, concluded that Revelation was "the work of some holy and inspired person," but that John was not an apostle (Eusebius, *Hist. Eccl.* 7.24.7). Most scholars today agree with Bishop Dionysius. At Rev 21:14, the author sees twelve foundation stones of the new Jerusalem upon which are written "the twelve names of the twelve apostles of the lamb." That way of referring to the twelve apostles suggests that John of Revelation was not one of them. In 1 Corinthians and Ephesians, prophets are ranked second only to apostles (1 Cor 12:28–31; Eph 2:20; 3:5; 4:11). At Rev 18:20, saints and apostles and prophets are referred to together, though not identified as the same group. In the *Didache* there seems to be some confusion between apostles (not the twelve) and prophets, for itinerant apostles who do not follow the rules are called false prophets (11.3–6).

[49] Most, but not all, visionaries live on the periphery of society, where they challenge the central values transmitted by institutions at the center.

[50] Bengt Holmberg, *Sociology and the New Testament* (Minneapolis: Fortress, 1990), 53. Also Gerd Theissen, *Sociology of Early Palestinian Christianity* (trans. John Bowden; Philadelphia: Fortress, 1978), 8–16. Matthew 10:41 mentions itinerant prophets. Compare Mark 6:6–13; Luke 10:1–12. The *Didache* refers to itinerant teachers, prophets, apostles, and other travelers (11–12). Revelation 2:2 refers to itinerant apostles, not to the twelve.

edge reflected in Rev 2–3. John does not indicate an intimate knowledge and personal engagement with a congregation such as Paul had. Although prophets were treated with great respect—Paul says they are second only to apostles (1 Cor 12:28)—their message had to be assessed, for sometimes it was false.[51]

Christian prophets could also be a settled member of a particular community, though they might prophesy outside that community (see Acts 11:27; 15:32; 21:9–12). In the *Didache,* an early-second-century manual for churches, directives are given for receiving an itinerant prophet into the community as a permanent member: "Every true prophet wishing to settle among you is worthy of his food. . . . they are your high priests. But if you do not have a prophet, give to the poor" (13.1–4). So a prophet could be an itinerant and then a settled community prophet. John was probably an itinerant prophet, though, as mentioned above, he may have settled in a Christian community on Patmos.

Whatever social and theological forces contributed to John's view, the double-edged policy of Roman authorities gave credibility to his position.[52] Anyone could be charged with being a Christian at any time, and the authorities executed those charged and found guilty. That was a reality that all Christians had to recognize. At the same time, those settled in the cities who made a living by "buying and selling," participating in the peace and prosperity of the empire and using their connections for spreading the Christian faith, would discount John's judgment that they carried the "mark of the beast," subject to evil Rome (Rev 13:17).

Consequences: John's Opposition to Settled Householders

Conflict between John and several of the settled householders in the Asian cities was inevitable, and it was a conflict that could have occurred at any time between 70 and 120. We see that conflict clearly in the messages to the separate churches recorded in chapters 2 and 3 of Revelation. The speaker exhorts Christians at Ephesus to keep to the exclusivism that they had at first.[53] Those at Smyrna and Philadelphia are praised for their poverty and powerlessness. To the former, Jesus, through John, says, "Be faithful until death, and I will give you the crown of life" (2:10); to the latter, "Because you have kept my word of patient endurance, I will keep you from the hour of trial that is coming on the whole world" (3:10).

---

[51] Cf., for example, Matt 7:15–20; 24:11, 24; 2 Pet 2:1; 1 John 4:1; *Did.* 11.7–12.

[52] There is no need to complicate the situation by importing problematic terms from sociology (perceived crisis, relative deprivation) or rhetoric (rhetorical situation different from the historical situation).

[53] They "abandoned the love" that they first had (2:4). Love expresses loyalty and attachment to Christ and the brothers and sisters, and detachment and aversion to those outside "our group" (cf. Rev 3:9). So it was at Qumran, "to love everything which [God] selects and to hate everything that he rejects; in order to keep . . . from all evil" (1QS 1.4).

Those at Laodicea were rich and prosperous, but, from John's and Jesus' point of view, they should be carrying on trade with Christ, not others (3:18).

At Pergamum and Thyatira, conflict occurred between the prophet John and other prophetic circles that he names Nicolaitans, followers of Balaam, and Jezebel.[54] If they were separate groups, they shared common views. The fundamental conflict is predictable: Should one participate in the economy and society of the empire, or is the empire an evil power against God that should be shunned by Christians?

John carries on that debate in what may appear to be odd terms: eating food offered to idols and practicing fornication (2:14, 20). Since meat in public civic gatherings, guild meetings of crafts, and private homes of non-Christians would be offered in sacrifice to local deities, those who participated in the economy and society of the cities and empire would inevitably find themselves in situations where they would eat such meat. The phrase "practicing fornication" refers not to sexual activity but to idolatry. It is another phrase that John uses to indict prophetic circles and other members of the seven churches for participating in civic and imperial society.[55]

John took the view of Christ *against* culture. Christians should withdraw from Roman imperial society in order to participate in the true imperium of God and his Christ enthroned in heaven (Rev 4–5). The enthroned Christ presently hovered close to Christians. They met him in worship and communicated with him through spirit possession (mediated through a prophet). Moreover, he will soon come down upon the earth with "the armies of heaven . . . to strike down the nations, and he will rule them with a rod of iron" (19:14–15). Then he will establish a true and righteous kingdom around the new Jerusalem (21:1–22:5).

John's emphasis on the imminent return of Jesus Christ is linked to

[54] We know nothing about the Nicolaitans, unless the name refers to followers of Nicolaus (Acts 6:5), who, according to Irenaeus, went astray (*Adv. Haer.* 1.26.3). John associates them with the Balaamites (Rev 2:14–15). Balaam caused the Israelites to go astray at Shittim by having sexual relations with the women of Moab and participating in the sacrifices of their gods (Num 31:16; 25:1–2; also Josephus, *Ant.* 4.137). He is referred to positively as well as negatively in later literature, so a prophetic school could have taken his name; see Thompson, *Revelation*, 71–72. Jezebel was the foreign wife of King Ahab (1 Kgs 16:31) and a follower of the god Baal. Her fornications involved not her sex life but her idolatry. See 2 Kgs 9:22; also Lev 17:7; Deut 31:16; Jer 2. It is possible that the different prophetic circles were attached to different house churches in those cities. Unfortunately, we know little about the relationship of the two.

[55] See chapter 4, "Wolves in Sheep's Clothing," and the discussion in Paul B. Duff, *Who Rides the Beast: Prophetic Rivalry and the Rhetoric of Crisis in the Churches of the Apocalypse* (New York: Oxford University Press, 2001), 51–59. He discusses alimentary and reproductive activities in Revelation more generally in chapter 8 of that book, in connection with gender stereotypes.

his condemnation of those who participated in the economy and society of the Roman Empire. At the end of Revelation, Christ says, "I am coming soon; my reward is with me, to repay according to everyone's work. . . . Blessed are those who wash their robes so that they will have the right to the tree of life and may enter the city [the new Jerusalem] by the gates" (22:12–14). Those who "wash their robes" have "made them white in the blood of the Lamb" (7:14). The Roman officials who kill Christians, when provincials have brought charges, are playing into the divine plan and hastening the return of Christ.

However contradictory the symbolism may be, Rome was the satanic beast who, by killing Christians, opened the way to Christian victory. In other words, Rome's proper role in the economy of God was to hold the dangerous edge of the double-edged knife over Christians. Therefore, Christians should not assimilate and acculturate to Roman ways. By participating in the Roman economy and Roman society, those Christians were implicitly denying the time of the end. Though their participation might allow them to attract others to Christianity, their actions implied ongoing history and normal times, an impossibility for John.

Conclusion

In a story that includes the abundance of history, no one actor can be identified as the moral center, as, for example, Eumaios the swineherd is in *The Odyssey*. Accounts of historical events are not crafted like epic narratives. The events are more happenstance and the actors more ambiguous. In the Book of Revelation, we hear from John's Christ. If we had prophecy from the woman John calls Jezebel, we would hear a different message. Abundance brings ambiguity, an ambiguity that John and the later process of canonization filtered out. In the New Testament, John is privileged over Jezebel. In Thyatira at that time, however, there was no New Testament. Prophetic authority alone legitimated those who opposed Roman society (John) and those who accommodated it ("Jezebel").

As with all young, grassroots organizations, the congregations in Asia had to strike a balance between maintaining high, impenetrable boundaries between themselves and non-Christians, on the one hand (John), and allowing social intercourse with non-Christians through lower, more porous boundaries, on the other ("Jezebel"). The former was necessary for group identity and religious solidarity. The latter was a necessity for pursuing craft and labor or food and dress in an urban setting. Both were essential for the survival of the congregations.

John's exclusivism kept religious identity in a prominent position. He reminded those who gathered in the house churches that they participated with angels in the heavenly court (cf. Rev 4–5) and that they were "looking for the city that is to come" (Heb 13:14). Rome was the wrong city; it was under the control of Satan. Christians must "come out" from her. John heightened their sense of identity and separation from the rest of the world by warning them of the imminent coming of Christ (Rev 2:5, 16, 21–23; 3:10–11, 16). John also gave theological significance to the negative edge of Rome's double-edged policy toward Christianity. Jesus gave the pattern to follow: victory through suffering and death.

Most Christians, however, had to live and work in the society and economy of the city and the empire. Moreover, that was not simply a necessary evil. According to other Christian writers, they were to "shine like stars in the world." They were to live as "children of God without blemish" (Phil 2:15). They should gently and reverently give a defense of their faith "to anyone who demands" (1 Pet 3:15).

If the end had come soon after John wrote Revelation, then his isolationism and opposition to the Roman Empire would have been vindicated. But it did not. History in its abundance continued and continues on. And eventually Christianity conquered Rome. The ordinary Christian effected that conquest. As Ernest Colwell observed some time ago, that triumph by the ordinary Christian "was made possible by their *failure* to live as separately and aloof as [many of] their leaders desired" (my emphasis).[56] In other words, were it not for the Jezebels and Balaamites and Nicolaitans who accommodated to the Roman world, shared life with non-Christians, and risked the wrath of their neighbors, Christianity might have disappeared from the Roman world.

The Roman authorities had their own reasons to be suspicious of Christianity: To them it seemed a deadly, wicked superstition, and its followers showed disdain and hatred toward the human race (Tacitus, *Ann.* 15.44; Suetonius, *Nero* 16.2). That is, Christians opposed the true gods who were the foundation of life and peace in the empire. Aelius Aristides put it well: As Zeus banished "faction, uproar, and disorder" when he began his rule, so when Rome began to rule, "confusion and faction ceased and there entered in universal order and a glorious light in life and government and the laws came to the fore and the altars of the gods were believed in" (*Oration* 26). By refusing to acknowledge Zeus and the other deities, Christians opposed that "universal order" and "glorious light in life." If they had their way, "confusion and faction" would once again rule. Thus, their "obstinacy and unbending perversity" deserved punishment (Pliny, *Ep.* 10.96). (John of course called that "steadfast endurance.") For more than two centuries, however, the authorities were tolerant and non-interventional. They allowed Christians to live peacefully and successfully in the empire, so long as charges were not brought against them.

I suggested at the beginning of this chapter that if I told the story really well and as truthfully as I could, then you would feel "a sense of spontaneous tolerance" toward all the actors: Romans, John, and "Jezebel." You may now also feel a sense of spontaneous frustration. You

---

[56] Ernest Cadman Colwell, "Popular Reactions against Christianity in the Roman Empire," in *Environmental Factors in Christian History* (ed. John Thomas McNeill et al.; Chicago: University of Chicago Press, 1939), 70.

may want the abundance and ambiguity strained out, so that the good guys are visible in their white hats and the bad guys are recognizable by the way they slouch and sneer. Stories like that are readily available, especially in the form of novels. But they are not truthful. They strain out too much of history's abundance and do not adequately encompass the range of interests among the actors. They make moral judgments, but the judgments are flawed because the story is flawed. I have offered an alternative. The times in which John wrote, as in all real life, were filled with an abundance, with actors and situations in which the good and the bad were mixed together. Sometimes, even, those speaking for God confused God's voice with their own interests. That alternative is admittedly more demanding of one's attention and thoughts. Moral judgments are made less easily, but that vision of the world and of the people in it is finally richer and more truthful.

3

The Beast from the Land

REVELATION 13:11–18 AND SOCIAL SETTING

Steven J. Friesen

Few texts have excited human imaginations like the Revelation of John. Nearly two millennia after its composition it continues to stimulate controversies, debates, analysis, and interpretation. One of the text's most celebrated characters is the beast from the land of Rev 13:11–18. The beast is described as having two horns like a lamb but a voice like the ancient dragon Satan (Rev 12). The beast from the land makes great signs and deceives the inhabitants of earth, causing them to worship the seven-headed beast from the sea, the great opponent of God and God's followers on earth.

Who or what does this beast from the land represent? Was it part of John's first-century world? Is it an abiding presence throughout history? Or will it be revealed in the future, at the end of the world? I accept the conclusion of most scholars that the beast from the land can be understood as a reference to the worship of the Roman emperors. The imagery does not require us to adopt a futuristic reading of the beast as an ecumenical spokesman who will appear in Israel and urge all the world to worship the antichrist.[1] Nor does the imagery require us to suppose that

---

[1] For popularizing interpretations, see Hal Lindsey, *The Late Great Planet Earth* (Grand Rapids: Zondervan, 1970), 111–13; Tim LaHaye, *Revelation Illustrated and Made Plain* (Grand Rapids: Zondervan, 1976), 184–89. LaHaye is also coauthor with Jerry B. Jenkins of the multivolume, mega-hit "Left Behind" series. Some specialists agree with this position in broad outline: Ernst Lohmeyer, *Die Offenbarung des Johannes* (2d ed.; HNT 16; Tübingen: J. C. B. Mohr [Paul Siebeck], 1953), 114–17; John F. Walvoord, *The Revelation of Jesus Christ* (Chicago: Moody Press, 1966), 197–98, 204–12; George Eldon Ladd, *A Commentary on the Revelation of John* (Grand Rapids: Eerdmans, 1972), 177, 183; Robert L. Thomas, *Revelation: An Exegetical Commentary* (2 vols.; Chicago, Moody Press, 1992), 2:154, 173.

the beast from the land represents an abiding presence in history such as the papacy of the Roman Catholic Church.[2] Most scholars conclude that the beast from the land is related in some way to the worship of the Roman emperors (also known as "imperial cults") and that this avenue provides a path to understanding.

The problem with the scholarly consensus is that it remains too vague about the connection between the beastly image and the worship of the Roman emperors. In this chapter I argue that close attention to the evidence from the social world of Revelation produces a more precise interpretation, because a better understanding of John's social setting allows us to understand better the text John wrote in that setting. The first section of this chapter provides an overview of the main imperial cult institutions in Roman Asia, the province in which John's audience lived. This lays the groundwork for the second section, which gives specific examples of the ways that imperial cults functioned in John's world and the people who were prominent in such institutions. This review allows us to name the beast (section three) and to understand more clearly the disturbing character of John's imagery.

Imperial Cults in Roman Asia: A Summary

The worship of political leaders is an unfamiliar phenomenon to most people in the English-speaking world. It is a fairly common phenomenon in some parts of the world, however, both in the present and at other periods in history.[3] This unfamiliarity has made it difficult for scholars in secularized Western societies to understand the significance of ancient imperial cults. There is a long tradition of Western scholars denouncing imperial cults in many ways. They have described them as everything from shameless flattery offered by subject peoples, to cynical legitimization by tyrants to support oppressive rule.

Such negative appraisals of imperial cults were scrutinized and rejected by Simon Price in the early 1980s.[4] He provided a general approach that emphasized the symbolic value of imperial cults in a polytheistic setting. He argued that the modern Western tendency of separating religion

---

[2] This is the position of some Protestant commentators, such as R. C. H. Lenski, *The Interpretation of St. John's Revelation* (Columbus, Ohio: Warburg, 1943), 388, 394, 413; and Carl M. Zorn, *Die Offenbarung St. Johannis* (Zwickau, Germany: Johannes Herrmann, 1910), 195–99.

[3] For example, see Clifford Geertz, *Negara: The Theater State in Nineteenth-Century Bali* (Princeton, N.J.: Princeton University Press, 1980); Valerio Valeri, *Kingship and Sacrifice: Ritual and Society in Ancient Hawaii* (Chicago: University of Chicago Press, 1985); Jacob Olupona, *Kingship, Religion, and Rituals in a Nigerian Community: A Phenomenological Study of Ondo Yoruba Festivals* (Stockholm Studies in Comparative Religion 28; Stockholm: Almqvist & Wiksell, 1991).

[4] S. R. F. Price, *Rituals and Power: The Roman Imperial Cult in Asia Minor* (New York: Cambridge University Press, 1984), 9–22.

and politics is inappropriate for a study of the Roman empire. Both religion and politics are ways of systematically constructing power. Thus we should not discount the worship of the Roman emperors as an inferior form of religion, nor as a covert form of politics. Imperial cults were a crucial expression of the significance of the emperor. Through these rituals the Greek subjects of the empire created a symbolization of the emperor in their own terms. The use of divine rituals, images, architecture, and vocabulary helped the subject peoples make sense of a foreign power that exerted so much authority in their world. The cults became "a major part of the web of power that formed the fabric of society."[5]

Price's general framework can be supplemented by a closer look at the worship of the Roman emperors in the area to which John wrote. In order to do this, though, a brief introduction to the relevant institutions in Roman Asia is needed. All of the churches mentioned in Rev 2–3 were located in major cities in the province of Asia (the western end of modern Turkey). The province of Asia was a Roman administrative unit within Rome's imperial domain. A Roman proconsul (governor of the province) was charged with oversight of the province's affairs. The proconsul often traveled to the various districts within his province to hear legal arguments and to render decisions on questions affecting cities, villages, groups of people, and even individuals. Since the proconsul normally served for only one year, the imperial bureaucracy in the province also exercised a good deal of influence. That no Roman legions were stationed in Asia suggests that this system of governance was relatively stable.

The province had a council that was known as the "koinon."[6] The *koinon* consisted of wealthy men who represented the cities of the province. This council probably had limited jurisdiction since cities could appeal directly to the proconsul or send delegations to Rome for a hearing before the emperor. One of the most prominent responsibilities of the *koinon* was the administration of provincial imperial cults. Such cults were highly valued. They were sponsored by the whole province and could only be established with the permission of the senate in Rome. If the request of the province to establish such a cult was granted, the cities of the province paid for a temple (sometimes with assistance from the imperial treasuries in Rome), and the *koinon* appointed a high priest or high priestess every year. High priests and high priestesses of Asia were required to pay for the animal sacrifices and festivities as a part of their office. The celebrations might last up to four or five days, and normally included competitions in athletics, music, and so on. These high priesthoods of Asia were among the most prestigious offices the province could bestow, and

    [5] Price, *Rituals and Power*, esp. 234–48. The quote is from p. 248.

    [6] Jürgen Deininger, *Die Provinziallandtage der römischen Kaiserzeit von Augustus bis zum Ende des dritten Jahrhunderts n. Chr.* (Vestigia 6; Munich: C. H. Beck, 1965), 16–19, 36–60.

they were filled by the most prominent members of the elite stratum of Asian society.[7]

By the end of the first century, the *koinon* was in charge of three provincial cults. One cult was established around 27 B.C.E. at Pergamon and was dedicated to the goddess Rome and to Augustus. Approximately fifty years later (c. 26 C.E.) the *koinon* received permission to establish a second provincial temple, this time at Smyrna. This provincial cult was dedicated to the emperor Tiberius, Livia (the widow of Augustus and mother of Tiberius), and the Roman senate. So, in format, the Smyrna cult was dedicated to the worship of the emperor and a corporate Roman entity in a manner reminiscent of—but distinct from—the earlier provincial cult of Rome and Augustus.[8] A third provincial temple that abandoned the earlier format was dedicated in the year 89/90 at Ephesus. This third temple was dedicated simply to the Sebastoi ("revered ones," which is the Greek equivalent of the Latin "Augustii"), that is, to several emperors and not to any other Roman entity. The objects of worship at this third provincial temple probably included the deceased emperors Vespasian and Titus, and the reigning emperor Domitian, and perhaps also his wife Domitia.[9]

Commentators on Revelation seldom take into account that these provincial cults were much different in number and character than the myriad local imperial cults that sprang up during the early imperial period. A local cult of the emperors could be established any place where local resources and politics allowed such an institution. No approval was needed from the Roman senate nor from Roman provincial officials. Local cults often included a temple with arrangements for priests, priestess, or other officials, all of which was underwritten by a wealthy family in the area. A local imperial cult could also be much more modest, comprising little more than an altar, a liturgical calendar, and a priesthood. Sometimes these rituals and objects were simply added to the ongoing cult of a more traditional god or goddess.

Participation in Imperial Cults in Asia

There are hundreds of references to imperial cults in the inscriptions of Roman Asia. These references provide us with specific examples of the roles that imperial cults played in the lives of the inhabitants of this area. More often than not, the inscriptions record the activities of the wealthy elite. They also give us occasional indications of the participation of the rest of society. The following paragraphs show some

---

[7] Price, *Rituals and Power*, 128–30; Steven J. Friesen, *Twice Neokoros: Ephesus, Asia, and the Cult of the Flavian Imperial Family* (Religions of the Graeco-Roman World 116; Leiden: E. J. Brill, 1993), 7–28. A database of these officials is accessible at http://www.missouri.edu/~religsf/officials.html.

[8] Friesen, *Twice Neokoros*, 7–21.

[9] Ibid., 35–36, 41–49.

of the ways that these inscriptions fill out our picture of John's social setting.[10]

The high priesthoods in the provincial imperial cults often comprised one important aspect of the broader public activities of wealthy families in the province of Asia. Enough information has survived about many of these people so that we can begin to reconstruct the significance of provincial high priesthoods for this elite sector of Asian society. During the years 80–130 C.E., the province of Asia required approximately 150 people to fill the provincial high priesthoods of Asia.[11] The names of seventeen of these high priests and high priestesses are known to us. Three individuals—an unmarried woman and a married couple—provide specific examples of the importance of high priestly service in the histories of wealthy families.

Vedia Marcia's career illustrates the importance of high priesthoods in the public life of elite families in the province. She lived in Ephesus, where her name was inscribed on a marble wall in the city's prytaneion.[12] The inscription was made between the years 97 and 100 C.E. to commemorate the end of her twelve–month service as prytanis of Ephesus. The prytanis was the most prestigious—and most expensive—municipal religious office. The inscription also mentions that she had served earlier as high priestess of Asia in one of the provincial cults of the emperors, which means that she held this imperial cult office right around the time of the composition of Revelation. She was probably older than her brother Publius Vedius Antoninus, because by 100 C.E. he had not served as a provincial high priest.[13] By 119, however, he had served a second time in the city's highest governmental office—the secretary (*grammateus*) of the *demos*—and had earned the prestigious title of Asiarch.[14] The Vedians

---

[10] For a more comprehensive handling of this theme, see Steven J. Friesen, *Imperial Cults and the Apocalypse of John: Reading Revelation in the Ruins* (New York: Oxford University Press, 2001).

[11] The years 80–130 were chosen to reflect the general period when Revelation is thought to have been written. The upper and lower limits were determined by the known dates of extant inscriptions and coins. The number of high priesthoods was calculated in the following way. Until the late 80s, there were two annual high priesthoods for the two cults: one in Pergamon and one in Smyrna. In 89/90, the Temple of the Sebastoi was dedicated at Ephesus, requiring a third high priesthood. A fourth temple and high priesthood was established in Pergamon around 115 C.E.

[12] *IvE* 4.1017. She was almost certainly single at the time. In this sort of inscription it would be unusual to identify a married woman without mentioning her husband, but Marcia is described only as the daughter of Publius. The prytaneion building in Ephesus served many functions. One important function was the administration of religious activities throughout the city.

[13] *IvE* 4.1016 commemorates his service as prytanis between 96 and 99 C.E., but no other titles are listed for him.

[14] *IvE* 2.429, from the years 117–119 C.E. The nature of the Asiarchate is contested, but it clearly was not another name for someone who had served in the

went on to become one of the most powerful families in Asia in the mid–
to late second century. An inscription from 164–169 C.E. lists the accom-
plishments of Antoninus's adopted son (Sabinus) and grandson (Sabini-
anus).[15] The son served as prytanis, secretary of the *demos* (twice), Asiarch,
panegyriarch of two major festivals, and ambassador to the Roman senate and to emperors. The grandson is listed with the same titles, as well as
alytarch and gymnasiarch. Thus, in Vedia Marcia's provincial high priesthood in the late first century, we see an early stage of a wealthy family's
rise to provincial prominence.

While the Vedians became prominent in Ephesus and in the province,
a couple from the city of Phokaia serves as an example of the role of high
priesthoods in a family that advanced beyond the provincial realm in the
service of the Roman Empire. Flavia Ammion Aristio and her husband,
T. Fl. Varus Calvesianus Hermokrates, each filled a provincial high priesthood at the Temple of the Sebastoi at Ephesus. Their terms of service took
place sometime between the dedication of the temple in 89/90 and 130 C.E.
Flavia was honored later by her tribe (*phylê*) in Phokaia with a statue. The
inscription on the statue base records her provincial high priesthood as
well as her service as municipal prytanis, *stephanephoros*, and priestess in
Phokaia.[16] Hermokrates, however, had ambitions beyond municipal and
provincial service. He was honored by the *boule* and *demos* of Phokaia for
the same municipal offices held by Flavia, for a regional liturgy (sacral
"king of the Ionians"), for an administrative position in the city of Rome,
and for two military posts outside the province of Asia.[17] The high priesthoods of Flavia Ammion and T. Fl. Hermokrates, therefore, represent one
facet of their illustrious careers in service of city, province, and empire. For
the husband, the provincial high priesthood was an intermediate honor
at the transition between provincial and imperial spheres of activity. For
Flavia—a woman married to a provincial aristocrat who was rising in the
imperial ranks—the high priesthood was the highest honor to which she
could reasonably aspire.

While it is true that such provincial high priesthoods would have increased one's status and influence, these sacral offices were by no means a
blank check for imperial favor. Two contrasting cases make this point. Tib.
Cl. Aristio was an early high priest at the Temple of the Sebastoi, founded
at Ephesus during Domitian's reign. He was probably the major Ephesian
influence in initiating Asia's third provincial cult, because he served as its

---

provincial high priesthoods. See Rosalinde Kearsley, "Asiarchs, *Archiereis*, and
Archiereiai of Asia," *GRBS* 27 (1986): 183–92; idem, "14. Some Asiarchs from Ephesus," *New Documents* (1987): 53–54; and Friesen, *Twice Neokoros*, 92–113.

[15] *IvE* 3.728. The names in the inscription are ambiguous because several generations were known by the same names, but the date of the inscription confirms
that we are dealing with the son and grandson.

[16] *IGR* 4.1325.

[17] *IGR* 4.1323.

high priest in 88/89 (the year before the official dedication of the temple) and then filled the role of *neokoros* of the same temple in 90/91 C.E.[18] From this time until about 125 C.E., Aristio held most of the major offices in Ephesus and in the province.[19] He is such an important figure that he is mentioned in more than two dozen existing inscriptions from Ephesus. When he was accused of an unspecified crime before Trajan (98–117 C.E.) by other Asians, the emperor ruled in his favor.[20] Whether the decision was influenced by his high priesthood cannot be ascertained with certainty, but his service as imperial high priest certainly did not hurt his case.

A provincial high priesthood in the imperial cults of Asia did not necessarily guarantee special consideration from the emperor, however, and this is suggested by what is known about Tib. Cl. Socrates and his wife Antonia Caecilia. These prominent Thyatirans held provincial high priesthoods of Asia sometime between the years 80 and 115 C.E. Their family followed a path similar to those of families mentioned above. Both were honored by the city of Thyatira for their service in high priesthoods, in the office of prytanis, in sponsoring athletic competitions, and in other capacities.[21] The city of Stratonikeia, however, lodged a complaint against Socrates with the emperor Hadrian (117–138). Socrates had not properly maintained his house in Stratonikeia, and the emperor's verdict went in favor of the city. The emperor ordered that Socrates either had to repair the home or sell it to an inhabitant of the city.[22]

Local imperial cults in Roman Asia provided a wider range of opportunities for members of wealthy families to serve in official capacities than did the provincial cults. I noted above that local imperial cults—in contrast to provincial cults—were dependent on their immediate religious and political situation, and were responsible to local authorities. This absence of centralization made these cults both more flexible and more creative. While provincial imperial cults involved high priesthoods that lasted one year,[23]

---

[18] A *neokoros* was probably an official who paid for the upkeep of temple facilities for a stipulated period of time; see Steven J. Friesen, "The Cult of the Roman Emperors in Ephesus: Temple Wardens, City Titles, and the Interpretation of the Revelation of John," in *Ephesus, Metropolis of Asia: An Interdisciplinary Approach to Its Archaeology, Religion, and Culture* (ed. Helmut Koester; HTS 41; Valley Forge, Pa.: Trinity Press International, 1995), 230–31.

[19] Kearsley, "Some Asiarchs"; Friesen, *Twice Neokoros*, 102, 162.

[20] The reference to the trial comes from Pliny the Younger, *Ep.* 6.31.

[21] *IGR* 4.1238–39. The later history of the family is strikingly similar to that of the Vedians in Ephesus. Their son Socrates Sacerdotianus later held several municipal offices and a high priesthood for life in a local cult of the emperors (*IGR* 4.1241); their grandson Menogenes Caecilianus became a provincial high priest, a priest of Apollo, a priest of Dionysos, and an *agonothete,* among other things (*IGR* 4.1238; the inscription is from the mid– to late second century C.E.).

[22] *IGR* 4.1156a.

[23] There is no evidence for "priests/priestesses of Asia," only for high priests/high priestesses.

local imperial cults sometimes included a high priesthood that lasted for life rather than for a year,[24] or they involved a priesthood rather than a high priesthood.[25] The diversity of officials in local cults is evident in other examples throughout this section and need not detain us further at this point.

Local imperial cults could be woven into a city's municipal religious institutions in novel ways that would not have been appropriate in provincial cult settings. We have evidence of such a development in Pergamon during the first half of the first century. A certain Otacilia Faustina was honored there as priestess of Athena at one of the city's most prominent temples. The title of her priesthood, however, indicates that she was also priestess of Julia Livilla, who was a daughter of Germanicus and the widow of both Gaius Caesar and of Drusus. In this Pergamene cult, Julia Livilla was "enthroned alongside (Athena)" as the "new Nikephoros."[26] In this way Livilla was associated with Athena, becoming an object of worship at major municipal festivals and in the temple of the goddess on the Pergamene acropolis. Again, there is no evidence to suggest that such local innovations were subject to regional control. These decisions were within the jurisdiction of Pergamon's municipal government in negotiation with the officials of the Athena temple.

One important observation for the interpretation of Rev 13 is that high priesthoods were not the only ways for members of the elite to participate in the imperial cults in Asia. We have already seen examples of priesthoods and the office of *neokoros*. Another important type of participation was that of municipal representative to a provincial cult festival. The names of such representatives are no longer known in most cases, but the Flavian Temple of the Sebastoi in Ephesus provides an important exception. Thirteen statue bases that once stood in that temple's precincts have been recovered, supporting statues donated by cities of the province. The bases also recorded the names of at least fifteen men who paid for their city's statues. A glance at the careers of these municipal representatives shows that participation in imperial cults was inextricably entangled in the public culture of the cities, precisely at the time when Revelation was written to churches in this area. From the thirteen inscribed bases we know that the representatives included several men who had held the chief civic offices of their respective cities: a first archon of Aizanoi;[27] two archons of Kaisareis Makedones Hyrkanioi;[28] a *strategos* of Klazomenai;[29] and another *strategos* of Silandos.[30] Other kinds of impor-

---

[24] Thyatira, *IGR* 4.1241; first half of second century C.E.

[25] Thyatira, *IGR* 4.1242; Claudia Ammion's father, Metrodoros Lepidas, lived during the Augustan period (31 B.C.E.–14 C.E.).

[26] *IGR* 4.464.

[27] *IvE* 2.232; 232a.

[28] *IvE* 5.1492.

[29] *IvE* 2.235.

[30] *IvE* 2.238.

tant officials are also attested among these municipal representatives. The inscription from Teos is fragmentary but the official was clearly a high financial official in the city.[31] Keretapa sent Glukon, son of Agathokleos, who had served as the municipal superintendent of works.[32]

The most informative of the thirteen bases is the one commissioned by the city of Tmolos, an inscription providing an example of a member of the municipal elite who was a supporter of a local imperial cult and also a city representative to a provincial cult.[33] One of the two representatives named in the text was clearly an eminent local leader who had served Tmolos in a variety of capacities. Aulus Livius Agron had held the city's highest governmental office—secretary of the *demos*. He had been the financial officer of the *boule* (city council) and had been accorded the title "son of the *boule*." Agron was also a prominent supporter of a local imperial cult, for he was described as priest and *neokoros* for life of a local cult of "[[Domitian]] Caesar, of Domitia Augusta and of their house, and of the (Roman) Senate."[34] He was apparently not able, for whatever reason, to attain the office of provincial high priest.

In contrast to the regional significance of the city representatives, a set of four Pergamene inscriptions from the Hadrianic period (117–138 C.E.) illustrates different kinds of participation in imperial cult activities.[35] The inscriptions are on the four sides of an altar and provide guidelines for the members of a male chorus known as the *hymnodes* of the god Augustus and the goddess Rome. These men sang sacred hymns to the emperors and sponsored various kinds of public imperial cult ceremonies. They met as well for private rituals restricted to members of the group. The front side of their altar is damaged but the existing text names at least thirty-four *hymnodes*, including the three men who paid for the altar. One of the three was a theologian for the group. The right side lists several festivals throughout the year, such as the birthday of Augustus and the birthdays of other emperors, and specifies which members need to contribute money, crowns, sacrificial cakes, incense, and lamps. A shorter inscription on the back side stipulates when the priest should provide wine, bread, and money, and when the uninitiated *hymnodes* should contribute money. Finally, the left side records responsibilities of the secretary (*grammateus*)

---

[31] The [ἀργυρ]οταμίας fulfilled the city's duty; *IvE* 2.239.

[32] *IvE* 2.234.

[33] *IvE* 2.241. The other inscriptions are *IvE* 2.233 (Aphrodisias); 237 (Stratonikeia); 240 (Kyme, fragmentary); 242 (badly damaged); and 6.2048 (Synaos, fragmentary).

[34] This local imperial cult had a very complicated structure: to Domitian, his wife, the imperial family, and the Roman Senate. The brackets in the quote indicate that the name of Domitian was chiseled out after his death when the Roman Senate condemned him posthumously and ordered his name stricken from public documents.

[35] *IGR* 4.353.

and other members of the group in providing for particular festivals. This set of texts presents us with an example of a closed group of men with special responsibilities for the celebration of local imperial cults. Some of their meetings would have been private and restricted; other meetings were part of public imperial cult ceremonies. In order to accomplish these tasks, several kinds of officials were needed besides priests or high priests.

The foregoing materials provide another observation about imperial cults in Asia: the worship of the Roman emperors and the imperial family permeated many aspects of society in Asia. The worship of the emperors was not an isolated facet of social interaction nor could it be easily disentangled from the fabric of the culture. At the local level, Agron and the other men involved in imperial cults were the same people who ran municipal governments.[36] They were also the same people who tended to hold offices in the cults of traditional deities. At the provincial level, the very wealthiest families served in high priesthoods. These high priests and high priestesses were the individuals who invested large amounts of money and energy in priesthoods, governmental offices, and other liturgies in order to keep urban life functioning. They were the people who sometimes attained imperial positions throughout the Mediterranean and occasionally even at Rome, the capital of the empire. Their lives flowed easily across the modern categories of "religion" and "politics," or "religion" and "economy," or "private" and "public."

One factor that tends to be overlooked in discussions of Revelation and the worship of Roman emperors is that the archaeological evidence implies that the imperial cult institutions involved far more than the elite sector of society.[37] Most of the evidence that has survived the intervening centuries provides names of the wealthy office holders, but many of the activities they sponsored included large segments of the populations of the given areas. One example mentioned above is the inclusion of Julia Livilla in the cult of Athena at Pergamon. The municipal processions and sacrifices for Athena Nikephoros and Livilla the new Nikephoros were not restricted to the elite of the city; they involved all the populace of the urban area.

Other examples of imperial cult institutions that clearly involved many levels of society can be adduced from the inscriptions. An inscription from the city of Assos from the first half of the first century C.E. honored Lollia Antiochos, the wife of a lifelong priest in a local cult of the em-

---

[36] Women did not usually hold governmental office. Their influence would normally have been wielded in other less direct ways as members of powerful families; see Riet van Bremen, "Women and Wealth," in *Images of Women in Antiquity* (ed. Averil Cameron and Amelie Kuhrt; Detroit: Wayne State University Press, 1983), 223–42; Mary Taliaferro Boatwright, "Plancia Magna of Perge: Women's Roles and Status in Roman Asia Minor," in *Women's History and Ancient History* (ed. Sarah B. Pomeroy; Chapel Hill: University of North Carolina Press, 1991), 249–72.

[37] Price (*Rituals and Power*, 107–13) is an important exception on this issue.

peror Tiberius. The reason for the honors was that she had built and furnished public baths, and had dedicated the baths to Livia (called "Aphrodite Julia") and to the *demos*.[38] An inscription from Mytilene mentions a secondary gymnasiarch of "Goddess Augusta Aeolian Karpophoros Agrippina," reminding us that imperial cults sometimes included athletic events and other kinds of competitions.[39] Or we can cite one last Pergamene inscription. This one honored Tiberia Claudia Melitine, whose mother was the priestess of Faustina who sponsored two days of bullfights. All of this suggests that imperial cults were not simply a game played by the elite to legitimize their dominance in society. Imperial cults were much more than that. Imperial cults were also bullfights, footraces, wrestling, public baths, concerts by male choruses, and festivals for a city's ancestral divine protector. Imperial cults were inscribed on public buildings, on altars, on statue bases, in gymnasia, in temples. They were proper expressions of reverence by "the small and the great, the rich and the poor, the free and the slaves" (Rev 13:16). In short, the worship of the emperors was a crucial part of Asian society in the first century c.e.

Naming the Beast from the Land

One of my goals in reciting so many inscriptions is to construct an image of imperial cults in first-century c.e. Asia. This in turn allows us to consider and evaluate commentators' interpretive options in discussing the beast from the land. We are in a better position to do this now that we have increased our understanding of topics that were common knowledge for John and his audience in late-first-century Asia.

The task of surveying commentators about the beast from the land is more difficult than one might think. Although there is widespread agreement that imperial cults are at the heart of the imagery, there is little agreement about the specifics of interpretation. I have placed the interpretations into two categories in order to show the diversity of the scholarly opinions.

One group of commentators asserts that the beast from the land is a symbol for the priests and priestesses who served in the imperial cults.[40]

---

[38] *IGR* 4.257.

[39] M. Granius Carbo served in this function according to *IGR* 4.100.

[40] For example, Wilhelm Bousset, *Die Offenbarung Johannis* (KEK; Göttingen: Vandenhoeck & Ruprecht, 1906); Isbon T. Beckwith, *The Apocalypse of John* (New York: Macmillan, 1919); Henry Barclay Swete, *The Apocalypse of St. John* (2d ed.; London: Macmillan, 1907); R. H. Charles, *A Critical and Exegetical Commentary on the Revelation of St. John* (2 vols.; ICC; Edinburgh: T. & T. Clark, 1920); Eduard Lohse, *Die Offenbarung des Johannes* (Göttingen: Vandenhoeck & Ruprecht, 1960); T. F. Glasson, *The Revelation of John* (Cambridge: Cambridge University Press, 1965). Elisabeth Schüssler Fiorenza could be considered in this category as well (*Revelation: Vision of a Just World* [Proclamation Commentaries; Minneapolis: Fortress, 1991], 85–86).

Two recent contributions within this group have given a more general interpretation of the beast as those people concerned with the regulation and maintenance of imperial cults, which might also include the imperial priests and priestesses (deSilva).[41] Caird and Bovon were more specific, naming the *koinon*—Asia's provincial council—as the group that regulated imperial cults.[42] Mounce, on the other hand, thought it should be one or the other; the beast represented either the *koinon* or the imperial cult priesthoods.[43] Weiss added regional Roman authorities to the mix when he suggested that the beast could symbolize either imperial cult priesthoods or Roman government in the province, because government officials like the proconsul were deeply enmeshed in the promotion of imperial cults.[44] Ramsay, however, argued that the image included both imperial cult officials and Roman government.[45]

On the basis of the biblical text and the inscriptions, several of these ideas can be dismissed as too narrow. We cannot restrict the symbol of the beast from the land so that it refers only to imperial priesthoods. There were many kinds of officials in imperial cults who cannot properly be called priests or priestesses. The *koinon* is also too narrow a referent for the symbol. The *koinon* had jurisdiction over a small number of the imperial cult activities in the area. The provincial cults for which they exercised oversight were prestigious institutions, but these cults comprised only one aspect of the much larger phenomenon. In the same way, the beast from the land included more than those who had jurisdiction over such cults.

Another possibility that can be dismissed is to read the beast as referring to the Roman governor (or Roman government) in the province. From the inscriptions it appears that the governor was not a prominent player in the public promotion of imperial cults. He would certainly have been a factor, but he was much less important than local proponents. The

[41] David deSilva, "The 'Image of the Beast' and the Christians in Asia Minor: Escalation of Sectarian Tension in Revelation 13," *TJ*, n.s., 12 (1991): 185–208. David E. Aune concluded that the beast symbolized the high priesthood of the provincial imperial cults (*Revelation* [3 vols.; WBC 52; Dallas: Word Books, 1996–98], 2:780.

[42] G. B. Caird, *The Revelation of Saint John* (Black's New Testament Commentaries; Peabody, Mass.: Hendrickson, 1966); François Bovon, "Possession ou enchantement: Les Institutions Romaines selon l'Apocalypse de Jean," in idem, *Révélations et écritures: Nouveau Testament et littérature apocryphe chrétienne* (Geneva: Labor et Fides, 1993), 131–46.

[43] Robert H. Mounce, *The Book of Revelation* (NICNT; Grand Rapids: Eerdmans, 1977).

[44] Johannes Weiss, *Die Offenbarung des Johannes: Ein Beitrag zur Lieratur- und Religionsgeschichte* (Göttingen: Vandenhoeck & Ruprecht, 1904).

[45] William Ramsay, *The Letters to the Seven Churches of Asia and Their Place in the Plan of the Apocalypse* (London: Hodder & Stoughton, 1904; updated by Mark W. Wilson, Peabody, Mass.: Hendrickson, 1994).

governor and his administrators should be included instead within the imagery of the beast from the sea who exercised hegemony over the world (Rev 13:1–10).

A second group of commentators has suggested variations on the theme that imperial cults were only a part of a bigger picture in the province of Asia during the first century C.E. Some argued that the beast represented pagan worship in general.[46] Others were satisfied to conclude that the beast from the land stands for every person and institution that was involved in imperial cults or imperial propaganda.[47] Boring, however, gave us the most inclusive interpretation of all:

> Since John is not communicating in code-language or steno symbols, it is useless to try to decide whether the beast from the land "represents" the Roman governors, the *commune* [i.e., the *koinon*], the Roman priesthood, or false Christian prophets and teachers. The beast has characteristics of all of these. All who support and promote the cultural religion, in or out of the church, however Lamb-like they may appear, are agents of the beast [from the sea].[48]

These proposals are too encompassing. The first option—that the beast from the land was a symbol for polytheistic religion, of which imperial cults comprised the most important aspect—overstates the religious dominance of imperial cults and overlooks the vibrancy of traditional cults. There is a tendency among some interpreters of this persuasion to describe polytheism as a discredited system and imperial cults in particular as the most degenerate form of polytheism. Moreover, this option would require a redefinition of the first beast as referring to something other than the Roman Empire, since polytheism predated (and outlived) Roman imperial power.

Boring's conclusion that the beast from the land might refer to gover-

---

[46] Heinrich Kraft, *Die Offenbarung des Johannes* (HNT 16a; Tübingen: J. C. B. Mohr [Paul Siebeck], 1974); Lucien Cerfaux and Jules Cambier, *L'Apocalypse de Saint Jean lue aux Chrétiens* (Lectio divina 17; Paris: Cerf, 1955). Leonard Thompson (*The Book of Revelation: Apocalypse and Empire* [New York: Oxford University Press, 1990], 164) implies that polytheism is the main issue as well but in a different way. While others see imperial cults as the liveliest part of polytheism and thus worthy of our full attention, Thompson considers imperial cults to be only one aspect of the larger phenomenon. Hence, he suggests we focus on the big picture, which is polytheism.

[47] Austin Farrer, *The Revelation of St. John the Divine* (Oxford: Clarendon, 1964); Pierre Prigent, *L'Apocalypse de Saint Jean* (CNT 14; Lausanne, Switzerland: Delachaux et Niestleé, 1981); Gerhard Krodel, *Revelation* (ACNT; Minneapolis: Augsburg, 1989); Jürgen Roloff, *The Revelation of John* (CC; Minneapolis: Fortress, 1993); G. R. Beasley-Murray, *The Book of Revelation* (rev. ed.; NCB; Greenwood, S.C.: Attic Press, 1979); David L. Barr, *Tales of the End: A Narrative Commentary on the Book of Revelation* (Santa Rosa, Calif.: Polebridge, 1998).

[48] M. Eugene Boring, *Revelation* (Interpretation; Louisville: John Knox, 1989), 157.

nors, *koinon,* priesthoods, Christian false prophets, or Christian false teachers is also too broad. The governors have been ruled out already, and it is hard to imagine any sense in which John could say that the beast from the sea had given all its authority to Christian prophets and teachers (13:12), or that these church members were deceiving all the inhabitants of the earth (13:12–15). The relatively more modest proposal that the beast from the land represented everyone or every institution involved in promoting the cults of the emperors is still too broad, for this would include the general populace, leaving no one for the beast to deceive.

In the final analysis, the position of Yarbro Collins on this issue is the most consonant with the biblical and the epigraphic data. Yarbro Collins shifted the focus and suggested that the beast from the land represented the wealthy elite in Asian society, since these were the people who served in the various priesthoods and offices.

> The vision about the beast from the earth (13:11–18) would have called to mind the leading families of Asia Minor, who had control of both political office and the various priesthoods. These families, as well as the general populace of the region, were very enthusiastic in supporting and even extending the worship of the emperor. In part such honor was a genuine expression of reverence and gratitude. In part it was a way of seeing the emperor's continuing friendship and potential special favors. In western Asia Minor, where the seven cities of the Apocalypse were located, political, religious, and economic activities were so intertwined that a Christian who refused to honor the emperor in a religious way would have been limited in economic and political options.[49]

The epigraphic evidence confirms the interpretation of Yarbro Collins and fills it out by clarifying the ways in which these people led the religious, cultural, and governmental life of the cities and the region. It provides examples of the ways in which imperial cults could enhance a family's fortunes and deepens our understanding of the variety of imperial cult institutions that gave coherence and color to public culture. Perhaps most important, the inscriptions show how thoroughly these cults were integrated into Asian society and how widespread was the involvement of the populace.[50]

The beast from the land was not simply a cipher for a certain group of individuals, though; it was much more provocative. Like all of John's images, the beast from the land operated at many levels. John's image was focused on the wealthy families of the cities and province as actors within a network of socioreligious institutions, including the *koinon,* priesthoods, local imperial cult offices, municipal representatives, choirs, athletic events, and so on. The image of the beast from the land was large

[49]   Adela Yarbro Collins, "'What the Spirit Says to the Churches': Preaching the Apocalypse," *QR* 4 (1984): 82.

[50]   G. R. Beasley-Murray comes close to this position in his statement that the promoters of imperial cult need to be understood in their wider institutional con-

enough also to include the web of institutions at work in John's world. This network supported the imperial vision of a peaceful province under Roman control, and this vision was expressed in part through imperial cult activities. The institutions flourished, withered, or survived over centuries, but the personnel were more or less interchangeable. Thus, John's attack was not simply directed against a particular institution or particular group of people, but ultimately against the Roman imperial way of life. John's portrait of the beast from the land challenged the values and practices that gave order to life in Roman Asia.

The Worlds of Revelation

One reason I have cited so many inscriptions in this chapter is to impress the reader with the great body of archaeological information about the worship of the emperors that has barely entered discussions of the interpretation of Revelation.[51] I do not intend to suggest, however, that archaeological materials are relevant for every topic in biblical studies or for every verse in Revelation. Archaeological materials, like all data in all disciplines, are limited resources that are appropriated within certain contemporary social contexts. They must be examined critically at many levels. They provide certain kinds of information but are silent on many topics.

Nor do I want to suggest that archaeological materials provide definitive answers to all questions about the meaning of the image of the beast from the land. The process of interpretation is much too complex to be circumvented by the mere citation of an inscription. Questions still remain about how inscriptions should be used in the interpretive process, and about the partial record they provide about the Roman Empire. To make matters even more precarious, I have made selections from this partial record of ancient evidence in order to build my case. It is important to remember that archaeology constructs certain kinds of knowledge about the past in particular contemporary contexts; it does not give us unmediated access to past realities. But that is true of any data or methods we employ. Handled with care, these can take us deeper into John's world.

My larger goal is to suggest that more attention to the social world of Revelation's audience will prove beneficial for Revelation studies in general, not just for Rev 13. There is widespread agreement these days that

---

text. His description of that wider context, however, was restricted to a few general statements of dubious value gleaned from the secondary literature (*Revelation*, 216–17).

[51] The monographs of William Ramsay (*Letters to the Seven*) and Colin Hemer (*The Letters to the Seven Churches of Asia in Their Local Setting* [Sheffield, England: Sheffield Academic Press, 1986]) employed archaeological materials extensively in the interpretation of Revelation, but I do not recommend them. The former is too dated to be useful, and the latter is plagued by severe problems of method and perspective.

John's Revelation articulated a way for his hearers and readers to understand their world, a way that was at odds with the basic tenets of public culture. The text reinterpreted the audience's experiences, transforming their perspective and creating the potential for conflict.[52]

Our understanding of this clash of worldviews has been heavily dependent on John's articulation of his minority opinion. In John's view of the world, members of the indigenous elite received their authority from Satan. They were secondary figures, subservient to the demonic power of Rome that exploited the world for its own purposes. Wealthy Asians executed the will of the great oppressor Rome. In John's view, the general populace was understood as pitifully mistaken. The participation of the masses in imperial cults was the result of the deceptions of the beast from the land. They had been misled by the spectacular signs, by the demonic authority, and by the threat of death for nonconformity. Their participation was leading them to destruction.

The inscriptions, on the other hand, give us access to the dominant symbolic universe in first-century Asia, where noble families were represented as fulfilling their pious responsibilities. From this perspective, the aristocrats demonstrated their benevolence, reverence, and virtue by their service on behalf of cities, the province, the empire, the imperial families, the gods, and the goddesses. They won praise and honor. Their names graced buildings, their statues adorned the streets and marketplaces. The citizens, the city council, and the provincial *koinon* made decisions on behalf of the people. The masses celebrated the festivals, they witnessed the sacrifices, they went to the bullfights and the baths, they benefited from the largesse of the elite.

Coming to terms with this collision of symbolic worlds has never been an easy task, both because of the nature of the biblical text and because of the distance between our time and Revelation's generative setting. Most commentators have addressed this problem on the basis of the literature from the first and second centuries. A more promising approach, I have argued, is one that is attendant to all the evidence that remains from John's world. If we are to make sense of enigmatic images like the beast from the land, we will need all the available information about John's social setting.[53]

---

[52] David Barr, "The Apocalypse as Symbolic Transformation of the World: A Literary Analysis," *Int* 38 (1984): 39–50; Adela Yarbro Collins, *Crisis and Catharsis: The Power of the Apocalypse* (Philadelphia: Westminster, 1984); Elisabeth Schüssler Fiorenza, *The Book of Revelation: Justice and Judgment* (Philadelphia: Fortress, 1985), 196–98; Thompson, *Book of Revelation;* deSilva, "'Image of the Beast.'"

[53] The research for this chapter was made possible by support from the University of Missouri Research Board; the Society of Biblical Literature's Research and Publications Committee; and the Research Council of the University of Missouri, Columbia.

4

Wolves in Sheep's Clothing
LITERARY OPPOSITION AND SOCIAL TENSION
IN THE REVELATION OF JOHN

Paul B. Duff

One expects an author to portray contrasting characters in contrasting ways, but one of the most fascinating and puzzling literary techniques employed by the author of the Book of Revelation is to describe contrasting characters in *similar* ways. The manner in which John depicts the various female characters in the Apocalypse provides an excellent example of this curious literary habit, for, according to John's vision, the virtuous and evil women appear as distorted reflections of one another. There must be a reason why the author positions antithetical figures in this way.

A close examination of the female figures in the Book of Revelation shows that their literary construction directly reflects the social tension that existed in the Christian communities of Asia in John's time. The literary construction also demonstrates the rhetorical dimension of John's writing. As we will see, John's Apocalypse is not merely a narrative recounting a heavenly vision. It is also a document whose purpose was to persuade its readers to abandon their understanding of the world as a relatively benign place and to come around to the author's more radical vantage point, which emphasizes the world's dangerous nature. In order to set the stage properly, I begin the investigation with an examination of the churches mentioned in the Book of Revelation.

The Churches of Revelation

We know, from the so-called letters in chapters 2 and 3 of the Apocalypse, that these churches contained factions of a kind of Christianity that was somewhat different from that of the author. The factions were especially evident in the churches at Ephesus, Pergamum, and Thyatira. John considered this variant form of Christianity a serious threat to the integrity of churches of Asia Minor.[1] That John mentions only one contemporary figure in connection with that variant form of Christianity suggests that this person was the leader of this faction in those churches. Although John does not give us this figure's name, he does provide us with a nickname. He calls this leader "Jezebel."[2] Why did John see "Jezebel" as such a threat to the churches? He himself answers that question in his letter to the Thyatira church (Rev 2:18–29), in which he tells us two things. First, he says that "[she] calls herself a prophet." Second, he accuses her of "teaching and beguiling [Christ's] servants to practice fornication and to eat food sacrificed to idols" (2:20).

If we remove the hostile edge from the first statement, we can see that "Jezebel" was respected in the Christian communities because of her prophetic abilities. Since John considered himself a prophet (cf. 1:3; 22:18; 22:19), this was obviously an important issue for him, especially since "Jezebel's" prophetic pronouncements were apparently incompatible with his own. Consequently, he scoffs at her prophetic office, implying with the phrase "[she] calls herself a prophet" that "Jezebel" has no legitimate claim to that status. John's charge that "[she] beguiles [Christ's] servants" in the second phrase informs us that "Jezebel" had a following and, given John's very strong reaction to her, it likely was a sizable one.

What precisely was the content of "Jezebel's" teaching by which she "beguiled" the churches? John points to two activities: practicing "fornication" and eating "foods sacrificed to idols."[3] The questions that we need to address concerning these issues are (1) what precisely are these activities and (2) what exactly was "Jezebel's" stance toward those practices?

Of the two practices, deciphering the issue of "fornication" (*porneia* in the original Greek) is the most problematic. *Porneia* usually meant some kind of sexually promiscuous behavior. However, in the Jewish tradition,

---

[1] I refer to the contents of chapters 2 and 3 as "so-called letters" because most scholars agree that what we see in these chapters are not letters at all. They look more like pronouncements by a sacred figure (like a deity) or a secular ruler. But because these pronouncements are typically referred to as "letters," I will also, for the sake of convenience, refer to them as such.

[2] Although some have suggested that "Balaam" mentioned in the letter to Pergamum was also a nickname of one of John's contemporaries, the way that the letter is phrased instead suggests to me that John is speaking of "Balaam," the figure from ancient Israelite history (Num 31:15–16), rather than someone alive in Pergamum at that time.

[3] It is important to note that these issues are enumerated in both the Pergamum and the Thyatira letters (2:14 and 2:20). In the former, John ties the activity to a group that he labels "Nicolaitans" (2:15). It is also noteworthy that John commends the Ephesian church for hating the works of the Nicolaitans (2:6). The works that he has in mind are probably also the same as in Pergamum and Thyatira, that is, committing fornication and eating meat sacrificed to idols.

it could be used metaphorically to refer to idolatry.[4] Consequently, it is possible that John was speaking not of sexual misdeeds in the Apocalypse but rather of some type of behavior that he considered idolatrous. How can we tell whether John was speaking literally or metaphorically? Since John gives us no specifics about "Jezebel's" (or anyone else's) alleged promiscuity, and since he uses sexual language metaphorically elsewhere in the text, it seems more likely that John intends a metaphorical meaning for the term *porneia* here. Unfortunately, it is impossible to know more precisely what John intended by this accusation. Perhaps he meant something specific,[5] but more likely this accusation simply indicates John's strong disapproval of Christian participation in the larger pagan society.[6]

The next practice, eating food sacrificed to idols, is also difficult to interpret with precision because it could cover a wide range of activities. On the one hand, it could refer to celebrating pagan festivals and eating the meat sacrificed to the pagan deities at these festivals. On the other hand, it could also mean simply eating the meat bought at the local meat market, since meat markets often sold sacrificial meat from the local pagan temples.

This issue of eating meat sacrificed to idols arose in Paul's time (roughly a half-century before the writing of the Book of Revelation), and, as his first letter to Corinth attests, the apostle was unwilling to rule definitively that the practice was always inappropriate (1 Cor 8–10). According to Paul, sometimes it was permissible and sometimes it was not. Where did "Jezebel" stand on the issue? Was she actively encouraging the practice regardless of the situation or was she, like Paul, merely allowing it in certain instances?

Although we cannot answer these questions with absolute certainty, the Pergamum and the Thyatira letters (2:12–17, 18–29) can provide us with some clues. It is important to note that John is cautious in each letter when he raises the issue of food sacrificed to idols. On the one hand, he never directly accuses the addressees of actually eating this food. Rather, he accuses them of tolerating those who do so (2:20). On the other hand, in the Pergamum letter, John seems concerned that the offensive character of this practice might not be readily apparent to his readers. As a result, he connects the activity to Balaam, a paradigmatic enemy of Israel from the distant past (2:14).[7] Both of these points give us clues about the

---

[4] We see this usage, for instance, in the biblical book of the prophet Hosea. In that ancient text, Israel is compared to a whore because she has abandoned God, her metaphorical husband. Other examples abound in both the Hebrew Scriptures (Old Testament) and also the later Jewish writings.

[5] In later Jewish writings a Hebrew term comparable to *porneia* could refer to a marriage between a Jew and a Gentile. Perhaps John refers here to marriages between Christians and pagans.

[6] John seems to want Christians to withdraw as much as possible from society, since he considers it utterly corrupt. We will see more on this below.

[7] See n. 2.

readership that John addressed as well as about "Jezebel's" stance toward sacrificial meat.

The first point—that he does not directly accuse his readers of eating food sacrificed to idols—suggests that John was not writing his apocalypse to convince "Jezebel" and her followers to change their views or their behavior.[8] Instead, John focuses on the uncommitted majority in the churches, the people who *tolerate* the behavior.[9] The second point—that John seems compelled to detail the offensive character of the activity—suggests that "Jezebel" had not been encouraging the consumption of sacrificial meat in all situations. Rather, like Paul, she had probably merely *allowed* it sometimes (like at dinner at a neighbor's or employer's house).[10] It is quite likely that eating sacrificial meat in some such circumstances was less an issue for many Christians in John's communities than it was for him. As a result, John was forced to demonstrate just how wicked eating sacrificial meat would be *under any circumstances*. He does this, as mentioned above, by tying the activity to Balaam's act of encouraging Israel in her idolatry.

All in all, John's cautious approach to both of these issues suggests that he was hesitant to address the specifics of the issues or to condemn them *too* directly lest he undermine his own standing in the communities. He holds back in his attacks because, it seems, he has little that he can use against his rival that would be taken seriously by many in the churches. If the people of the churches were not particularly bothered by the practice of eating food sacrificed to idols in certain situations, John's strong opposition could backfire and damage his own authority. This would be a particular danger in the case where "Jezebel" held what many might have considered a more reasonable position.

In sum, it is fair to say that from John's perspective, "Jezebel's" main "offense" was her openness to Greco-Roman society, an openness that many in the churches seemed to share. Consequently, in order to oppose her John was forced to resort to a more subtle approach. We can see this approach in the way that he ties "Jezebel" to the other women of the Apocalypse.

---

[8] From John's vantage point, "Jezebel" had already had her chance. Note that in 2:21, the speaker says, "I gave her time to repent but she refuses to repent of her fornication."

[9] Perhaps these people accepted the prophetic legitimacy of *both* John and "Jezebel." To the best of my knowledge, this was first suggested by David Aune in "The Social Matrix of the Apocalypse of John," *Biblical Research* 28 (1981): 28–29. See also chapter 2 above, pages 36–43.

[10] It is hard to imagine that John would have to struggle to convince many in the community that eating food sacrificed to idols was wrong if, for example, "Jezebel" was encouraging her followers to fully participate in pagan festivals.

The Women of Revelation

There are four female characters mentioned in John's Apocalypse: "Jeze-bel" in 2:18–29; an unnamed "woman clothed with the sun" in chapter 12; the whore named "Babylon" of chapter 17; and, finally, the bride "Jerusa-lem" of 21:1–22:6. These female characters—whether mythological, meta-phorical, or flesh-and-blood women—are all comparable to some degree. The author has taken great pains to link the four passages that contain these women by using similarities in imagery, words, phrases, or ideas found within them.

The importance of these women in the Apocalypse is attested by their placement throughout the work. That is, John juxtaposes the female fig-ures symmetrically as well as linguistically. "Jezebel" and "Jerusalem" frame virtually the whole of the work (appearing near its beginning and end, in chapters 2 and 21–22, respectively), whereas the woman "clothed with the sun" and the woman "Babylon" appear toward the work's cen-ter (in chapters 12 and 17, respectively). In addition, the figures alternate between evil and good, the first and third figures being evil and the sec-ond and fourth good.

Certainly the most prominent of the figures in the narrative are the two women who appear in chapters 12 and 17, that is, toward the center of the work. Given the importance of these figures, I first examine them in their respective literary contexts. I then look at the way that the author makes literary connections between these two figures. Finally, I consider these female characters as they compare and contrast with "Jezebel."

The Woman "Clothed with the Sun" and the Whore "Babylon"

Chapter 12 of the Apocalypse describes a vision that consists of three scenes revolving around a woman described as "clothed with the sun, with the moon under her feet, and on her head a crown of twelve stars." In the first scene of this chapter (vv. 1–6), the woman's about-to-be-born son is threatened by the hungry jaws of a waiting dragon. The death of the child is averted however, for when the woman's son is born, he is "snatched away and taken to God." The woman then flees into the wilderness where she is nourished (presumably by God).

This opening scene is followed by an account of a heavenly war in which Michael and his forces battle the dragon and his minions (vv. 7–9). The dragon—identified in this text with "the Devil" and Satan—is thrown to earth. A hymn celebrating the victory of God over Satan follows this second scene (vv. 10–12).

In the third scene, we see a dragon—angered by his fall from heaven—pursuing the woman, who ultimately escapes with the aid of God (vv. 14–16). Finally, the dragon leaves the woman and goes off to make war on "the rest of her children," identified as "those who keep the commandments of God and hold the testimony of Jesus" (v. 17).

Chapter 17, on the other hand, shows a great prostitute seated upon a scarlet beast that has seven heads and ten horns. The first part of the chapter describes the prostitute as

> clothed in purple and scarlet, and adorned with gold and jewels and pearls, holding in her hand a golden cup full of abominations and the impurities of her fornication; and on her head was written a name, a mystery: "Babylon the great, mother of whores and of earth's abominations." . . . [The woman was] drunk with the blood of the saints and the blood of the witnesses to Jesus. (17:4–6)

This description is followed by an enigmatic interpretation of the various features of the beast (vv. 7–14), and this interpretation, in turn, is followed by a narrative explaining the significance of several elements in the passage (vv. 15–17). Finally, the chapter ends with a seemingly clear identification of the whore: "The woman you saw is the great city that rules over the kings of the earth" (v. 18). Any reader of John's time would certainly understand "the great city that rules over the kings of the earth" as a reference to Rome.

The various literary links between the figures of chapters 12 and 17 can be listed as follows:

Chapter 12	Chapter 17
• woman depicted as a mother (v. 2)	• woman depicted as a mother (v. 5)
• woman located in wilderness (v. 6)	• woman located in wilderness (v. 3)
• woman eats/drinks in wilderness (v. 6)	• woman eats/drinks in wilderness (v. 6)
• eating/drinking connected with death (v. 4)	• eating/ drinking connected with death (v. 6)
• woman "clothed (peribeblēmenē) with the sun" (v. 1)	• woman clothed (peribebēlmenē) in splendid attire (v. 4)
• beast: red dragon with seven heads and ten horns (v. 3)	• beast: scarlet beast with seven heads and ten horns (v. 3)
• reference to "those who hold the testimony of Jesus" (tōn echontōn martyrian Iēsou, v. 17)	• reference to witnesses of Jesus (hoi martyroi Iēsou, v. 6)

As the above chart indicates, there are a significant number of connections between the two texts:

1. *In each of the texts the women are depicted as mothers.* The woman in chapter 12, although not called a "mother," is described in the process of giving birth—the maternal act par excellence. The woman of chapter 17, on the other hand, is specifically labeled a

"mother," but she is identified as a "mother of whores and of earth's abominations" (v. 5).

2. *The women in each text are associated with a common location.* Each passage places its respective woman in the wilderness (*erēmon*; 12:6, 14; 17:3).

3. *Each woman is tied to the act of eating/drinking. Eating and drinking is also connected with the wilderness (12:6; 17:4–6).* In chapter 12, the woman's child (and presumably the woman herself) narrowly escapes being eaten by the dragon (12:5, 13). Furthermore, after her escape from the dragon, the woman is fed in the wilderness (12:6, 14). The woman of chapter 17, on the other hand, consumes the blood of the holy ones in the wilderness (17:6).

4. The act of eating/drinking (whether by one of the women or by another character) is connected with death in each of the passages. As mentioned above, in chapter 12 the dragon attempts to devour the child and the unnamed mother. In chapter 17, on the other hand, the woman "Babylon" drinks the blood of the witnesses of Jesus.

5. *Each passage highlights the splendid attire of its respective woman* (12:1; 17:4). Furthermore, the same participle (*peribebēlmenē*) is used in each text.

6. *Each passage depicts surprisingly similar beasts.* Revelation 12:3 speaks of a great red dragon with seven heads and ten horns which threatens the woman and her child. Revelation 17:3 depicts a scarlet beast with seven heads and ten horns upon which the woman is seated.

7. Each passage concerns itself with the "testimony of/witnesses to" Jesus (12:17, [*tōn*] *echontōn martyrian Iēsou*; 17:6, *hoi martyroi Iēsou*). The language is similar in the original Greek, although the English translation obscures the connection somewhat.

Despite these many literary links, it is apparent that the figures of these two passages are meant to be contrasted. The woman in the one passage obviously presents an intentionally distorted reflection of the other, the one belonging to the realm of the godly (the unnamed woman of chapter 12) and the other to the satanic domain ("Babylon" in chapter 17).

These two women function in the Book of Revelation as contrasting feminine paradigms. Each of the two remaining female figures—the flesh-and-blood figure "Jezebel" and the metaphorical bride "Jerusalem"—*corresponds* to one of these women and *contrasts* with the other. In the interest of brevity, I will not examine the role of "Jerusalem" here. Instead, I look only at the figure of "Jezebel" and her points of contact with the figures of chapters 12 and 17.

"Jezebel"

John refers to his flesh-and-blood rival "Jezebel" in a few short verses of the letter to the church at Thyatira (2:18–29). There, the seer reports the words of the Son of God:

> I have this against you that you: you tolerate that woman "Jezebel," who calls herself a prophet and is teaching and beguiling (*plana*) my servants to practice fornication and to eat food sacrificed to idols. I gave her time

to repent, but she refuses to repent of her fornication. Beware, I am throwing her on a bed, and those who commit adultery with her I am throwing into great distress, unless they repent of her doings; and I will strike her children dead. (2:20–23)

This text presents us with several major points of contact with both chapters 12 and 17. In the first place, the above passage depicts the woman "Jezebel" as a mother (for 2:23 speaks of the fate of her children), just as chapters 12 and 17 portray their respective women as mothers. Second, the same three passages (Rev 2:18–29; Rev 12; and Rev 17) are some of the few places in all of Revelation in which sexual imagery and imagery focused on eating and nourishment converge. Finally, the verb *planaō* (usually translated as "to lead astray" or "beguile") is used to describe the evil activity of "Jezebel" in chapter 2, of the dragon (the unnamed woman's adversary) in chapter 12, and of the beast that the woman rides in chapter 17.[11] The literary links among these three passages make it clear that John invites his readers to consider his rival "Jezebel" in connection with the two women found in chapters 12 and 17. I consider the links that John draws between "Jezebel" and the woman of chapter 12 first.

"Jezebel" and the woman of chapter 12. The points of comparison and contrast between "Jezebel" and the unnamed woman of chapter 12 can be outlined as follows:

"Jezebel" in Thyatira Letter	Unnamed Woman of Chapter 12
Woman depicted as a mother whose children are threatened by the Son of God (2:23)	Woman depicted as a mother whose children are threatened by Satan (12:4)
Allusion to Ps 2:8 in passage (2:27)	Allusion to Ps 2:8 in passage (12:5)
"Jezebel" "leads astray" (*planaō*, 2:20)	Opponent of woman "leads astray" (*planaō*, 12:9)
Woman depicted as aggressive	Woman depicted as passive
Illicit sexual activity attributed to "Jezebel" (2:20, 22)	Proper sexual activity connected to woman
Dangerous eating/drinking activity practiced by "Jezebel" and her followers (food sacrificed to idols; 2:20)	Dangerous eating/drinking activity directed against woman and child (12:4, 15)

[11] We should note that the verb *planaō* does not occur in chapter 17 but rather in 18:23. However, it is indisputable that the later passage's discussion of the beast looks back to and comments on chapter 17.

As we have already seen, both "Jezebel" and the woman of chapter 12 are depicted within their respective contexts as mothers. There is a further similarity, however, in the case of these two women. Both are described as mothers whose children are at risk. In the case of the woman of chapter 12, the risk is neither brought on by the mother, nor can the mother lessen it by herself. On the other hand, in chapter 2, the risk to the children has been brought on by the mother "Jezebel" herself. Furthermore, this risk could at any time in the past have been neutralized (by the repentance of the mother; 2:21).

Another example of contrast between "Jezebel" and the woman of chapter 12 appears in the seer's use of Ps 2:8 in each passage. Revelation 2:27—the eschatological promise to the faithful of Thyatira—describes "the one who conquers" (here clearly identified as members of the community who shun "Jezebel") as the one who will "rule [the nations] with a rod of iron." In 12:5, however, it is the child born to the unnamed woman who "is to rule all the nations with a rod of iron."

John's use of the verb *planaō* ("to beguile" or "to lead astray") also presents the reader with a contrasting point of contact between "Jezebel" and the unnamed woman of chapter 12. In 2:20 it is "Jezebel" herself who "leads astray" (*planaō*) the community. But in chapter 12, it is the dragon, the opponent of the unnamed woman, who is responsible for "leading astray" (*planaō*) the whole earth.

The issue of gender likewise provides an implicit contrast between 2:18–29 and chapter 12. In 2:20, "Jezebel" apparently defies John's expectations of proper feminine behavior by her active and aggressive deportment.[12] John responds by structuring verse 20 (the verse in which he introduces "Jezebel") to highlight her active role. This verse shifts the burden of guilt for her followers' crimes onto "Jezebel" herself by suggesting that she is the real cause of their evil activity.[13]

In the same spirit, John speaks a few verses later (2:22) of the sins of her followers not as their own sins but as "Jezebel's" sins: "Beware, I am throwing ['Jezebel'] on a bed, and those who commit adultery with her I am throwing into great distress unless *they* repent of *her* works" (2:22). The blame for the transgressions of the Asia Minor Christians is laid, almost exclusively, at the feet of the active agent "Jezebel." However, John is not content to describe "Jezebel" merely as an active figure. He also depicts her as a sexually aggressive individual. She is both an adulterer (v. 22) and a prostitute (v. 21).

On the other hand, John depicts the woman of chapter 12 as a passive feminine figure. She is the subject only of the verbs connected with

---

[12] John's understanding of the "proper" role of women largely matches that of the larger Mediterranean society of the time.

[13] "'Jezebel' . . . teaches and beguiles my servants *with the result that they* commit fornication and eat food sacrificed to idols" (my translation, emphasis added). This contrasts with the grammar of Babylon; see n. 16.

birthing and fleeing. It is perhaps fair to say that she does not usually act in this text but rather is acted upon. She is threatened by the beast, and consequently she has to flee "into the wilderness, to a place which had been prepared for her by God" (v. 6). The next part of the scene reinforces the passive nature of the woman. In the wilderness, the woman is fed and protected by God. Later in the text she is pursued, again by the beast, and again she is saved, this time by the earth (vv. 13–16). Note that the active roles in this text belong to the beast, the deity, and the earth. Not surprisingly, the woman's sexuality appears only in an oblique way in this text. No explicit mention is made of any sexual activity on her part. Rather, the text highlights birth, the fruit of what John would probably consider "proper" sexual activity (i.e., sex solely for the purpose of procreation; cf. 14:4).[14]

Besides gender issues, the topics of eating and drinking also figure prominently in the two passages (and we will see that they also appear in chapter 17). In Rev 2:20, the act of eating, specifically eating food sacrificed to idols, presents itself as a dangerous activity. It is dangerous because it alienates those involved from the "Son of God" (v. 18) and ultimately from salvation. However, it also—at least when combined with *porneia*—carries a physical threat, for if it continues it will cause harm (and possibly even death) to those that participate (2:22–23). In chapter 12, the imagery connected with eating and drinking is also tied closely with immediate physical danger. In that chapter, the child of the unnamed woman and, it seems, the woman herself are both depicted as potential food for the beast (12:4, 13f.).

Interestingly enough, chapter 12 connects further danger (as well as salvation) not with food directly but with the mouth, that part of the body responsible for ingesting food. In verse 15, the dragon spews forth a torrent of water from its mouth which threatens to destroy the unnamed woman. It is noteworthy that the woman's salvation depends upon the mouth of the earth, which opens and swallows the deadly flood.

In sum, gender and food issues loom large in each of these passages. In fact, sexual imagery and the imagery of eating and drinking account for the majority of the points of contact that the two passages share. In the next section, we see that the same issues surface in the points of contact between the "Jezebel" passage and the section of Revelation depicting the whore "Babylon."

"Jezebel" and the woman "Babylon." The points of contact between "Jezebel" and the figure "Babylon," whose portrayal begins in chapter 17, are as follows:

---

[14] Jewish and pagan moral teaching at John's time viewed sexual activity as legitimate only if its purpose was to conceive children.

"Jezebel" in Thyatira Letter	"Babylon" in Vision of Chapters 17–18
Woman depicted as a mother who engages in fornication (2:23)	Woman depicted as a mother of "whores and abominations" (17:5)
Woman identified with a negative name from Israel's past: "Jezebel"	Woman identified with a negative name from Israel's past: "Babylon"
Woman "leads astray" (planaō, 2:20)	Woman "leads astray" (planaō, 18:23)
Woman depicted as active	Woman depicted as active
Woman depicted as sexually aggressive	Woman depicted as sexually aggressive
Woman consumes defiling food (food sacrificed to idols, implied in 2:20)	Woman consumes defiling food (human blood, 17:6)
Passage predicts her destruction (2:22)	Passage predicts her destruction (17:16)

If the relationship between the women of 2:18–29 and chapter 12 is one of contrast, the connection between "Jezebel" and "Babylon" is one of compatibility. Like the woman in chapter 12, "Babylon" is depicted as a mother. However, unlike the unnamed woman of chapter 12 who is portrayed as a nurturing mother (i.e., a mother giving birth to a child), chapter 17 describes its character as the "mother of whores (pornōn) and of the abominations of the earth." As such she looks much like "Jezebel," who, according to John, encourages fornication (porneia, 2:20) and engages in adultery (2:22).

John's disdain for both "Jezebel" and "Babylon" is further highlighted by the fact that he associates them with evil figures from Israel's past. John connects his rival with the evil queen of Ahab, the wicked Israelite king from the ninth century B.C.E. He ties the woman of chapter 17 with Babylon, the city responsible for the destruction of Jerusalem and her temple as well as the exile of her citizens in the sixth century B.C.E.

The verb planaō ("to lead astray"), which John has tied to "Jezebel," also appears in conjunction with the character "Babylon."[15] In both cases, the women are characterized as "leading astray" their victims. In contrast, it is the opponent of the unnamed woman in chapter 12 ("the great dragon, that ancient serpent who is called the 'Devil and Satan'") who plays the role of the beguiler (planōn, v. 9).

When we turn to the gender issue, we can see that "Jezebel" again closely resembles "Babylon," while both "Jezebel" and "Babylon" contrast with the portrait of the woman of chapter 12. In chapter 17, "Baby-

[15] In 18:23 (a passage that clearly refers back to the woman of chapter 17) the text states: "and all the nations were [led astray] (eplanēthēsan) by [Babylon's] sorcery."

lon" is not a passive victim. Rather, she is an active player in the drama. She rides the evil beast (17:3), she drinks the blood of the holy ones (17:6), she sleeps with the kings of the earth (17:2), and she provides the "wine of *porneia*," which intoxicates the dwellers of the earth (17:2).[16] The only place where she is a passive agent occurs in verse 16, in which she is stripped, devoured, and burned by the ten horns of the beast. However, rather than suggesting her passive nature, this passage communicates a particularly ironic fate for one who has been so active up to this point.

Closely tied to "Babylon's" active nature is her sexual depravity. The text labels her a "whore" (*pornēs*, 17:1) and the "mother of whores" (v. 5). Her actions are described with the noun *porneia* ("fornication") and with the verb *porneuein* ("to engage in fornication," v. 2). Like "Babylon," "Jezebel" is also associated with promiscuity, specifically fornication (*porneia*, 2:20, 21) and adultery (*moicheia*, 2:22).

Imagery dealing with eating and drinking also plays an important role in chapter 17, in which the woman "Babylon" guzzles the blood of the holy ones. The consumption of any blood, of course, is taboo in the Jewish tradition (and possibly also in John's community). However, in this case the blood is doubly defiling because it is *human* blood.

Finally—presumably as a result of their active demeanor as well as their eating habits and their sexual practices—both women face destruction. "Jezebel" will be thrown onto a bed (specifically, a "sickbed") to waste away until the time of her death.[17] "Babylon," on the other hand will be made "desolate and naked," her flesh will be devoured, and finally she will be "burned up with fire" (17:16).

In sum, John closely ties "Jezebel" with "Babylon," the evil figure of chapter 17 and contrasts both of those figures with the female character of chapter 12. Were we to bring "Jerusalem" into the analysis, we would see that John depicts these four women of Revelation in such a way that two of the comparable characters are set in opposition to the other two figures (who are themselves comparable). "Jezebel" and "Babylon" stand over against the unnamed woman of chapter 12 and "Jerusalem." How do these literary comparisons and contrasts tie into the leadership struggle within the churches that was mentioned earlier? It is to this matter that I now turn.

[16] It is important to note that although the grammatical structure of the passage often describes the woman using the passive voice (as opposed to 2:20, which depicts "Jezebel" using the active voice), nevertheless it is indisputable that "Babylon" plays an active and even aggressive role here.

[17] Although the text does not explicitly predict her death, it is a safe assumption since death awaits her "children" (2:23). It is hard to imagine that her punishment would be less than that of her followers. If we assume, on the other hand, a protracted death (after a long illness, for instance), her punishment is more severe, which is what we would expect.

Insiders and Outsiders

In the pages above, I noted that John found himself in a precarious leadership position in his communities. His rival "Jezebel," another Christian prophet—one who advocated a conciliatory stance toward Greco-Roman society—was apparently gaining popularity at John's expense. John countered by drawing a picture in the Book of Revelation of a sharply polarized, apocalyptic world. In his highly symbolic vision of a universe poised upon the brink of devastation and renewal, we have seen that four female characters stand out, two good and two evil. It is somewhat surprising that John sets his rival "Jezebel" on the side of evil for, regardless of his disagreements with her, she nevertheless remained a fellow member of the church. Given this fact, we need to ask, why would John equate his fellow Christian prophet with the forces of evil? Was he just being petty and malicious or was there something else going on that would provoke such a strong reaction in him?

According to the anthropologist Mary Douglas, certain types of social groups (especially those with little internal self-definition)[18] see the world as follows:

[It] is divided between warring forces of good and evil. Leadership is precarious in such groups, roles ambiguous and undefined. The group boundary is the main definer of rights: people are classed either as members or strangers. . . . evil is a foreign danger introduced by foreign agents in disguise.[19]

This sounds remarkably like John's view of the world. His universe is clearly divided into warring forces of good (God) and evil (Satan), and his leadership role is under assault. In order to distinguish between those who are good and those who are evil, John focuses on the group boundary. On one side of the boundary are the "saints" and the "witnesses." On the other are the beasts and the other forces of evil. Unfortunately, the line differentiating insiders from outsiders is not as hard and fast as one might hope. All who look like insiders are not necessarily so. Instead, within the ranks of the good can be found hidden agents who work for evil powers. Through them, evil is able to enter into the community.

Seen in this way, John's strong reaction to "Jezebel" is more than the petty complaint of a small-minded individual. Rather, his reaction is based upon a perception of the universe typical of apocalyptic groups. John's worldview, which perceives the threat of insidious outsiders (who

[18] The church at the end of the first century seemed to have little in the way of internal structure or definition. The letters of Ignatius of Antioch, written in the same area a decade or so later than the Book of Revelation, mention bishops in the churches. But those same letters indicate that such bishops were not necessarily well regarded by the members of the churches.

[19] Mary Douglas, *Natural Symbols: Explorations in Cosmology* (New York: Vintage, 1973), 169.

look like insiders), not only explains John's hostility towards "Jezebel," it also provides an explanation for many of the odd literary juxtapositions found in the Book of Revelation.

As we know, throughout the work, evil forces and individuals look surprisingly like their benign opposites. From John's perspective, "Jezebel" is one such evil character. Although she appears to be an insider, she is actually a disguised outsider, an operative of Satan. Her role, as John sees things, is to infiltrate and corrupt the community of God. In order for John to expose "Jezebel" and to put her teaching into what John sees as the proper perspective, John shapes his literary portraits of the female characters in the Book of Revelation so as to emphasize the danger that his rival presents to the churches. He does this, in part, by using odd juxtapositions to focus on her teachings, most notably her teaching about food.

When we look at these chapters in the light of John's perception of who "Jezebel" really is, we can easily see the reason that John constructed these narrative passages in the way that he did. He attempts to compare what he considers to be "Jezebel's" promotion of food sacrificed to idols with other abominable eating and drinking acts committed by evil characters, such as cannibalism (17:6) or the dragon's attempted consumption of the child (ch. 12). Meanwhile, John contrasts the food sacrificed to idols with the God-given food that nourishes the unnamed woman (ch. 12) in the wilderness.[20]

Although we have not focused on the fourth female character ("Jerusalem") in this study, a few words about her now will demonstrate her role in the author's strategy. Revelation 22:2 shows the connection between the fruit from the tree of life and "Jerusalem." The imagery of the tree of life and its fruit, derived from the early chapters of Genesis, provides the reader with a vision of a future, uncorrupted world, which contains life-giving food only. John compares this food in "Jerusalem" with the nourishing food provided to the unnamed woman in the wilderness. Both of these positive references to food probably allude to the Christian Eucharist.[21] Conversely, John contrasts these positive images of food with the abominable food in Rev 2:20, 12:4, and 17:4–6.

John thereby presents his readers—Christians living in the communities of the Apocalypse—with a choice between the defiling food of death (which now includes food sacrificed to idols) and the incorruptible food of life (the Eucharist). "Jezebel" and her followers, having already chosen

---

[20] The nourishing food provided to the woman in the wilderness calls to mind the miraculous feeding of Israel in the wilderness during the exodus.

[21] For more on this, see Paul B. Duff, *Who Rides the Beast? Prophetic Rivalry and the Rhetoric of Crisis in the Churches of the Apocalypse* (Oxford: Oxford University Press, 2001), 102–5. For more on Eucharistic allusions in the Book of Revelation, see David L. Barr, *Tales of the End: A Narrative Commentary on the Book of Revelation* (Santa Rosa, Calif.: Polebridge, 1998), 171–72.

to participate in the life of the larger society (which can include the social occasions where food sacrificed to idols is present), have made their choice. Their choice of defiling food, John implies, sets them over against the Eucharistic fellowship of the Christian community. They have chosen the food of death rather than the food of life. It remains to be seen where John's readers will cast their lot.

One cannot help but admire the seer's deft use of imagery here. What he has done in these passages is, in effect, to intensify the charges against "Jezebel" and those who have been swayed by her. John may have realized that his protestations against "Jezebel's" openness to the consumption of sacrificial meat could easily have gone unheeded. In fact, the seer's denunciation of this practice might even have been viewed by some in the community as trivial.[22] Consequently, he approaches the subject subtly.

By approaching the issue indirectly, John is able to proceed with impunity while at the same time "upping the ante" significantly. Hence, he answers what we can imagine to be his opponent's justification for eating food sacrificed to idols, a justification like the one heard in a Pauline community roughly a half-century earlier: "What does it matter what we eat, for 'food will not bring us close to God'" (cf. 1 Cor 8:8). John shapes his narrative in such a way to point out that what is eaten can indeed matter a great deal.

Summary

Throughout the Book of Revelation, John ties significant characters to evil doubles. This practice is nowhere more evident that in his portrayal of the female figures in the Apocalypse. His juxtapositions of good and evil characters reflect the seer's understanding of the world as a dangerous place in which evil forces disguise themselves as godly characters so as to dupe humanity into siding with Satan in the impending apocalyptic struggle. When John sets two of the women of the Apocalypse in opposition to the other two, he does so in order to provide a subtle yet effective polemic against his rival "Jezebel" and her policy of integrating the Christian communities into mainstream pagan society. By pitting the women of chapters 12 and 17 against one another and by closely tying his rival to the latter and contrasting her with the former, John blurs the distinctions between "Jezebel" and "Babylon." By doing this he hopes to tar his rival with the same brush that he has used on the bloodthirsty whore "Babylon." Ultimately, John expects (or at least hopes) that his audience will turn their backs on "Jezebel," reject her openness to pagan society, and embrace him as the true prophetic leader of the Christian congregations of western Asia Minor.

[22] It is noteworthy that these churches lay in the area originally proselytized by Paul. As seen above, Paul himself did not construct hard-and-fast rules about the eating of meat sacrificed to idols (see especially 1 Cor 8–10). Perhaps the churches in this area were open to such eating practices from the time of the apostle and would have had little tolerance for John's hard-line stance.

5

A Tale of Two Cities and (At Least) Three Women

TRANSFORMATION, CONTINUITY, AND CONTRAST
IN THE APOCALYPSE

Edith M. Humphrey

. . . there were loud voices in heaven, saying, "The kingdom of the world
has become the kingdom of our Lord and of his Christ, and he will reign
forever and ever." (Rev 11:12)

"Behold, I am coming soon! . . . Behold, I am coming soon! . . . Surely, I
am coming soon!" (22:7, 12, 20)

It may surprise students of the NT to learn that the Apocalypse is the
most frequently read book of the Bible in North American correctional institutions. This fascination stems, no doubt, from the popular (mis)con-
ception that the book makes pronouncements in the manner of a sacred
medium, her gaze firmly fixed upon the future: surely *here* one may
move, unlimited by prison bars, into the realm of a more promising, more
interesting future! Yet, as the two short citations above show, the mysteries of Revelation are as much about the present and past as about the future.

Its name in Greek is Apocalypse, meaning "unveiling" or "uncovering," and the uncovering has to do with mysteries that encompass the
whole scope of human time (imagine a horizontal time line), even push-
ing the limits of the beginning and the end. The unveiling also has a ver-
tical (spatial) dimension, probing mysteries in the heavens above and in
the abyss below,[1] although the lower regions are only intimated. (Some
later Christian apocalypses will, however, feature vivid explorations of

---

[1] See *Semeia* (Chico, Calif.: Scholars Press) 14 (1979), an issue edited by John J.
Collins with the theme "Apocalypse: The Morphology of a Genre."

81

hell.) So Revelation is not just about the future; its scope is both temporal (past, present, and future) and spatial (what takes place *"up* here," 4:1). The seer John—and so the reader—is invited to explore these mysteries through the mediation of heavenly voices and figures from that realm, and is especially addressed by the One who is named the "First and the Last."

Not surprisingly for a piece directed toward a relatively young community, and which eventually found itself within the NT collection of community writings, there is also a focus on the issue of identity. Even this concern for identity is presented as a mystery, or set of mysteries, to be revealed: Who are God's people, in relation to the world, in relation to their forbears, in relation to angelic beings, in relation to God? This theme is so insistently sounded, so integrally woven into the rich tapestry of symbols, actions, vision, and structures, that it appears to vie for attention alongside the temporal and cosmic mysteries vouchsafed to the reader(s). The book signals itself not only as a revelation of the mysteries of heaven, of past, present, and future, but as a mysterious retelling of the story of God's new humanity. In providing such a perspective, the Johannine Apocalypse answers not only to the *what* of this mysterious cosmos, and the *when* of these mysterious events, but also to the question of *who*—how God's people are to be understood. A significant aspect of this identity is made present in feminine imagery.

Intimations of the City and the Women

And so, we come to a tale of two cities and (at least) three women. Obviously, the Apocalypse is a complex book, and the city/women images are only one or, perhaps, two threads in the fabric. The purpose of this study is to follow this thread and to use it to consider the entire sweep of the Apocalypse. We will be tracing the descriptions and intertextual allusions, the locales and actions, associated with the city/women figures, and analyzing the manner in which these symbols are rendered effective within their immediate structural contexts (smaller units) and within the overall structure of the book.

In any reading, particularly a literary study, it is helpful to approach the book with some understanding of its overall plan. However, the intricate nature of the Apocalypse has made mapping a structure very difficult.[2] There is much to be said for considering the book, as has Elisabeth Schüssler Fiorenza,[3] as a series of inclusive brackets, comparable to the

---

[2] For a consideration of several representative structural suggestions, see Edith M. Humphrey, *The Ladies and the Cities: Transformation and Apocalyptic Identity in Joseph and Aseneth, 4 Ezra, The Apocalypse, and the Shepherd of Hermas* (Sheffield, England: Sheffield Academic Press, 1995), 82–83.

[3] Elisabeth Schüssler Fiorenza, "Composition and Structure of the Book of Revelation," *CBQ* 39 (1977): 344–66; idem, *The Book of Revelation: Justice and Judgment* (2d ed.; Minneapolis: Fortress Press, 1998), 159–80.

nesting dolls that come from Slavic countries. Thus the framework of the beginning and end mirror each other (A, 1:1–8 // A', 22:10–22:21), the promise of the seven letters mirrors the fulfillment of judgment and salvation (B, 1:9–3:22 // B', 19:11–22:9), the seven seals and trumpet events mirror the seven bowls, together comprising the contents of the "sealed scroll" (C, 4:1–9:21 // C', 15:5–19:10), and we find a central section, the "little prophetic scroll," at exact center (D, 10:1–15:4). Moreover, there are a few bits that seem misplaced, which function to interlock the parts, binding them together rather than separating.[4] But this picture is too static, for there is also a dynamic, forward movement, leading to the climax and conclusion. The interconnected women and city figures emerge with full force in the second half of the book, that is, from chapter 12 on. Attention to the structure of intercalated sections (ABCDC'B'A') suggested above gives these symbols even more prominence, with one female actor taking a prominent role in the very center of the Apocalypse (D) and both cities and women coming to the forefront of the action as the book moves toward its grand finale.

Some have assumed that these figures appear from nowhere, beginning at chapter 12, but there is in fact an intimation of them even during the first few chapters. It is as if the two great cities and femininely pictured actors are waiting in the wings, ready to emerge at the dramatic moment. In continuity with a long tradition of biblical and extrabiblical writings, the *polis* and the woman stand for human communities or groups, either in faithful relationship to God, or in rebellion and infidelity. The early description of the faithful community as the work of Jesus Christ ("he has made us to be a kingdom, priests serving his God and Father," 1:6) and the initial vision of Jesus (in which he walks among the lampstands, speaking to his churches, 1:12–20) set the scene for a relationship later developed in masculine/feminine imagery. Among the promises in the letters to the seven churches (chs. 2–3), we catch a glimpse of the final city, the New Jerusalem, with which the Apocalypse will conclude in chapters 21–22. The letters offer tantalizing images of "the tree of life . . . in the paradise of God" (2:7b), "a new name" (2:17b), "walk[ing] with [him] in white" (3:4b), and "sit[ting] with [him] on [his] throne" (3:21)—all notes and chords that will be recapitulated in the final cadences of the book, when the New Jerusalem is described. In the letter to Philadelphia, the city is not merely suggested, but makes a brief cameo appearance: "I will make him a pillar in the temple of my God; never shall he go out of it, and I will write on him the name of the city of my God, the new Jerusalem which comes down from my God out of heaven, and my own new name" (3:12). At this point the feminine imagery to be used later does not emerge. The individual believer is addressed by the masculine

---

[4] For further details, see the references in n. 3 and Humphrey, *Ladies and the Cities*, 91–100.

pronoun (used inclusively, in the custom of the times, for female faithful, as well); it is the *city* of New Jerusalem (not yet the bride) who makes a debut: yet do we catch sight of her bridal skirts, so to speak, in the picture of one who "comes down from God," endowed "with a new name"? All is allusive and elusive: we are in the realm of promise at this point in the Apocalypse, not fulfillment.

More concrete—in fact, quite earthy!—is the description of "the woman Jezebel" in the letter to Thyatira (2:20). She finds her counterpart in the male figure of "Balaam," who is presented to the reader in the immediately preceding letter to Pergamum. Both churches have been infected with "immorality" and the eating of "food sacrificed to idols" (cf. Num 24 and 1 Kgs 16). Even more striking is the language used to describe "Jezebel" and her awaited judgment. If, at this point in his writing, the seer is content merely to intimate the glories of the bride, he is more willing to fill in a picture of present debauchery and fast-approaching judgment. It is, of course, not clear whether the infidelities of Jezebel—or for that matter, of those "holding to the teachings of Balaam"—are intended literally. Within the "grammar" of the imagery, "immorality" may be a figure for spiritual adultery, that is, infidelity to God. In this case, "immorality" would form a parallelism with the charge of idolatry, rather than a separate item.

At any rate, Jezebel, a self-styled prophet(ess), is presented as a leader of evil who has seduced the servants of God with promises of the "deep things of Satan." Her refusal to repent means that she will be forcibly removed from the bed of infidelity and "thrown on a sickbed," to receive, along with her co-adulterers, great tribulation and judgment at the hands of the One who rules with a rod of iron. Rather than treating her simply as an unknown prophetess, we should consider the network of imagery surrounding "Jezebel," whose very name is a cipher. This means that, alongside the more obvious symbolic female figures (New Jerusalem and the prostitute Babylon), the picture of Jezebel addresses the Christian community in general, and not merely the seven churches. The language used for her both echoes the Old Testament judgments of "the daughter of the Chaldeans" (Isa 47:1–15; cf. Ezek 28:2) and sets up overtones to be rung again more fully in the description of "Babylon's" downfall at the climax of the drama. The references to those who "commit adultery with her" and to "her children" not only establish these connections but also picture "Jezebel" (seemingly a local manifestation of "Babylon") as intimately connected with a community. Even the initial polemical reference to her as "*that woman* Jezebel, who calls herself a prophet" sets up this corporate dimension—while also surprising the biblically literate reader who expects the title "Queen." A complicating factor is the suggestion that while "Jezebel's" fate is sealed, her collaborators may still repent. The judgment of unrepentant evil is unambiguous; the position of those implicated is not.

In this initial major section of the Apocalypse (the seven letters), we therefore find tantalizing glimpses of the women/city figures to follow. While these are brief, they are in no way minor accents, nor tangential to the discourse. Subtle allusions to New Jerusalem, scattered across the letters, crystallize in the letter to the most faithful of the congregations, Philadelphia (3:11–12). The danger of infidelity and warnings of judgment, similarly scattered across the letters, set up themes that will be sounded more fully in the descriptions of Babylon. At this early point in the Apocalypse, the figure of Jezebel emerges like a threatening cancer in the center of the letter section, Thyatira taking middle place among the seven churches. Within the heart of God's community, there is a pretender who is to be searched by the One with "eyes like a flame of fire" and found wanting; yet there is also the promise of glory for those who have endurance, and who listen to what the Spirit says to the churches. Both dynamics of faithfulness and faithlessness have a present reality. That the presence of infidelity is by no means marginal is suggested by the central placement of Jezebel's description. Still, there is the vision of purity, not *yet* brought to fulfillment in a final victorious statement, but held out as promise in the message to Philadelphia. For now, the seer will close on a darker note ("Therefore repent!") to Laodicea: the end is not yet.

At chapter 4, we leave the imagery of city and women for a while and are snatched up with John into heaven to behold the throne, the Lion/Lamb, the ongoing divine liturgy, the scroll with its seven seals, the unsealing of a scroll which unleashes plagues upon earth, the sealing of the 144,000, and the praise of the multitude. And we hear sounds and voices: the sounding of seven trumpets, voices of declaration, the uninterpreted and mysterious seven thunders. The momentum of action increases, and the inevitability of judgment and fulfillment seems assured, as we come to the measuring of God's temple, the victorious ascension of God's two servants, the long-delayed sounding of the seventh trumpet and a declaration of victory: "the kingdom of the world *has become* the kingdom of our Lord and of his Christ . . ." (11:15). But the end is not yet. Throughout the seals and the trumpets, we have experienced a sequence, or unfolding, of sight and sounds which shows deliberate signs of order, and of disrupted order. As we hear the sounding of the seventh trumpet, and look in awe at the pyrotechnics accompanying its final note (11:19), the end again eludes us. Instead, the prophet turns our attention to a new and different story. He has eaten a little scroll of prophecy, direct from the hand of God (10:11), and means to tell us about it, from his perspective in heaven (4:1; the scene is recalled at 11:16–19).

The Refugee Queen

Enter another woman (12:1–6). She is a great portent, a sign, clothed with the sun, the moon under her feet, and a crown of twelve stars on her head. *Here* is a queen (where "Jezebel" only pretended), about to give birth. A second sign is introduced, an enormous red dragon, with seven heads, ten horns, and seven crowns. He sweeps a third of the stars out of heaven, and blocks the woman, attempting to devour her child, a child who will "rule all the nations" and who is snatched up to heaven, while the woman flees to the desert. An evil dragon, a rescued prince, a refugee queen. "Speed, bonnie boat . . . ," and all that. The stuff of stories!

Abruptly, with only the dragon as a link, John switches scenes. There is war in heaven, with Michael and his angels fighting against the dragon and his evil crew, and they are cast down to earth. Finally, our dragon is identified as the ancient serpent, or Satan, who leads the whole world astray. After the expulsion of the diabolic forces, we hear a positive declaration by the loud voice in heaven:

> Now have come the salvation and the power and the kingdom of our God and the authority of his Christ, for the accuser of our comrades has been thrown down, who accuses them day and night before God. But they have conquered him by the blood of the Lamb and by the word of their testimony, for they did not cling to life even in the face of death. Rejoice then, you heavens, and those who dwell in them! But woe to the earth and the sea, for the devil has come down to you with great wrath, because he knows that his time is short! (12:10–12)

Notice here that the declaration gives us another insight into the battle. Michael and his angels fight against the dragon; yet the dragon has been overcome "by the blood of the Lamb, and by the word of their testimony." It seems that the one born to be king has not *exactly* been rescued after all, but that he has fought the good fight, and in being slaughtered, has won. Yet what does the casting down of Satan mean for those on earth? It means suffering, because the dragon is in hot pursuit.

What are we to make of this? The accuser of God's people, the one who wants to devour the child and hurt the woman, is God's enemy. In one sense, he has been conquered: the decisive battle has been fought through the death of Jesus, the Lamb. *Now* has come the authority of God's Messiah, the Lion who is a Lamb. No longer will God listen to the accusations of the adversary, no longer does Satan have access to the throne, because of what the Lamb has done. *Now* have come God's power, and kingdom, and salvation. Yet this very conquest means the unleashing of Satan upon the world, upon those associated with the woman. Suffering is a necessary *result* of the conquest of Satan, as much as it is the means to his defeat: "[T]hey overcame him by the blood of the Lamb, and the word of their martyrdom. . . . woe to the earth and the sea, for the devil has come down to you." Here is a convoluted but powerful "logic." The enemy has been conquered by suffering, yet the very conquest of Satan in heaven means the suffering of God's people here and now.

Again, the seer switches scenes, returning to the conflict between the dragon and the woman in 12:13–17. No longer able to devour the child (for the child is the One who wields true authority), the dragon pursues the woman. And she is given help. Help comes from the earth itself, which swallows the flood coming from the dragon. Yet first, help comes from heaven: she is given eagle's wings, a help to the woman but also to the reader. By allusion to Exod 19:4, John cues us as to the identity of this refugee queen, reminding us of the children of Israel, carried by God on eagle's wings out of Egypt. The image of eagle's wings recalls also the great "Song of Moses" (Deut. 32:11), a metaphorical retelling of Israel's story (Deut 32:1ff.) that takes place at a climactic point in the Book of Deuteronomy, prior to the blessing of the twelve tribes by Moses. Here the differences are as instructive as the parallels. In the Song of Moses, the Lord discovers the foundling Israel in the desert, rescues him with eagle's wings, and leads him into a land of plenty. In John's vision, the woman is rescued on eagle's wings and flies *to the desert*, to a place prepared for her by God. The desert also is included in God's design, dismal and dangerous as it may be. It is a place of preparation (v. 6) and nourishment (v. 14). This dual theme of preparation/nourishment, of course, again recalls Israel, wandering for a probation period in the wilderness and fed by manna and quails before the tribes entered the promised land.

Thus, the queen is a kind of Israel, an Israel associated with the Messiah, and an Israel associated with other offspring who "keep the commandments of God and hold to the testimony of Jesus" (v. 17). This heavenly woman, introduced as one crowned with *twelve* stars, is bound up with both the people that brought forth the Messiah and with the children against whom the adversary fights. Not yet come to a throne or a city, she is the epitome of humility. In refuge, and requiring protection, she is nonetheless a queen by birth. Her two places of residence, heaven and the desert, are pictures of her identity.

Let us pause for a moment to consider the desert sojourn and the time references connected with it. Notice that two times are given for the woman's stay in the desert, at 12:6 and 12:14. In fact, they are the same, since 1,260 days is equivalent to "time, times, and half a time" (i.e., three and a half years)—and also equivalent to forty-two months (cf. 11:2). While we do well to disregard the ink spilled regarding these numbers in popular dispensational tomes, the numbers are not irrelevant. They are best understood in concert with other time references in the Apocalypse, since 7 is a recurring number, and the $1,260 = 42 = 3\frac{1}{2}$ times is found also at 11:2, 3, and 11, as well as at 13:5. This is the time period that the holy city will be trampled upon; this is the time period during which two paradigmatic witnesses of God will prophesy in sackcloth; this is the time period during which the demonic beast, who deceives the world, will be allowed to blaspheme and exercise authority. *This* is the time period in which the woman, in a desert place, will be cared for and prepared.

John's visions pile image upon image, suggesting that suffering and the seeming victory of evil are temporary, but allowed by God. The desolation, the humiliation, the oppression will all be used by God to God's glory—they are part of the care of God's people, a prepared time of three and a half that fits into the perfect "7" (or renewed, re-created "8") of this drama.

In considering the seven letters, I noted the placement of Jezebel at the very heart of that section—a dramatic description of infidelity requiring judgment. In the sequence of chapter 12, the disposition is equally effective, but to a different end. Consider again the outline of the chapter: the two major characters are introduced; the woman is persecuted and flies; there is war in heaven; there is a grand declaration of conquest (12:10–12); we return to the woman's persecution and flight; and there is war on earth:

a The woman and the dragon
b The persecution and flight of the woman
c War in heaven
d Declaration of victory
c' War in heaven
b' The persecution and flight of the woman
a' War on earth (the dragon and the women's children)

This is a chapter, following a pattern of inclusive brackets, that describes and is enveloped by conflict and suffering. We return to the two major players (plus the women's children) in the final section, but the story is not brought to resolution, and the war continues. Yet in the midst of this, there is a confident declaration of victory (d), an oracle that connects the suffering of the Lamb with victory over the dragon and that declares even suffering to be a part of God's purpose. Those in solidarity with the Lamb (and the woman) are directed to understand that God's ways are often mysterious. The time in the desert, only half the story, is superintended by God. If there is a cancer in the heart of God's community, a state that requires judgment, there is also a victory in the midst of suffering. Things are not always as they seem: an apocalypse, an uncovering, is needed.

John continues his saga, telling us more about the dragon and his two beasts, reminding us of the final bliss of the Lamb and his followers, and giving a preview of the final judgment of God. Just as the New Jerusalem is allowed to make a quick appearance in the letters sequence (chs. 2–3), so Babylon receives a quick acknowledgment in the prophet's little scroll (chs. 10–14): "Fallen, fallen is Babylon the great! She has made all nations drink of the wine of the wrath of her fornication" (14:8). The preview of final judgment (14:14–19), with which the little scroll closes, finally merges into the sequence of the seven plagues (chs. 15–16), with which the drama comes to its climax.

The Mad Mistress and the City

Enter Babylon, city and woman (chs. 17–18). Like Jezebel and the refugee queen, she is a mother, and she, like the queen, is associated with a scarlet beast who has seven heads and ten horns (12:3; 17:3; also 13:1). The parallels highlight the contrasts: she is not the mother of the Messiah, nor of those who hold to the testimony, but the "mother of prostitutes," of those who sell themselves. (Remember again the "grammar" of fidelity/infidelity in this book.) Nor is she in enmity with the beast, but she is, rather, its consort, riding upon it. Ironically, her very alliance with the beast will bring about her downfall, and she will be brought to ruin by the beast and the ten authorities who once "committed adultery" with her. Over against the refugee queen, this mad mistress takes the stance of luxury and pride (18:7), recalling again the archetypal pride of Babylon in the prophetic literature of the Hebrew Bible. Pride before fall. The description of Babylon merges with a dirge sung over the city/woman: she who has been great has been humiliated and brought low. This dirge stands in contrast with the song of joy in heaven (12:10–12), sung at the occasion of the dragon's downfall. Three times we hear the refrain of woe, "Fallen, fallen, is Babylon the great. . . . woe, woe, O great City!" (18:2, 9, 16, 19).

Babylon emerges, then, as the flip side of the refugee queen. She is proud, where the refugee is humble; she seems to prosper where the refugee is in exile; she rides on a beast, where the refugee is pursued by a beast; she is a pretending queen, where the refugee is a deposed (or fleeing) queen; she is the mother of evildoers, where the refugee gives birth to those who are faithful to the testimony of Jesus. Babylon's end is destruction, while, it seems, the refugee will sooner or later be reinstated. The refugee displays a holy dependence upon God, where Babylon wields an evil dominion, seeking her independence from God. Babylon's wilfulness and madness will eventually lead to ruin, despite a present time of prosperity.[5]

And so, along with the lamenters in chapter 18, we behold Babylon, the city now desolate, the woman now isolated, taking her true place not on the beast, nor on many waters or on seven mountains, but in the wilderness. Her final, desolate end—despite her outward grandeur—has, indeed, been signaled beforehand by the locale in which the seer was first introduced to her (17:3). She whose place is the desert is deserted. If the locale of this vision is the desert (over against the dual locale of heaven/wilderness in chapter 12), the dramatic action is that of a death and funeral (where in chapter 12 we heard of persecution and warfare).

---

[5] For more on these similarities and differences see chapter 4 in the present volume, "Wolves in Sheep's Clothing: Literary Opposition and Social Tension in the Revelation of John."

To be precise, chapter 18 is set up to provide the parody of a funeral, since the lament is prefaced and concluded by exultant angelic announcements of Babylon's fall and final end. Moreover, the mourners themselves, once intimate with the woman, do not come close in their distress, but "stand far off, in fear of her torment" (18:10, 15, 17). The tone throughout is that of irony, created by contrasts of Babylon's first and last state, and distancing of the mourners from the city. The final lament, in fact, mutates into a call for joy to heaven, and to the saints, apostles, and prophets (18:20), modeling even in the mouths of the mourners the preferred response to this judgment scene.

Yet the tone is not that of unmitigated triumph. In the initial picture (17:5) we were introduced to the woman with a sign on her forehead, proclaiming "a name, a mystery." Part of the mystery is that the woman is bound up with the life of the witnesses. How is this signaled? First, we consider the locale of this woman "in the wilderness" (17:3). The last time we looked, it was the refugee who was there. Second, the woman is "drunk with the blood of those who bore testimony to Jesus": the cup of impurities and abominations in her hand indicates that the faithful have had intimate and hurtful contact with her. Finally, there is the commanding voice, sounding as we have full view of Babylon, and urging: "Come out of her, my people, so that you do not take part in her sins, and so that you do not share in her plagues" (18:4).

The command assumes that God's people must be instructed to come out of Babylon. How is this possible, given the stark contrasts of the Apocalypse—Jezebel against the faithful, two witnesses against two beasts, Babylon against the refugee queen? Yet we recall from the letters that the division has never been absolute: in the words of Leonard Thompson, the boundaries in this book are "soft."[6] We have heard about Ephesus "forsaking her first love," of Pergamum and Thyatira tolerating "immorality," of Sardis's near-morbidity and "uncleanness," of Laodicea's pride and blindness. The command suited to each situation is the refrain, "therefore, repent!" For these very communities are called to the tree of life, the paradise of God, to eternal life and not a second death, to eat of hidden manna, to receive the morning star, to be known by a new name of intimacy with God, to have their name written in the book of life, to be dressed in white, to sit on thrones, to bear the name of the city New Jerusalem. The members of the community are called to glory, born to glory, and so they must come out of the one pretending to glory. At the heart of the identity of God's people is a mysterious infection with the power to negate their identity.

The second connection of the mad mother with the people of God is that contact which produces suffering, or martyrdom. The mystery of

---

[6] Leonard L. Thompson, *The Book of Revelation: Apocalypse and Empire* (Oxford: Oxford University Press, 1990), 100.

Babylon, as laid bare in the funeral lament (and heavenly joy) over her downfall, also involves the paradox that at present there is greatness where there should be judgment, life where there is no solid form of sustenance, light where all is darkness, fruitfulness where there should simply be barrenness. Babylon is fit only to be a home for demons, evil spirits, unclean birds of prey: and this, of course, is its final end. Yet in this city opposed to God, the unthinkable goes on: the round of joyful weddings, fruitful trade and commerce, festivity, fun, music. The seer here takes up the well-established theme of the prophets, exilic psalms, and later literature (e.g., 4 Ezra's laments)—the observation that the righteous perish while the arrogant seem to succeed. For the psalmist and the prophets, the dilemma was broached by complaint and the question, "How long, O Lord?" For John, this problem is cast in a different mode by going directly to the scene of judgment, and describing the greatness as something that is, from the perspective of justice, already weighed and found wanting.

It might seem that John's treatment suffers in comparison with the prophetic cry, lacking its depth and realism, and moving too facilely to triumphalism. Yet taken in its completeness, the drama of the Book of Revelation does not function like a math book, with answers in the back for the impatient or lazy student. Its approach may seem less subtle than that of the struggling psalmist who envies the arrogance of the wicked, and who receives an unimparted encouragement from God in the sanctuary (Ps 73:16–17). In fact, the reader of the Apocalypse is not called to hear the lament, and to rejoice, without also being compelled to read the visions as a whole, and thus to participate in scenes that consistently portray the mixed character of human living. The balance of lament on earth (18:10ff.) and joy in heaven (18:20) found in chapter 18 mirrors the complexity of chapter 12, in which earth and heaven are called to contrasting responses over the downfall of the adversary (12:12). This complexity is consonant with John's sketch of an ambiguous present: the community of God itself is in more than one sense connected, even implicated with Babylon, and must learn separation. Chapter 17, with its view from the desert, does not allow the reader to forget that the present faithful community is still a refugee, still in preparation, beset by trials, and prone to seduction. There is here no false or cold comfort, for behind these scenes, too, lie the visions of chapter 5 and chapter 12: the weeping of John over unresolved mystery on earth, with the mystery's uncomfortable resolution in the Lion who is a Lamb; and the ongoing persecution of the refugee's children who are, nevertheless, in the care of God. Chapter 18 is also carefully balanced. The final word of the angel, "in you was found the blood of prophets and of saints, and of all who have been slaughtered on earth" (18:24), rings in the ears of the reader, just as the emotive "Come out of her, my people" (18:4) initially sets a sober tone for this scene of judgment and "lament."

The Bride of the Lamb and the New Jerusalem

The closing angelic declaration of judgment (18:24) moves to a threefold cadential "Hallelujah!" (19:1–8) offered by "what seemed to be the loud voice of a great multitude" (19:6) and by the inner circle of worshipers around the throne. This tentative language of "seemed to be" or "like" or "as" is typical of revelatory reports and mystical writings. Its roots go back at least to the prophet Ezekiel, who writes about beholding "the *appearance* of the *likeness* of the *glory* of the Lord" (Ezek 1:28) and who prefaces most of his related visions with a qualification. Using this same technique, which became a commonplace in apocalyptic (and mystical) writing, John signals to the reader that the multitude of the redeemed creation, as well as the mysterious twenty-four elders and four living creatures, are the stuff of revelation. Not only does the faithful community await and derive comfort from the unveiling of the Lord: the community is an *item* of the unveiling, one of the mysteries! Thus, the comment on Babylon and the hallelujahs merge into the presentation of a final woman figure, with which John's vision will close. The somber but final notes of "the smoke goes up from her" (19:3) give way to the sound of servants, great and small, praising God. Included within that praise is a glimpse of the "bride" who has "made herself ready" and who has "been granted to be clothed with fine linen, bright and pure" (19:8).

More than a glimpse we do not yet receive, however, for in the final chapters the emphasis is placed first on the One to whom this bride is to be given. Before the marriage supper comes a swiftly moving series of dramatic events: the defeat of adversaries; the binding and final defeat of the dragon; the establishment of thrones for the righteous; the appearance of the great throne that displaces all, in heaven and in earth; the judgment of the dead; and the opening of the books (chs 19–20). It is only then that John sees a new heaven and a new earth, and glimpses the holy city, "prepared as a bride," while he hears the proclamation of how God will make "all things new" (21:1–5).

John (and so the reader) had viewed the refugee queen, deposed from heaven into the desert, from the perspective of heaven, where he had been invited in 4:1; he had viewed the Babylon/mistress from the perspective of the desert, where the angel had carried him in the spirit (17:3). Now he is taken, like Moses (Deut 34), to a "great, high mountain" from which he (and we) will view the "bride, the wife of the Lamb . . . the holy city Jerusalem, coming out heaven from God" (21:10). From the heavenly perspective, in the vision of the deposed queen-mother, we saw the panorama of a huge war, a determinative battle in heaven, followed by an ongoing, if limited, series of skirmishes on earth. From the perspective of the desert, in the vision of fallen Babylon, we witnessed a funeral, or rather, a funeral parody, since the "far-off" stance of the mourners, and the framing of their lament by angelic declarations, distanced the reader from the event. Yet, even in parody, the vision remained complex, re-

minding the faithful community of their mysterious implication and connection with that city. These visions masterfully evoke a dual perspective
of confidence and humility: God's people are intended for glory, despite
(or perhaps *because of*) their present exile and preparation. Again, the vision of Babylon calls for a sober evaluation of evil in the world, and even
in the community of God, as did the fleeting reference to "that woman"
Jezebel. The reality and presence of evil is qualified only by the insistence
that its time is limited.

Our final woman figure contrasts both with Babylon and with the
refugee queen. In contrast with Babylon, we see white versus red, inno-
cence versus worldly wisdom, purity versus jaded connections. In contrast to the harried and persecuted mother, we see a glorious and fortified
bride Jerusalem, protected and illuminated by God. Earlier readers encountered such contrasts immediately, and without controversy. No
doubt the early-twenty-first-century reader has already begun to feel
"edgy" about the subordination implied in the use of female figures.
Adela Yarbro Collins speaks of these symbols as "limited and limiting for
women"[7] because they are so male-centered; Tina Pippin insists that "the
Apocalypse is not a safe space for women";[8] Elisabeth Schüssler Fiorenza
has warned that the ethical reader must not "surrender the imagination"
to the dramatic action of the Apocalypse, because "Revelation engages the
imagination of the contemporary reader to perceive *women* in terms of
good or evil, pure or impure, heavenly or destructive, helpless or powerful, bride or temptress, wife or whore."[9] From such perspectives, the presentation of the bride, a female figure in a positive mode, is no less trou-
blesome than the presentation of the evil Babylon, for it is represents an
unrealistic and therefore vicious, or at least dangerous, assumption about
women. The bride is only pure insofar as she remains subordinate; Babylon is impure precisely because of her drive for independence.

It is a truism by now to notice that symbols not only speak about reality, but that they shape it. It is also true that symbols, because of their
"polyvalence" (their potential for many meanings), may be hijacked or
robbed of their deepest impact by the unscrupulous or the ideologue. But
a sympathetic reading of the Apocalypse will acknowledge that this book
paints its pictures not only for women, but also for men—indeed, for both
together as a group, and not separately. There is as much scandal for the
male reader of the Apocalypse, who is, from time to time, called to picture
himself in a female role, as for the female reader, who must distinguish
between a call to complete dependence upon God, and a call to "reign,"
along with others of the faithful community, with Christ. The eschatolog-

---

[7] Adela Yarbro Collins, "Feminine Symbolism in the Book of Revelation," *Biblical Interpretation* 1 (1993): 33.

[8] Tina Pippin, *Death and Desire: The Rhetoric of Gender in the Apocalypse of John*
(Louisville: Westminster John Knox, 1992), 80.

[9] Schüssler Fiorenza, *Book of Revelation*, 199.

ical scene of chapter 20 is instructive: thrones are set up and authority is
"given to those seated on them" (20:4; cf. Dan 7:9); yet before the great
throne, earth and heaven flee away (20:11). The pictures are, on the level
of sheer logic, contradictory: Does the Almighty establish thrones for the
righteous so that they participate in ruling? Or does any human power
pale before God's authority? The strange logic of the vision asserts that
both are true. The subordination of the female figure of the bride (and of
the refugee queen) in Revelation is, in the first place, a reflection on the
supreme authority of the Alpha and the Omega. It is not as if Revelation
were concerned with an elaborate chain of being, from God through angels, through males, through females, down to the inanimate created
order. For John is twice forbidden to do obeisance to the mediating angel
(19:10; 22:9), and all, great or small, find a level place before the throne of
God and the Lamb (19:12). Moreover, if we read not solely for gender, but
rather acknowledge the complex network of associative metaphors in
Revelation, we see that the bride and queen are cast as strong as well as
humble figures. The queen is mother, martyr, and warrior; the bride is a
fortified city. As these figures are subordinate to God, so they retain
strength over against their detractors. The book does not concern itself in
the first place with empowerment, but with humility, suffering, and re-
liance on a mighty God. Yet strength, too, has its place in the human community, and so we move on to consider the transformation of humanity
in the image of the bride Jerusalem, a picture that emerges out of pointed
contrast with Babylon and the refugee queen.

In contrast with Babylon, the image of the bride Jerusalem is bound
up with fecundity and fruitfulness. Here is a "bride" of radiance juxta-
posed with an enormous metropolis, described in terms of maternal and
fertility imagery: the life-giving water flowing down the middle of the
major street, the tree of life, yielding its fruit every month, and providing
healing. Just as the imagery of 22:1–3 recalls Eden, a reverse Eve (and,
perhaps, Adam) is suggested by the removal of "every curse." (The allusion in *pan katathema ouk estai eti* is not well-expressed by the NRSV's "nothing accursed.") The specificity of this language suggests that the effects of
Adam and Eve's disobedience are to be undone, and thus deepens the
declaration of 21:4, that there will be "no mourning and crying and
pain"—neither in work nor in childbirth (contrast Gen 3:16–17). Such joyful fruit-bearing is in contrast to Babylon, who considered her children a
sign of her own greatness, but who was brought low so that "the fruit for
which [her] soul longed has gone from [her]" and "the voice of the bride-
groom and the bride will never be heard in [her] again" (18:14, 23b). Similarly, the vicious and parasitic association of Babylon with others contrasts with the organic description of Jerusalem, built on the apostles and
prophets, working for the benefit of the nations, and illumined by God.
Bride, garden, city, and society come together in a picture of fullness and
cooperation.

In contrast with the queen of chapter 12, the bride Jerusalem is found not in the desert, but seen from a mountain, descending from heaven, and associated with garden imagery. The menacing river from the dragon's mouth (12:15) is replaced by the river of life. Where the queen was associated with stars and moon, the holy city derives her light and glory from God. The twelve-starred crown of the queen gives way to a battlement gate, supervised by twelve angels. The first woman labors under childbirth, giving a loud cry, while with the second woman every curse is gone. All has been transformed! The refugee along with her offspring "deck the bridal garments of joy."[10] Hidden glory becomes evident glory, as the time in the wilderness is seen to have been a time of preparation. The community's suffering, like the blood of the Lamb, emerges as a strength, rather than as weakness.

The final scene presents—more than a mere mending—a complete remaking of the human community and the cosmos. This is indicated in John's adaptation of Genesis imagery to a city-temple scenario that surpasses in scope even the grand pictures offered by the closing chapters of Isaiah and Ezekiel. The promises to the seven churches find their fulfillment: tree of life, hidden manna, new name, morning star, white clothing, the right to sit on the throne. The picture is multifaceted, piling image upon image to show the immensity of the blessing of those "invited to the wedding supper of the Lamb," not as spectators, but as participants. The corporate nature of these pictures cannot be overemphasized, since the three major female figures of refugee queen, mad mistress/Babylon, and bride/New Jerusalem speak of and to communities or groups, faithful and otherwise. Nevertheless, Revelation, as it began with a symbol of specificity, Jezebel, returns to speak directly to the individual reader. The Spirit and the bride issue their invitation to "the one who hears," asking her, or him, to join in the corporate call "Come," and to be satisfied by the water of life. Again, the warning is given to anyone who tampers with the revelation that they will miss their part in the "tree of life" and the "holy city."

The reader of the Apocalypse can hardly come to the closing passages without the awareness that this book issues a challenge. Taken on its own terms, the book resists the role of literary object that we have assigned to it and asserts a rhetorical power. It invokes the reader(s), first of all, to change perspective, to "come" (4:1) and see what things look like from the vantage point of heaven, from the desert, from a mountain. The summons is also to consider the implications of, among other scenes, three striking visions: visions of an ongoing but limited war, of a fall and "funeral," and of a paradisial wedding. Where there is mystery, there is also realism, and thus the visions come uncomfortably close to both community and reader at certain points. One of the major questions broached by

---

[10] Martin Kiddle, *The Revelation of St. John* (London: Hodder & Stoughton, 1940), 417–18.

these corporate figures, and by the reference to individuals such as "Jeze-bel," "the one who is filthy," and "the one who is righteous," is the issue of the identity of God's community. The reader is encouraged to ask, not only what God has done, is doing, and will do, not only what is the na-ture of reality here, and in the heavenlies, but also, *who* are the people of God—in differentiation from Babylon, in connection with the angelic hosts, in connection with the cosmos, in connection with angels. And the answer suggested is twofold: the community of God is called both to hu-mility and to God-endowed greatness. Readers of our time may have dif-ficulty not only with the choice of imagery, but with the unveiling itself. The femaleness of the figures may be discomfiting to us, in the end, not because of its "chauvinist" implications, but because of its power to pic-ture human frailty and promise. Could it be that the extremes of lowliness and authority, the realism and the aspirations, of the Apocalypse consti-tute a liquor too strong for our palates, too disturbing to our constitu-tions?

6

Doing Violence

MORAL ISSUES IN READING JOHN'S APOCALYPSE

David L. Barr

It will be a long time before we know how much violence will flow out of the terrorist attack that destroyed the World Trade Center, damaged the Pentagon, and murdered thousands of individuals, mostly U.S citizens, but including citizens of eighty other countries. The violence of that attack has traumatized the nation and horrified the world. Calls for retaliation—even war—are common. I cannot predict what will happen, but I will hazard two guesses, based on history.

First, there will likely be much more violence as the United States seeks redress for this evil. And while this violence will be intended for those who committed this crime, it is likely that many innocent people will be caught up in it. And this will lead to further violence, as some seek to avenge that injustice. Such is the cycle of violence. Violence begets violence.

Second, some will use the events of September 11, 2001, to interpret the Book of Revelation, claiming that September 11 corresponds to one or the other of the disasters predicted there. They will be wrong. At least every single prediction of the future based on identifying aspects of Revelation with historical events so far has been wrong—and there have been hundreds of them.[1] But they will be wrong in a more basic sense, for it is wrong to read John's story as if it were about divinely sanctioned violence.

This chapter is based on a paper read at the Society of Biblical Literature meeting in 1997 and published as David L. Barr, "Towards an Ethical Reading of the Apocalypse: Reflections on John's Use of Power, Violence, and Misogyny," in *Society of Biblical Literature Seminar Papers* (Atlanta: Scholars Press, 1997).

[1] See the historical summary in Arthur Wainwright, *Mysterious Apocalypse: Interpreting the Book of Revelation* (Nashville: Abingdon Press, 1993), esp. 49–103.

This chapter will examine the Apocalypse ethically, first challenging the ethics of many elements of the story, then asking after the ethical stance of the story itself, and finally suggesting the value of an ethical critique for reading the story. In summary, I argue that the use of coercive power is always wrong and is judged to be wrong by the Apocalypse itself. In fact, in John's story what most distinguishes the rule of God from that of the devil is that the latter uses coercive force. Of course, it is common to read Revelation as if evil is overcome only through violence, by unleashing the power of God.

The Ethical Problem of Coercion

There is much in the Apocalypse that lends itself to a theory of divine violence. The extremity of the destruction of the whore of Babylon should shock every reader: "[T]hey will make her desolate and naked; they will devour her flesh and burn her up with fire" (17:16). The warrior appears from heaven with a blood-dipped robe and slays the army of the beast, seemingly after the battle is over, leaving them on the battlefield so that "all the birds were gorged with their flesh" (19:21). He treads the winepress of God's wrath (19:15), from which comes blood "as high as a horse's bridle for a distance of 1600 stadia" (14:20). He, or God, consigns all not found enrolled in the book of life to the lake of fire (20:14). Commenting on the eternal torment of the worshipers of the beast, and this in the presence of the Lamb, one writer has remarked:

> Had such a statement been written about the beast, commentators would no doubt have described it as the epitome of malice, vindictiveness and evil.[2]

The ultimate value in this story seems to be power, power exercised ruthlessly. One even has the sense that God is willing to engage in torture in an effort to induce humanity to repent. Notice how John describes the final torments:

> The fourth angel poured his bowl on the sun, and it was allowed to scorch them with fire; they were scorched by the fierce heat, but they cursed the name of God, who had authority over these plagues, and they did not repent and give him glory. The fifth angel poured his bowl on the throne of the beast, and its kingdom was plunged into darkness; people gnawed their tongues in agony, and cursed the God of heaven because of their pains and sores, and they did not repent of their deeds. (16:8–11; see also 9:21)

Suffering does not lead to repentance, so it seems inevitably to lead to destruction. This is the deplorable logic of the Inquisition, but the moral problem goes even deeper. For if God triumphs over evil only because

---

[2] Steve Moyise, "Does the Lion Lie Down with the Lamb?" in *Studies in the Book of Revelation* (ed. Steve Moyise; T. & T. Clark, 2001).

God has more power than evil, then power—not love or goodness or truth—is the ultimate value of the universe. Human free will counts for nothing if obedience is finally to be coerced by force.

Stephen Moore puts his finger on the moral issue: "If the slaughter of the 'ungodly' should be permissible at the Parousia, then why not before?"[3] Indeed, it is a short step from the literary justification of violence, to the political justification of violence, to the use of violence against the enemy. Yet here some doubts must arise, for nearly all commentators recognize the rejection of violence by the Apocalypse:

> If you are to be taken captive, into captivity you go; if you kill with the sword, with the sword you must be killed. Here is a call for the endurance and faith of the saints. (13:10)

John does not call for violence but for endurance (Greek: *hypomonē*, which I think will easily bear the more active sense of *consistent resistance* that Elisabeth Schüssler Fiorenza assigns it.)[4] Our reading of the Apocalypse must account for both elements: the use of violent images and the rejection of violent action. Before exploring violence more carefully, we need to consider a related issue, for the story raises a further moral issue by portraying the deferral of divine action.

The Ethical Problem of Delay

There is much suffering in the world. Innocent people are killed by terrorists. Children die of malnutrition because government leaders divert money to the leaders' own use. Much of the world's population is forced to live in extreme poverty. Many have asked how God can allow this suffering, and the usual answer involves two parts. First, suffering is caused by humans, not by God, for humans have free will. And second, God will someday bring all such suffering to an end. We have seen that the portrayal of divine violence calls the question of human free will into question, but there is an additional moral issue.

For if God has the power to end suffering and evil, and intends one day to use that power, by what logic can God allow innocent suffering to continue? A police officer, a judge, even a social worker would be held liable in such a case. Imagine you know that a certain child is being abused, imagine you have the legal power to remove the child from the home, but you refuse to act. Are you not then responsible for whatever happens to that child?

John seems to recognize this issue in the telling of the story, for just this question is raised by the martyrs whose lives have been poured out on the altar:

---

[3] Stephen D. Moore, "Revolting Revelations," in *The Personal Voice in Biblical Interpretation* (London: Routledge, 1999), 192.

[4] Elisabeth Schüssler Fiorenza, *Revelation: Vision of a Just World* (Minneapolis: Fortress Press, 1991), 51.

> "Sovereign Lord, holy and true, how long will it be before you judge and avenge our blood on the inhabitants of the earth?" (6:10)

That such an issue is raised within the story suggests that the author is not unaware of these moral concerns. We can begin to analyze John's ethical stance by examining the way he portrays the divine answer to this question.

John's Ethical Stance: No Delay, No Coercion

The divine response to the martyrs is first to give them a white robe (signifying their victory) and then to tell them that they have to

> rest a little longer, until the number would be complete both of their fellow servants and of their brothers and sisters, who were soon to be killed as they themselves had been killed. (6:11)

If we probe the possible meaning of this portrayal, two aspects of John's ethics become clear. First, the answer has to do with the quantity of the martyrs. Now it would be silly to imagine that John portrays God has having some magic number, acting only when that number is reached. No, there is a logic at work, and it is the logic of the accumulation of evil.

Every society can bear up under small amounts of social disorder, but when the disorder reaches a sufficient amount, disastrous consequences ensue. To take a trivial example, as long as only 2 or 3 percent of the students on campus park illegally, parking can be regulated. But if half the students were to do so, chaos would result. The system would break down. Before we pursue this logic further, we need to consider a second aspect of John's ethics: victory does not obviate the need for suffering. Just the opposite: victory comes through suffering.

The crucial scene for portraying victory through suffering occurs in chapter 5. In that scene John is perplexed that no one can be found to open the sealed scroll; he is so distressed that he cries:

> Then one of the elders said to me, "Do not weep. See, the Lion of the tribe of Judah, the Root of David, has conquered, so that he can open the scroll and its seven seals." Then I saw . . . among the elders a Lamb standing as if it had been slaughtered, having seven horns and seven eyes, which are the seven spirits of God sent out into all the earth. (5:5–6)

There could not be a more stark symbolic contrast between the figure announced by the angel and the character actually seen by John: conquering lion/slaughtered lamb. Now on one level this is a portrayal of early Christian experience: they had heard that the Messiah would come with justice and vengeance, but what they actually saw in Jesus was quite the contrary: one who suffered. And it is precisely this suffering that makes him worthy to open the scroll.

It is quite surprising that it is this Lamb who gathers the 144,000 holy warriors on Mount Zion (14:1); it is the Lamb on whom the armies of evil make war (17:14); it is even the Lamb who marries and rules after the war

(19:7; 22:3). In this story, evil is conquered by the death of the Lamb, not by the exercise of divine power.

Even when the story seems to portray divine violence, the opposite (innocent suffering) is said to be the real force at work. This is seen clearly in the miniature scene in chapter 12, in which we are told the story of a war in heaven:

> And war broke out in heaven; Michael and his angels fought against the dragon. The dragon and his angels fought back, but they were defeated, and there was no longer any place for them in heaven. (12:7–8)

This is the traditional language of holy war; but the language, story, and moral situation are inverted by John's coda:

> But they have conquered him by the blood of the Lamb and by the word of their testimony, for they did not cling to life even in the face of death. (12:11)

Again we find a radical symbolic inversion: images of power are replaced by images of suffering. Similar inversions occur at every point in the story—even in the climactic scene in which the heavenly warrior kills all his enemies, for his conquest is by means of a sword that comes from his mouth, not by the power of his arm (19:21). Thus the victory over evil is procured not by physical violence but by verbal power. Surely this story is built on the mythology of holy war (and that itself may be ethically problematic), but just as surely John consistently demythologizes the war—or perhaps more accurately, remythologizes the warrior with the image of the suffering savior so that the death of the warrior and not some later battle is the crucial event. At every juncture in this story where good triumphs over evil a close examination shows that the victory is finally attributed to the death of Jesus.[5]

This then leads us back to the first point about the delay. Why is postponement necessary? By what logic must retribution await further suffering? The logic of judgment is articulated by the angel of the waters when the third bowl causes the earth's water to turn to blood:

> "Because they shed the blood of saints and prophets, you have given them blood to drink. It is what they deserve!" (16:6)

Notice both the appropriateness, the justice, of the retribution (blood because of blood) and also the inevitability of the retribution. The best analogy to this thinking can be found in our own impending ecological crisis. Because we have polluted our rivers we will have polluted water to drink. Retribution does not require some divine, tyrannical power over us; nor can any amount of divine mercy save us from it. This is the same logic of justice that undergirded Amos's visions of Israel's destruction, which

---

[5] For a consistent reading of Revelation as narrative, see David L. Barr, *Tales of the End: A Narrative Commentary on the Book of Revelation* (The Storytellers Bible 1; Santa Rosa, Calif.: Polebridge Press, 1998).

would come as a result of social injustice. Amos first saw a vision of locusts, but when he prayed God stopped the locusts. Amos then saw a vision of fire, but when he prayed God stopped the fire. Amos then saw a
vision of a crooked wall, and Amos could not pray for relief. For crooked
walls—and unjust societies—fall. (See Amos 7:1–9.)

So in our story the martyrs have to wait till their "number would be
complete" (6:11). This is not because God waits in some dispassionate indifference to the suffering of the innocent, but because in John's story
God acts *through* the process of suffering. There comes a time in every oppression when the amount of coercion needed to maintain a system will
itself destroy the system, as we ourselves have seen in Russia and South
Africa. So the great whore has become drunk with the blood of the saints
(17:6); Rome's very act of killing becomes her own death. Such is John's
vision. In this story evil is overcome by suffering love, not by superior
power, and the apparent delay in judgment of the wicked is not due to divine indifference but to John's basic understanding that human acts cause
human downfall. Still, we must face the reality of John's violent language.

While it is possible to appreciate the meaning of John's violent language, the language itself remains a problem. There is too much violence.
There is violence against mythic characters, violence against humans allied
with these characters, and verbal violence against other community members. There is also a subversion of violence, especially in connection with
the Lamb, as seen above. This subversion is not complete, however, and
we are left with the question of what to do with this surplus of violence.

The Ethical Problem of John's Language

Divine violence is portrayed as coming in four ways: in cosmic upheavals,
war, harvest scenes, and judgment scenes. Numerically, the cosmic upheavals—earthquakes, hail, fire, and water—predominate. Both the
seven trumpets (8:7ff.) and the seven bowls (16:2ff.) embody this violence,
which is directed at physical earth (trees, grass, water) and general
human victims (with only a couple of references to differentiate between
the wicked and the righteous, as in the sealing of the servants of God in
7:2–3; 9:4).

More powerful if less numerous are scenes of war. Already intimated
in 2:16 (where Jesus is said to be ready to come and war against a faction
of the church at Pergamum), war dominates the last half of the book. In
every case, the dragon starts the war and even prevails in one case (the
two witnesses [11:7, and see 13:15]), but ultimately loses the war to the
Lamb or the heavenly warrior. Little actual violence is portrayed in these
scenes, for no battle scene is ever dramatized.

The real problem stems from the scenes of judgment that follow bat-
tles. For example, in the battle scene in which the rider on the white horse
(whose name is "the Word of God") conquers all by the sword in his
mouth, we are told:

> [T]he beast was captured, and with it the false prophet who had per-
> formed in its presence the signs by which he deceived those who had re-
> ceived the mark of the beast and those who worshiped its image. These
> two were thrown alive into the lake of fire that burns with sulfur. And
> the rest were killed by the sword of the rider on the horse, the sword that
> came from his mouth; and all the birds were gorged with their flesh.
> (19:20–21)

One might justify the punishments of the leaders as stemming from their
crimes of war, but what of the rest? Is it right to kill combatants after the
war is over? In the same way, the dragon's later destruction in the lake of
fire (20:10) seems defensible, but what of the rest? For after all the fighting, the dead are assembled before one seated on a great white throne, to
be judged by what is recorded in the divine record books. Then,

> anyone whose name was not found written in the book of life was
> thrown into the lake of fire. (20:15)

This same problem attaches to two other scenes of judgment built on the
symbol of the harvest, first of the grain (14:15) and then of the wine
(14:20). The two scenes are introduced with a wine-making symbol that is
perhaps the most disturbing portrayal of divine violence in the book, involving as it does the participation of the Lamb:

> Then another angel, a third, followed them, crying with a loud voice,
> "Those who worship the beast and its image, and receive a mark on their
> foreheads or on their hands, they will also drink the wine of God's wrath,
> poured unmixed into the cup of his anger, and they will be tormented
> with fire and sulfur in the presence of the holy angels and in the presence
> of the Lamb. And the smoke of their torment goes up forever and ever.
> There is no rest day or night for those who worship the beast and its
> image and for anyone who receives the mark of its name." (14:9–11)

That such torture can be envisioned is horrible; that the Lamb can be envisioned as a spectator to it is beyond horror.[6] And one must raise here the
specter of coercion. Humanity seems left in the impossible situation that
the beast will kill all those who do not worship it (13:15), and God will kill
and torture all those who do. It seems a fine line between killing to induce
worship and killing because of worship.

This problem with a surplus of violence can also be found in the portrayal of the destruction of Rome under the image of a prostitute. The
ethics of this scene have been most thoroughly challenged by Tina Pippin.[7] And while I disagree with the way she resolves the problem, I thor-

---

[6] Chris Frilingos, "Making Males in an Unmade World: A Manly Paradise in
the Book of Revelation" (unpublished paper, 2000), to be published in revised
form as "Sexing the Lamb," in *Semeia*.

[7] Tina Pippin, *Death and Desire: The Rhetoric of Gender in the Apocalypse of John*
(Louisville: Westminster John Knox, 1992). See also idem, *Apocalyptic Bodies: The
Biblical End of the World in Text and Image* (London: Routledge, 1999).

oughly agree with the problem she sees.[8] The story of the destruction of the whore of Babylon is told in Rev 17 and interpreted in chapters 18 and 19. After a dramatic scene of the woman clothed in scarlet riding on a great beast and accompanied by ten kings, John is told:

> [T]hey and the beast will hate the whore; they will make her desolate and naked; they will devour her flesh and burn her up with fire. (17:16)

Pippin interprets this scene thus:

> The object of desire is made the object of death. The Whore/Goddess/ Queen/Babylon is murdered (a sexual murder) and eaten and burned. This grotesquely exaggerated vision of death and desire accentuates the hatred of the imperial power—and of women. This story of death and desire is the most vividly misogynist passage in the New Testament. The Apocalypse is cathartic on many levels, but in terms of an ideology of gender, both women characters in the narrative and women readers are victimized.[9]

Pippin is absolutely right to confront the way women are portrayed in this text. Contemporary men can justify their mistreatment of women by such ancient texts; contemporary women draw self-images from such stories. No one can be allowed to feel that what happens to John's whore in this story could ever be justified for any woman. It is dangerous that John used a human image here. We must challenge the text at this point (as we must challenge its comfort with violence generally). Still, careful reading is called for.

Thus in the scene of the destruction of the whore of Babylon that Pippin highlights, it is human brutality that is portrayed. The ten kings and the beast destroy her. Even so, this is because "God has put it into their hearts to carry out [God's] purpose" (17:17). Thus in some way God must be held accountable for all the violence in the world, even human violence, for God is responsible for creation. But this is surely morally different than imagining divine violence. In fact, John signals this dialectical tension by immediately adding, "The woman you saw is the great city that rules over the kings of the earth" (17:18). Those who seek to dominate others will themselves be devoured by the process; it is, John says, what God has ordained. While the image of violence is problematic for me, the understanding of violence is not. As Pippin herself observed:

> Having studied the evils of Roman imperial policy in the colonies, I find the violent destruction of Babylon very cathartic. But when I looked into the face of Babylon, I saw a woman.[10]

And this is the moral dilemma I find in the Apocalypse: I rejoice at its vi-

---

[8] I treated this disagreement at some length in the original version of this essay (see n. 1).

[9] Pippin, *Death and Desire*, 58.

[10] Ibid., 80

sion of the overthrow of evil, the elimination of oppression, the destruction of the destroyers of the earth; yet I cannot accept the images and actions that are used to portray this overthrow. While much of this portrayal is traditional—earthquake, war, harvest, final judgment—the degree of violence, involving eternal torture and the participation of the Lamb, at least as spectator, raises acute moral concerns. Rather than resolving these issues, the final section of this essay attempts to understand them more fully by placing them in their contexts, both the context of Roman Asia Minor and the context of John's story.

The Setting of John's Language

We have seen that it is no longer possible to explain John's language as the emotional outburst of a persecuted minority; it seems unlikely that the community faced any systematic Roman persecution.[11] John is concerned that his readers learn to identify Rome with evil; he must teach them how wicked Rome is because they are all too easily tempted to compromise with that evil. So rather than deal with the actual historical situation, I want to explore John's perception of that situation.

John makes two paradoxical assertions in his story. He asserts both that God rules this world (11:15) and that this world is still ruled by evil (17:18). Consider, for example, the little cameo scene in which there is a war in heaven and Satan is defeated. This is a cause for both rejoicing and for lamenting, for now Satan is loosed on the earth (12:7–12).

Perhaps we can see this situation more clearly if we return to one of John's opening sentences by which he introduces himself to the audience:

> I, John, your brother and partner in the affliction and reign and consistent resistance in Jesus, came to be on the island called Patmos on account of the word of God and the testimony of Jesus. (1:9, my translation)

First, notice that John expresses his solidarity with the audience in the strongest possible familial terms: brother and partner. In fact, the idea of partnership in Roman law derived from the need for brothers to inherit jointly their father's estate; thus, a partner is a virtual brother, but one with a shared investment. The surprise comes from how John describes the partnership; he uses three terms that do not fit readily together.

The first I have translated "affliction" (*thlipsis*). *Thlipsis* belongs to the language domain of trouble and suffering; it generally means "that which causes pain" (see 2:22).[12] It is regularly used to refer to the period of tribulation imagined to come at the end of the age (e.g., Matt 24:21). The sec-

---

[11] See chapters 2, 3, and 4 in this volume.

[12] Johannes P. Louw and Eugene A. Nida, eds., *Greek-English Lexicon of the New Testament Based on Semantic Domains* (2d ed.; New York: United Bible Societies, 1989).

ond term I have translated "reign" (*basileia*, pronounced baa-sa-LAY-a). *Basileia*, by contrast, belongs to the domain of power and rule—nearly the antithesis of *thlipsis*. Then to this oxymoronic pair, John adds a third, which I translated "consistent resistance" (*hupomonē*, pronounced hoopo-MON-ay). This term is usually translated "endurance"; it signifies the ability to bear up under difficult circumstances.[13] It is for John, I think, the active quality of standing up to evil; it is one of the works of the faithful (2:19).

Now the pairing of *hypomonē* and *thlipsis* makes perfectly good sense, but what of *basileia*? Only an apocalypse can show life as simultaneously *thlipsis* and *basileia*, for an apocalypse allows the audience to look behind the veil of ordinary experience (an unredeemed world, *thlipsis*) and see the true order of life (God's rule, *basileia*). John's audience is imagined to live in two worlds, corresponding to the basic dualism of John's world. But this is not a dualism of spirit and flesh or even of secular and spiritual, for the way to live in both is *hypomonē*. Or perhaps it is more accurate to say that life in the *basileia* provides power to live the resistance to evil (*hypomonē*) that is necessary in the time of *thlipsis*. (See 2:2–3; 3:10; 13:10; 14:12.)

I do not mean the actual audience (a historical question) but the "listener" *in* the story. We are all accustomed to thinking about the narrator, the voice through which an author tells a story, but what of the one to whom the story is told? Scholars have invented a name for this aspect of the story: the narratee.[14]

I see John's story moving at three basic narrative levels, each with its own narrator and narratee. The three levels of narration are the telling of the whole work by a public reader (1:3); the telling of the stories of the visions by John on Patmos (1:9); and the telling of things by characters in these stories (for example, the voice addresses the souls under the altar in 6:11). To whom does the narrator speak at each level; who are the narratees?

At the outermost level the narrator is the reader and the narratee is the audience gathered to hear the reading (1:3). This narratee corresponds most closely to the implied audience of the work, but we know almost nothing about this audience. The story leaves this narratee largely undefined, except to imagine them gathered to hear this work read.

The second-level narratee, however, is carefully defined, for that is the listener to whom John narrates his vision of the risen Christ. This narratee is explicitly named as the seven churches and extensively characterized in the messages to the churches (chs. 2–3). This narratee is a complex group, both rich and poor, both zealous and lax, both loving and cold. They are carefully distinguished from the people John calls Jezebel and

---

[13]   Ibid.

[14]   Seymour Chatman, *Story and Discourse: Narrative Structure in Fiction and Film* (Ithaca, N.Y.: Cornell University Press, 1978), 146–51.

Balaam, precisely because they are folk who might be tempted to follow such accommodating leaders.[15]

At the third narrative level, the narratees are the people addressed in the stories told to these second-level narratees—that is, the saints and martyrs who struggle to conquer the beast (see 6:10, 15:2, and the constant references to saints and servants). They are characterized as suffering and oppressed. These saints and martyrs are the focal points of the story, and both the second- and first-level narratees are encouraged to identify with them, leading one narrative critic to assert that ideal audience takes on the role of the martyr.[16] This is something of a poetical exaggeration, but it is clear that by telling the story through the point of view of those abused by Roman power, the discourse persuades the audience to resist such power.

So whatever the historical reality when viewed objectively, John tells this story to show Rome as the embodiment of evil. John portrayed a community at war, fighting for their very lives. This is not the actual experience of the community (narrative-level one) but the experience of the heavenly counterparts to the community (narrative-level three). John seeks to give the historical community the resources to fight that battle by portraying the utter conquest of evil. He portrays this conquest in vivid, bloody, even immoral extreme. These are dangerous images, for they can support the idea of a righteous violence, a redemptive violence.

What must be always kept in mind, however, is that these images of the conquest of evil, however immoral they may appear, always correspond to the innocent suffering of Jesus and of those who hold the testimony of Jesus. John consciously discourages the use of violence and calls rather for faith and consistent resistance (13:10). John's vision is not an easy solution, nor is it easy to accept. Events like September 11 and suicide bombings call out for retaliation, violence begetting violence in an endless round. John's vision peers behind the violence of this world, offering a glimpse of the cosmic war between good and evil, a war only won through suffering.

The purpose of the Apocalypse is to tell again of the vile things that Rome has done and is doing. It was Roman power, after all, that crucified Jesus; it is Roman power that constitutes the totalitarian state in which the audience now lives. If, as the saying goes, politics makes strange bedfellows, John wanted his audience to know just whom they were getting in bed with. John's Apocalypse is a revelation of the true nature of Roman

---

[15] I do not regard Jezebel and Balaam as part of the intended narratee because John's characterization of them is through insult and name-calling, devices designed to make them appear as outsiders. See Adela Yarbro Collins, "Vilification and Self-Definition in the Book of Revelation," *HTR* 79 (1986): 308–20.

[16] See the excellent, if technical, discussion of the reader as martyr in chapter 4 of Michael A. Harris, "The Literary Function of the Hymns in the Apocalypse" (Ph.D. diss., Southern Baptist Theological Seminary, 1989), 227–301.

power and Roman culture. Seeing Rome in this light could lead to despair, but it is a measure of John's achievement that he has created a story that both reveals the mistake of accommodating to Rome and provides a rationale for resistance. In this story the prayers, the patience, the persistent resistance of the saints overthrow the powers of evil and bring God's kingdom into reality.

7

Undercurrents and Paradoxes

THE APOCALYPSE TO JOHN IN PROCESS HERMENEUTIC

Ronald L. Farmer

The drama of the Apocalypse, set forth in what to modern readers is bizarre symbolism, can be characterized as a clash of powers. The Dragon (Satan), working through his henchman the Beast (the Roman government), wages war against the people of God. The power the Beast exercises is coercive, controlling, and unilateral. That God overcomes the Beast and the Dragon is clear. Also clear is that John exhorts his readers to overcome or conquer in the same manner that Jesus conquered. What is not so clear is the nature of this divine/human overcoming power.

The issues at stake can be brought into focus by reflecting upon D. H. Lawrence's assessment of the Apocalypse as a betrayal of the Christian ideas of grace and love. He felt that there were two kinds of Christianity: one focused on Jesus and the command to love even our enemies, and the other focused on the Apocalypse and its portrayal of vengeance on and power over our enemies. Thus for Lawrence, Revelation is the "Judas" of the New Testament because its portrayal of God's overcoming power— God as an absolute and brutally vengeful despot—betrays Jesus and his call to love.[1] But is this the only, or even the best, way to read the Apocalypse? This chapter will read the Apocalypse using a *process hermeneutic;* both terms need to be defined.

A Process Hermeneutic

Hermeneutics (the word comes from a Greek word meaning "interpretation") is the study of how people create meaning. Although the discipline of hermeneutics is concerned with how people discern/impose meaning in all of their experiences, the present chapter focuses on one very important activity: how people derive meaning from a written text.

[1] D. H. Lawrence, *Apocalypse* (n.p.: Penguin Books, 1974), 14–15.

A process hermeneutic is a theory of interpretation derived from process philosophy, which is based on Alfred North Whitehead's view of language.[2] One aspect of Whitehead's view is that language does not so much describe a reality as it lures us into particular ways of thinking and feeling about it. Because a text lures the reader, one of the goals of a close reading is to identify the lures at work in a text. Some lures are readily identifiable; these more prominent lures are labeled *surface lures*. Other lures operate below the surface of the text at the presuppositional level; that is, they reflect the author's assumptions and so typically are implied rather than stated. Because they underlie the surface lures, they are termed *basal lures*. At times basal lures may operate in a manner quite at odds with a straightforward reading of the surface lures. In such instances one may speak of these basal lures as an *undercurrent*.

Unlike some hermeneutical models, a process hermeneutic does not excise aspects of a text that are incompatible with the process worldview or that conflict with one another; on the contrary, a process hermeneutic encourages special attention to those dimensions of a text. What some hermeneutical models see as contradictions, a process hermeneutic attempts to view as *contrasts*. Careful consideration of lures foreign to the interpreter's own sensibilities, or lures that are at odds with other lures in the text, may result in the emergence of a novel pattern large enough to include both the foreign and the familiar in a harmonious contrast. A contrast is the unity had by the many components in a complex phenomenon, for example, perceiving many colors in a unified pattern (as in a kaleidoscope) as opposed to perceiving only a single color. Contrast is the opposite of incompatibility, for an incompatibility is resolved by the exclusion of one or more elements to achieve a more trivial harmony. According to process philosophy, however, the more a subject can hold the items of its experience in contrasts, and contrasts of contrasts, the more it elicits depth and intensity of experience. When this occurs, the subject (e.g., an interpreter) experiences *creative transformation*.[3]

A Paradox: Conflicting Portraits of Divine Power

A process-informed reading of the Apocalypse sets in bold relief a paradox (one of several) that exists in the text. John presents us with two very different portraits of divine power. Some passages clearly lure the reader

---

[2] See especially Alfred North Whitehead, *Adventures of Ideas* (New York: Macmillan, 1933; reprint, New York: Free Press, 1967); idem, *Process and Reality: An Essay in Cosmology* (ed. David Ray Griffin and Donald W. Sherburne; corrected edition; New York: Macmillan, 1929; reprint, New York: Free Press, 1978); and idem, *Symbolism: Its Meaning and Effect* (New York: Macmillan, 1927; reprint, New York: Fordham University Press, 1985).

[3] For a detailed presentation of a process hermeneutic, see Ronald L. Farmer, *Beyond the Impasse: The Promise of a Process Hermeneutic* (Macon, Ga.: Mercer University Press, 1997).

to think of God's power as coercive, controlling, and unilateral. Surprisingly, other passages just as clearly lure the reader to perceive divine power as persuasive, influencing, and relational.[4]

The Dominant Imagery: Coercive, All-Controlling, Unilateral Power

Generations of commentators assumed that the original readers of the Apocalypse were experiencing *official, government-sponsored* persecution under the Roman emperor Domitian. Present-day scholars point out that no reliable evidence exists supporting the long-held hypothesis.[5] This does not mean, however, that the late-first-century Christians of Asia Minor were not experiencing troubles. They were, and on several fronts. They were being ostracized and occasionally accused before the authorities by their Jewish neighbors. Gentiles despised Christians because of their suspicious beliefs and practices and, like the Jews, occasionally accused them before the magistrates. Moreover, tensions between rich and poor frequently erupted during times of stress and food shortages. Christians, generally poor and disenfranchised themselves, probably sympathized with the poor in these conflicts, which again brought them into confrontation with the authorities. As a result of these situations, Roman magistrates increasingly looked with disfavor upon Christians. One way the magistrates tested the loyalty of people brought before them was willingness to participate in the imperial cult (worship of the goddess Roma and the emperor). If Christians persistently refused to participate, refused to confess "Caesar is Lord," they could receive a death sentence; their endurance was perceived as stubborn disobedience and disloyalty to the state.[6]

Faced with this multifaceted crisis in which their opponents' power was clearly coercive, controlling, and unilateral, Christian leaders proposed two quite different responses. One group of leaders—whom John unflatteringly calls Nicolaitans, Balaamites, and Jezebel—advocated participation in civic life to counter the suspicion and hostility Christians were experiencing. For example, Christians should feel free to participate in trade-guild banquets, even though such banquets were dedicated to the patron deity of the guild. Likewise, on civic holidays they should feel free to engage in the festivities and eat the food, even though the festivals and food had been consecrated to a deity. After all, these deities did not really exist. Similarly, the emperor's claim to divinity was really just a po-

---

[4] For a discussion of another paradox—that of two conflicting notions of salvation, universal and limited—see chapter 9 of Farmer, *Beyond the Impasse*. My forthcoming commentary (*The Revelation to John: A Commentary for Today* [St. Louis: Chalice Press]) analyzes the entire Apocalypse from a process viewpoint.

[5] See chapter 2 in this volume, "Ordinary Lives: John and His First Readers."

[6] Adela Yarbro Collins, *Crisis and Catharsis: The Power of the Apocalypse* (Philadelphia: Westminster, 1984), 84–110; and Leonard Thompson, "A Sociological Analysis of Tribulation in the Apocalypse of John," *Semeia* 36 (1986): 147–74.

litical device used to promote loyalty to Rome. Why should they refuse to pay this honor to the emperor? Had not the Apostle Paul given similar advice many years ago (see 1 Cor 8–10; Rom 14:13–23)? "This theological stance had great political, economic, and professional advantage for the Christians living in the prosperous trading cities of Asia Minor."[7]

In John's opinion, however, such counsel amounted to acquiescing to (at best) or embracing (at worst) their opponents' conception of the highest form of power and to being assimilated into Roman culture. Representing the other group of Christian leaders, John called for a Christian communal life of social radicalism. Because the value systems of the two "kingdoms" were incompatible, no accommodation to Roman culture was allowed. John appealed to his readers to reject their oppressors' conception of power in favor of a radically different understanding of power. By means of a radical rebirth of images (stated overtly in chapter 5 and expressed as an undercurrent running throughout the Apocalypse), he set forth a new understanding of reality, one in which a slaughtered Lamb conquers, and faithful testimony—accompanied by voluntary, redemptive suffering, even to the point of martyrdom if need be—results in the overthrow of evil and the establishment of the rule of God.

In typical apocalyptic fashion, the Dragon and the Sea Beast wage war against John's readers, while the Earth Beast and the Great Whore attempt to seduce them from loyalty to God. These four are not, however, the only characters in this cosmic drama whose power could be described as coercive, controlling, and unilateral. These three adjectives are also conjured up by many of the Apocalypse's portraits of God and the Risen Christ. As early as 1:8 we encounter the first of nine descriptions of God as *pantokrator*, a term variously translated "almighty," "all-powerful," "omnipotent," and "ruler of all things." Likewise, the Risen Christ is described as "the ruler of the kings of the earth" (1:5) who has "dominion forever and ever" (1:6). Expressions such as "King of kings and Lord of lords" (17:14; 19:16), and ruling the nations (11:15; 15:3) "with a rod of iron" (19:15), occur frequently. But doubtless it is the central section of the book, chapters 6–20, that leads many readers to agree with Lawrence's assessment of the Apocalypse as the Judas of the New Testament.

In Rev 6, the Lamb begins opening seven seals, each one unleashing an unspeakable horror. The infamous four horsemen of the Apocalypse ride through the land unleashing military conquest, civil unrest, famine, and death. An enormous earthquake shakes even the mountains and islands from their places. The heavens have their own cosmic equivalent of an earthquake as the sun becomes black as sackcloth, the moon turns blood-red, the stars fall to the earth, and the sky vanishes like a scroll rolling itself closed. So terrified are "the inhabitants of earth" that they hide in caves,

    [7] Elisabeth Schüssler Fiorenza, *Invitation to the Book of Revelation* (Garden City, N.Y.: Image Books, 1981), 65.

calling on the mountains and rocks, "Fall on us and hide us from the face of the one seated on the throne and from the wrath of the Lamb; for the great day of their wrath has come, and who is able to stand?" (6:16–17). (The careful reader will note that "the inhabitants of the earth" are those who follow the Beast, wear his mark, and hence have their citizenship on earth. In sharp contrast, "the heaven dwellers" follow the Lamb, wear the mark of God, and consequently have their citizenship in heaven.)

In chapters 8 and 9, seven angels blow trumpets with devastating results. A fiery hailstorm burns up one-third of the earth's plant life. A burning mountain falls into the sea, causing one-third of the sea to turn to blood, killing one-third of the creatures in the sea and destroying one-third of the ships in the process. A blazing star falls from heaven, poisoning one-third of the earth's fresh water. One-third of the light of the sun, moon, and stars is extinguished. Scorpion-like locusts ascend from the bottomless pit to torment people with painful stings. And finally, from across the Euphrates River two hundred million demonic cavalry troops invade, killing one-third of humankind. The mention of the Euphrates River carried special significance for the original readers because it marked the eastern extent of Roman influence. Across it lay the Parthians, who had twice defeated the Roman army (53 B.C.E. and 62 C.E.). The Romans lived in fear that one day the Parthians would pour across the Euphrates in a massive invasion. The terror of the Parthian army lay in its mounted archers, who shot one volley as they charged and another volley over their horses' tails as they retreated, a tactic reflected in John's description of the demonic horde.

In chapter 16, seven angels pour out bowls containing the wrath of God. Painful sores erupt on the skin of all those who follow the Beast; the sea becomes blood, killing all marine life; the fresh waters also turn to blood; the sun scorches the earth with intense heat; and the Beast's kingdom plunges into utter darkness. The Euphrates River dries up so that armies from the east can pass over, assembling for battle at a place called Harmagedon. And finally, there is a violent earthquake, such as had never occurred, accompanied by huge hailstones weighing one hundred pounds.

As if these three cycles of terror were not enough, we also witness the devastating judgment of the Great Whore (Rev 17–18), the gory winepress of God's wrath, which expels a river of blood almost two hundred miles long (14:19–20; 19:15), and the gruesome great supper of God, where birds gorge themselves on the flesh of God's enemies (19:17–18, 21). And last but certainly not least, we encounter the well-known image of the sulfuric lake of fire into which are cast not only the Dragon, the Sea Beast, the Earth Beast, Death, and Hades, but also all those whose names are not written in the book of life (19:20; 20:10, 14–15; 21:8). In light of the gruesome horrors so vividly depicted in chapters 6–20, is it any wonder that many commentators feel that the Book of Revelation is the Judas of the New Testament?

The Undercurrent: Persuasive, All-Influencing, Relational Power

That interpreters have no difficulty in marshaling texts portraying divine power as coercive, all-controlling, and unilateral should come as no surprise given the general tone of apocalyptic writings. What readers do not expect to discover in Revelation are passages that picture divine power operating in quite a different manner.

Chapters 4 and 5 are pivotal to the understanding of the book as a whole and the issue of power in particular. In a manner reminiscent of the Hebrew prophets, John is invited (4:1) to observe the heavenly council, where the purpose of God is revealed. In keeping with his prophetic office, John then reveals to God's people the divine purpose and what part they play in its implementation.

As the drama unfolds, John receives four crucial revelations, which, as will be demonstrated, form an undercurrent to the dominant surface imagery: (1) the necessity of a worthy human agent to reveal and implement God's purpose for creation; (2) the image of the slain Lamb as the wisdom and power of God; (3) the call for the Lamb's followers to adopt the Lamb's lifestyle, rather than the lifestyle of the Beast, in order to insure the continuance of God's purpose; and (4) the portrayal of earthly events as not only reflected in heaven but also affecting heavenly dispositions. I will expand on each of these revelations in turn.

1. *The necessity of a worthy human agent to reveal and implement God's purpose for creation.* Chapter 5 opens with a scroll lying on God's right palm (5:1). Commentators generally agree that this sealed scroll represents the redemptive plan by which God's purpose will be achieved. Although the scroll rests in God's open hand, its opening awaits the emergence of a human agent willing *and worthy* to break the seals, thereby revealing and implementing the content of the scroll (5:2). The announcement that no one in all creation was found worthy to open the scroll moves John to uncontrollable weeping (5:3–4). Will God's purpose fail to be revealed and enacted for lack of a worthy agent?

2. *The image of the slain Lamb as the wisdom and power of God.* That not a single person was found worthy sets in bold relief the announcement that "the Lion of the Tribe of Judah, the Root of David" has conquered so that he can open the scroll (5:5). These titles are couched in the traditional messianic imagery of the Hebrew Bible and have a martial ring to them.

In reading Revelation, one should carefully examine the dialectical relationship between what John hears and what he sees, as these auditions and visions explain one another. John looks for the Lion of the audition but sees instead a Lamb bearing the marks of sacrificial slaughter (5:6). The audition explains the vision: the death of Jesus is not weakness and defeat but power and victory. Likewise, the vision explains the audition: God's power and victory lie not in brute force but in suffering, redemptive love. This radical rebirth of images (Lion/Lamb) contrasts sharply with the portrayal of demonic power. The Earth Beast may look like a lamb, but it speaks like a dragon (13:11); the Earth Beast is a deliberate parody of Christ the Lamb! Throughout the Apocalypse, Christ's only power is that of the sword that issues from his mouth (1:16; 2:12, 16; 19:15), that is, words that pierce people's souls. This imagery suggests that God conquers by means of a war of words—through persuasion, not coercion.

In addition to the marks of slaughter, the Lamb has two other striking characteristics: seven horns and seven eyes (5:6). Horns frequently symbolize power in Jewish literature. The presence of seven horns indicates that the Lamb is perfect in power. Eyes frequently symbolize wisdom or knowledge; consequently, the presence of seven eyes signifies that the Lamb is perfect in wisdom. By means of this vivid imagery John asserts that suffering, redemptive, persuasive love is the most powerful force in the universe, an expression of the perfect wisdom of God.

3. *The call for the Lamb's followers to adopt the Lamb's lifestyle, rather than the lifestyle of the Beast, in order to insure the continuance of God's purpose.* John goes on to state that the horns and eyes of the Lamb are "the seven spirits of God sent out into all the earth" (5:6). Apparently, John has interpreted Isa 11 by Zech 3:8–4:10, in which seven lamps are "the eyes of the Lord which range through the whole earth," and the point is, "not by might, nor by power, but by my Spirit." The earlier symbolism of the seven churches as seven lamp stands (1:12, 20) would have prepared John's readers to understand the seven flaming spirits of God (1:4; 4:5), which symbolize the manifold energies of God's Spirit, in terms of their own mission and witness. They are, or at least have the potential of being, Spirit-filled followers of the Lamb. Thus, John asserts that the continued activity of God in the world depends upon the followers of the Lamb acting as the horns and eyes of the Lamb sent out into all the earth.

At this point, knowledge of the literary structure of Revelation plays a key hermeneutical role. Several structural analyses[8] have noted that the visions of destruction (Rev 6–20) are bracketed by the vision of God the Creator and Redeemer (Rev 4–5) who makes all things new (21:1–22:5). Moreover, the whole drama (4:1–22:5) is itself bracketed by exhortations to faithfulness addressed to the readers (chs. 1–3 and 22:6–21). Thus, the structure of the book is:

$$1\text{–}3 \left[4\text{–}5 \left[6\text{–}20 \right] 21{:}1\text{–}22{:}5 \right] 22{:}6\text{–}21$$

Now if chapters 6–20 stood alone it would be hard to see them as any-

---

[8] For example, J. P. M. Sweet, *Revelation* (Westminster Pelican Commentary; Philadelphia: Westminster, 1979), 13, 47, 51, 126; David Barr, "The Apocalypse as a Symbolic Transformation of the World: A Literary Analysis," *Int* 38 (1984): 46; and idem, "The Apocalypse of John as Oral Enactment," *Int* 40 (1986): 252–56.

thing other than a gruesome portrait of divine coercive power. Reading
chapters 6–20 in light of this bracketing, however, significantly alters the
interpretation of the passage. The wrath and victory of the Lamb (Rev 6–
20) are to be understood in light of the slain Lamb, who redeemed a people to serve as priests with the task of unifying the cosmos in the worship
of God (5:1–14). Moreover, the nations and their kings—the victims of the
horrors of chapters 6–20—will walk by the light of the New Jerusalem's
lamp, which is the Lamb (21:23–27), and the leaves of the tree that grows
in the city's streets serve to heal the nations (22:1–3). But this new creation
(21:1) is not accomplished by divine fiat. The whole cosmic drama (4:1–
22:5) is itself bracketed by exhortations to faithfulness addressed to the
readers (1–3 and 22:6–21). For the Word of God to accomplish the new
creation, the followers of the Lamb must bear faithful testimony (the persuasive word). Thus, the testimony of the Lamb's followers functions not
merely as *witness* to the reality and nature of God's power; their testimony also functions as the *instrument* through which the divine power
accomplishes its purposes. In this manner, they demonstrate that they are
indeed followers of the Lamb, for one of John's first descriptions of Jesus
is "the faithful witness" (1:5).

4. *The portrayal of earthly events as not only reflected in heaven but also affecting heavenly dispositions.* As noted previously, God's ability to implement the divine purpose depends upon finding a willing and worthy
human agent. When John wrote that Jesus' sacrificial death enabled God
to do what could not be done before—that is, open the scroll—he indicated that God's power is relational, not unilateral. But John did not limit
this interdependent relationship to God and Jesus. In the Apocalypse, the
scene continually shifts from earth to heaven and back. As J. P. M. Sweet
noted, in heaven one finds "both the origin and the reflection of earthly
events. . . . [Moreover,] heaven's will waits on earth's response." He further observed that in worship, "the heavenly will is communicated and
becomes fruitful in earthly doing and suffering; [then] the earthly victory
is registered . . . and becomes effective in new heavenly dispositions."[9] An
excellent example of this interdependent relationship can be seen in the
prayers of the saints on earth, which have their heavenly counterpart
(5:8) and produce an effect on heavenly dispositions (8:3–5). Not only are
good earthly deeds reflected in heaven, that is, deeds in which the divine
will has been accomplished, but also reflected in heaven are earthly deeds
resulting from the rejection of the divine will. Examples of evil being reflected in heaven include the sea before the heavenly throne (4:6),[10] the
souls of the martyrs, who had been slaughtered because of their testi-

---

[9] Sweet, *Revelation*, 113–14.
[10] On the symbolism of the sea, note John Day, *God's Conflict with the Dragon
and the Sea in the Old Testament* (Cambridge: Cambridge University Press, 1985).

mony, under the altar (6:9–11), and the war in heaven (12:7–12). These bad deeds also are registered and effect new heavenly dispositions. Consequently, John exhorts his readers to reject the counsel of the Nicolatians, Balaamites, and Jezebel—counsel that amounts to embracing Roman society's definition of power. That understanding of power results only in evil and therefore hinders God's purpose for creation.

Throughout the Apocalypse, John exhorts his readers to conquer in the same fashion as Jesus conquered (for example, the promise to those who "conquer" at the end of each of the seven letters in chs. 2–3; see also 12:11 and 20:4, 6). Jesus' sacrificial death may have enabled God to *inaugurate* the divine purpose, but the *continued* implementation of God's purpose depends upon the followers of Jesus making his lifestyle their lifestyle. Obviously, heeding John's exhortation requires a radically new understanding of reality, one in which a slaughtered Lamb conquers, and faithful testimony—accompanied by voluntary, redemptive suffering, even to the point of martyrdom if need be—results in the overthrow of evil and the establishment of God's purpose for creation.

Concluding Hermeneutical Reflections

The preceding analysis has uncovered a cluster of basal lures in which John provides his readers a new perspective on power, both divine and human. The power that will triumph—that is, the power that will result in God's purpose being achieved—is persuasive not coercive, influencing not controlling, relational not unilateral. But even if the preceding analysis has convincingly demonstrated the existence of this undercurrent, undoubtedly some readers will insist, and rightly so, that the undercurrent is not the whole picture. The dominant imagery of the Apocalypse (the surface lures) presents God's power as coercive, all-controlling, and unilateral. Indeed, interpreters throughout the ages have felt that the major textual lures operate in this deterministic fashion. Thus, the preceding analysis has revealed a strong undercurrent working against the text's dominant surface imagery by means of basal lures, suggesting that divine power be understood as persuasive, all-influencing, and relational. What is a reader to make of this paradox?

As previously noted, a process hermeneutic does not excise textual lures that are incompatible with the process worldview or that are at odds with other lures operating in the text; on the contrary, it encourages special attention to these "problematic" dimensions of the text. The entertainment of lures foreign to the interpreter's sensibilities may result in the emergence of a novel pattern large enough to include both the foreign and the familiar in a harmonious contrast, so that the reader's understanding of the text undergoes a creative transformation. How might this occur with respect to the discordant lures at hand: that God's power be viewed as coercive, all-controlling, and unilateral (the surface lures) and that God's power be viewed as persuasive, all-influencing, and relational (the basal lures)?

To begin with, the reader should note that it is a matter of conjecture as to John's level of awareness of the tension he created by means of this undercurrent. Being a child of the first century may have prevented him from perceiving what appears obvious—obvious at least in light of the preceding analysis—to modern interpreters operating with a radically different worldview. Thus, it is possible that John was unaware of the problem he created with (1) his insistence on the necessity of a worthy human agent to reveal and implement God's purpose for creation; (2) his image of the slain Lamb as the wisdom and power of God; (3) his call for the Lamb's followers to adopt the Lamb's lifestyle, rather than the lifestyle of the Beast, in order to insure the continuance of God's purpose in the world; and (4) his portrayal of earthly events as not only reflected in heaven but also affecting heavenly dispositions. But whether John created this undercurrent intentionally or inadvertently, these basal lures nevertheless stand in tension with the deterministic worldview implied by the surface lures.

Whether John viewed the language of the surface lures literally or imaginatively is also a matter of conjecture. But even if John intended it to be understood literally, present-day readers may view it imaginatively because all language, especially mythopoetic language, is relatively indeterminate. Moreover, a process hermeneutic proposes that when the basal lures of a text function as an undercurrent to the surface lures, then the surface lures should be read imaginatively rather than literally. The reason for this hermeneutical proposal is that the basal lures form the deepest metaphysical assumptions undergirding the text as a whole (and thus are the most important lures), even if these implied assumptions were not consciously entertained by the author.

Therefore, when held in the unity of a contrast with the basal lures, John's deterministic language can evoke non-deterministic lures. The deterministic language of the surface lures can evoke the firm *conviction* that God and God's people will eventually overcome evil, while the non-deterministic language of the undercurrent can evoke the *manner* of overcoming: persuasive love that is willing to suffer if need be (the basal lure) will eventually triumph (the surface lure), for such redemptive love (the basal lure) is the most powerful force in the universe (the surface lure). Thus, a process hermeneutic enables the Apocalypse to speak powerfully and relevantly to today's reader by issuing a transforming challenge to the modern world's understanding of the nature of supreme power.

8

Taking a Stand on the Sand of the Seashore
A POSTCOLONIAL EXPLORATION OF REVELATION 13

Jean-Pierre Ruiz

Like the dragon poised on the sand of the seashore in Rev 12:18, from its place at the extreme end of the New Testament canon the Book of Revelation has long exercised a strange fascination among readers out of "every tribe and people and language and nation." In this study I explore what happens when the Apocalypse is read from the margins, by first taking a look at liberationist perspectives on the Apocalypse, and then by considering the challenges that postcolonialist reading strategies pose to liberationist and mainstream perspectives alike.

Embracing Apocalypse: Liberationist Readings of the Apocalypse

Fernando F. Segovia traces the origins of liberationist hermeneutics in the following terms:

> For Latin American theologians and biblical critics, the fundamental question of massive material poverty, with its roots in the conflict between socioeconomic classes, became the point of departure for a new way of doing theology. This was readily extended to the realm of biblical studies in the form of a search for the stance of the Bible and its proper interpretation. As this search unfolded, a consensus gradually emerged. On the one hand, the Bible was seen as a text against oppression and for liberation; on the other hand, a twofold interpretation was posited: The Bible can be read either from the perspective of continuing oppression, as it has been, or from the perspective of liberation, as it should be. Consequently, the interpreter was called upon to read the Bible on the side of the oppressed and thus for their liberation from socioeconomic oppression.[1]

I owe special thanks to Dr. Carmen Nanko for her insightful comments on several drafts of this piece.

[1] Fernando F. Segovia, "Reading the Bible Ideologically: Socioeconomic Criticism," in *To Each Its Own Meaning: An Introduction to Biblical Criticisms and Their Ap-*

Beginning in the 1970s with the work of Peruvian theologian Gustavo Gutiérrez in Latin America and with the work of African American theologian James Cone in the United States, liberation theology and liberationist biblical hermeneutics rapidly expanded in the 1980s and 1990s to include a variety of emancipatory discourses, ranging from African and Asian liberationist hermeneutics, to Native American, African American, Asian American, and Hispanic American perspectives, as well as a variety of feminist emancipatory perspectives.[2] Hand in hand with the advocacy stance of liberationist hermeneutics, that is, the decision to read the Bible *with* and on the side of the oppressed and marginalized, came liberationist encouragement of the appropriation of the Bible *by* ordinary readers.[3]

---

plication (ed. Steven L. McKenzie and Stephen R. Haynes; rev. ed.; Louisville: Westminster John Knox Press, 1999), 285–86.

[2] Gustavo Gutiérrez, *A Theology of Liberation* (1973; Maryknoll, N.Y.: Orbis Books, 1988); James H. Cone, *A Black Theology of Liberation* (1970; Maryknoll, N.Y.: Orbis Books, 1990); Aloysius Pieris, *An Asian Theology of Liberation* (Maryknoll, N.Y.: Orbis Books, 1988); Itumeleng Mosala, *Biblical Hermeneutics and Black Theology in South Africa* (Grand Rapids: Eerdmans, 1989); Ali Ashgar Engineer, *Islam and Liberation Theologies* (New Delhi: Sterling, 1990); Virginia Fabella and Mercy Amba Oduyoye, eds., *With Passion and Compassion: Third World Women Doing Theology* (Maryknoll, N.Y.: Orbis Books, 1988); Virginia Fabella and Sun Ai Lee Park, eds., *We Dare to Dream: Doing Theology as Asian Women* (Hong Kong: Asian Women's Resource Centre, 1989; Maryknoll, N.Y.: Orbis Books, 1990); Mercy Amba Oduyoye and Musimbi R. A. Kanyoro, eds., *The Will to Arise: Women, Tradition, and the Church in Africa* (Maryknoll, N.Y.: Orbis Books, 1992); María Pilar Aquino, *Our Cry for Life: Feminist Theology from Latin America* (Maryknoll, N.Y.: Orbis Books, 1993). For examples of the rich and diverse readings of biblical texts that have emerged from the margins, that is, from and by readers outside the academic settings of Western Europe and English-speaking North America, see Fernando F. Segovia and Mary Ann Tolbert, eds., *Reading from This Place*, vol. 1: *Social Location and Biblical Interpretation in the United States* (Minneapolis: Augsburg Fortress, 1995); Fernando F. Segovia and Mary Ann Tolbert, eds., *Reading from This Place*, vol. 2: *Social Location and Biblical Interpretation in Global Perspective* (Minneapolis: Fortress Press, 1995); R. S. Sugirtharajah, ed., *Voices from the Margin: Interpreting the Bible in the Third World* (rev. ed.; Maryknoll, N.Y.: Orbis Books, 1995).

[3] See, for example, Ernesto Cardenal, *The Gospel in Solentiname* (4 vols.; Maryknoll, N.Y.: Orbis Books, 1982); Carlos Mesters, "The Use of the Bible in Christian Communities of the Common People," in *The Bible and Liberation: Political and Social Hermeneutics* (ed. Norman K. Gottwald; Maryknoll, N.Y.: Orbis Books, 1983), 119–33; idem, *Defenseless Flower: A New Reading of the Bible* (Maryknoll, N.Y.: Orbis Books, 1989); Pablo Richard, "The Hermeneutics of Liberation: Theoretical Grounding for the Communitarian Reading of the Bible," in *Teaching the Bible: The Discourses and Politics of Biblical Pedagogy* (ed. Fernando F. Segovia and Mary Ann Tolbert; Maryknoll, N.Y.: Orbis Books, 1998), 272–82; Gerald West, *The Academy of the Poor: Towards a Dialogical Reading of the Bible* (Sheffield, England: Sheffield Academic Press, 1999).

In the canon-within-the-canon of liberationist hermeneutics, the Apocalypse of John holds an especially prominent place. Elisabeth Schüssler Fiorenza notes that

> the imagery of chapters 13 and 17–18 as well as chapters 20–21 is very popular with the peasants and the poor of Central and South America who are reading the Bible in Christian base communities. Since Revelation depicts the exploitation of the poor and the concentration of wealth in the hands of the powerful, the injustices perpetrated by the colonialist state, and a society that has grown obscene by perpetrating stark contrasts between rich and poor, they can read it as speaking to their own situation of poverty and oppression.[4]

Their reading strategy seeks a "correspondence of relationships between Revelation in its context and their own sociopolitical context" so that Revelation serves as "a canonical prototype and as a utopian language resource for illuminating present situations of suffering and injustice."[5] Pablo Richard, a Chilean priest who works in Costa Rica, illustrates this correspondence of relationships: "Revelation arises in a time of persecution—and particularly amid situations of chaos, exclusion and oppression. In such situations, Revelation enables the Christian community to rebuild its hope and its awareness. Revelation transmits a spirituality of resistance and offers guidance for organizing an alternative world."[6] In the same vein, Brazilian biblical scholar Gilberto da Silva Gorgulho explains, "The Book of Revelation is the favorite book of our popular communities. Here they find the encouragement they need in their struggle and a criterion for the interpretation of the official persecution in our society. The communities plumb the depths of the book that is revelation, witness and prophecy (Rev 1:1–6), a book whose purpose is to encourage and maintain the prophetical praxis of the new people—this priestly, royal and prophetic people."[7]

---

[4] Elisabeth Schüssler Fiorenza, *Revelation: Vision of a Just World* (Proclamation Commentaries; Minneapolis: Augsburg Fortress, 1991), 11.

[5] Ibid. For a brief review of Latin American liberationist readings of the Apocalypse and a sketch of a U.S. Hispanic American liberationist reading, see Jean-Pierre Ruiz, "Biblical Interpretation from a U.S. Hispanic American Perspective: A Reading of the Apocalypse," in *El Cuerpo de Cristo: The Hispanic Presence in the U.S. Catholic Church* (ed. Peter Casarella and Raúl Gómez; New York: Crossroad, 1998), 78–105. Also see Jean-Pierre Ruiz, "The Bible and U.S. Hispanic American Theological Discourse: Lessons from a Non-innocent History," in *From the Heart of Our People: Latino/a Explorations in Catholic Systematic Theology* (ed. Orlando O. Espín and Miguel H. Díaz; Maryknoll, N.Y.: Orbis Books, 1999), 100–120.

[6] Pablo Richard, *Apocalypse: A People's Commentary on the Book of Revelation* (Maryknoll, N.Y.: Orbis Books, 1995), 3.

[7] Gilberto da Silva Gorgulho, "Biblical Hermeneutics," in *Mysterium Liberationis: Fundamental Concepts of Liberation Theology* (ed. Ignacio Ellacuría and Jon Sobrino; Maryknoll, N.Y.: Orbis Books, 1993), 146.

Insisting that "the mystery revealed in the book of Revelation is actually more current today than ever, and merits our close attention," Enrique Dussel works out a correspondence of relationships between the first-century sociopolitical context of the Apocalypse and that of late-twentieth-century Latin America. Dussel formulates the "Babylon principle" on the basis of Rev 17–18 as a metaphor for the death-dealing ethos of exploitative accumulation that characterizes "this world."[8] On the basis of Rev 20–21, he formulates an opposing "Jerusalem principle" as the metaphor for "a utopian Christianity that believes in the reign of God, hates the Prince of 'this world' and his reign, and inaugurates a praxis of liberation where all will receive 'on the basis of each one's need.'"[9] In his own study of Rev 18, Argentinian biblical scholar Néstor Míguez elaborates on Dussel's "Babylon principle" to suggest that "behind the mask of luxury and progress lies the true visage of human destruction. The repulsive spirits of violence, racial hatred, mutilation, and exploitation roam the streets of our Babylon in Latin America (and the globe)."[10]

Latin America is not the only setting that has given rise to liberationist readings of the Apocalypse. Amidst the violence of apartheid-era South Africa, activist pastor Allan A. Boesak proposed that

> The clue to understanding the Apocalypse as protest literature . . . lies, I think, in Revelation 1:9: "I John, your brother, who share with you in Jesus the tribulation and the kingdom and the patient endurance [of suffering]." This is the key. Those who do not know this suffering through oppression, who do not struggle together with God's people for the sake of the gospel, and who do not feel in their own bodies the meaning of oppression and the freedom and joy of fighting against it shall have grave difficulty understanding this letter from Patmos. . . . It is the struggling and suffering and hoping together with God's oppressed people that open new perspectives for the proclamation of the Word of God as found in the Apocalypse.[11]

In the end, both in Latin America and elsewhere, the liberationist optic reads the Apocalypse as a hopeful book, an empowering utopian manifesto that redefines the innocent suffering to which the faithful are subjected as a participation in the paradoxical victory of Christ as the slaughtered Lamb. The book is read as an unflinching prophetic proclamation of justice that speaks the truth to power no matter the cost, and as a divine

[8] Enrique Dussel, *Ethics and Community* (trans. Robert R. Barr; Maryknoll, N.Y.: Orbis Books, 1988), 28.

[9] Ibid., 52.

[10] Néstor Míguez, "Apocalyptic and the Economy: A Reading of Revelation 18 from the Experience of Economic Exploitation," in Segovia and Tolbert, *Reading from This Place*, 2:260.

[11] Allan A. Boesak, *Comfort and Protest: The Apocalypse from a South African Perspective* (Philadelphia: Westminster, 1987), 38.

declaration that the violent designs of the powers of "this world" will result in their own undoing.

Rethinking Revelation: A Postcolonial Turn

"Until now liberation hermeneutics has been seen as the distinctive contribution of Third World biblical interpreters. Recently another critical category, postcolonialism, has emerged as its rival, and has staked a claim to represent minority voices."[12] Who is this newcomer? With the emergence of postcolonial criticism, according to Indian critic Harish Trivedi, "For the first time probably in the whole history of the Western academy, the non-West is placed at the centre of its dominant discourse. Even if it is in part a sort of compensation for all the colonial material exploitation, the academic interpretation now being paid to the post-colonial is so assiduous as to soothe and flatter."[13] Like liberationist criticism, postcolonial criticism emerged in the so-called Third World.[14] With its theoretical underpinnings sketched out in the work of cultural critics Edward Said, Gayatri Chakravorty Spivak, and Homi K. Bhabha,[15] postcolonial criticism shares the emancipatory commitment of liberationist criticism inasmuch as it "offers a space for the once-colonized. It is an interpretive act of the descendants of those once subjugated. In effect it means a resurrection of the marginal, the indigene and the subaltern. . . . It is an act of reclamation, redemption and reaffirmation against the past colonial and current neo-colonializing tendencies which continue to exert influence even after territorial and political independence has been accomplished."[16]

[12] R. S. Sugirtharajah, *The Bible and the Third World: Precolonial, Colonial, and Postcolonial Encounters* (Cambridge: Cambridge University Press, 2001), 244.

[13] Harish Trivedi, "India and Post-colonial Discourse," in *Interrogating Post-Colonialism: Theory, Text, and Context* (ed. Harish Trivedi and Meenakshi Mukherjee; Shimla, India: Indian Institute of Advanced Study, 1996), 232, as cited in R. S. Sugirtharajah, "A Postcolonial Exploration of Collusion and Construction in Biblical Interpretation," in *The Postcolonial Bible* (ed. R. S. Sugirtharajah; The Bible and Postcolonialism 1; Sheffield, England: Sheffield Academic Press, 1998), 92.

[14] Virginia Fabella explains that the expression "Third World" was coined "in 1952 by the French demographer Alfred Sauvy, who saw similarity between the nations moving toward independence from colonial powers and the Third Estate in France demanding freedom and equality during the French Revolution" and that the expression continues to be used "as a self-designation of peoples who have been excluded from power and the authority to shape their own lives and destiny" ("Third World," in *Dictionary of Third World Theologies* [ed. Virginia Fabella and R. S. Sugirtharajah; Maryknoll, N.Y.: Orbis Books, 2000], 202).

[15] Edward W. Said, *Orientalism* (New York: Pantheon, 1978); idem, *Culture and Imperialism* (New York: Knopf, 1993); Gayatri Chakravorty Spivak, *In Other Worlds: Essays in Cultural Politics* (New York: Methuen, 1987); idem, *The Postcolonial Critic: Interviews, Strategies, Dialogues* (ed. Sarah Harasym; New York: Routledge, 1990); Homi K. Bhabha, *The Location of Culture* (London: Routledge, 1994).

[16] Sugirtharajah, *Bible and the Third World,* 250.

Postcolonialism has been described as "a mental attitude rather than a method," a critical stance that finds expression "in such wide-ranging fields as politics, economics, history and theological and biblical studies."[17] Fernando F. Segovia sets out the broad (inter)disciplinary reach of postcolonial studies as:

- The study of imperialism and colonialism, which I understand as follows: while the former focuses on all that pertains to the center or metropolis, the latter marks all that pertains to the margins or periphery.
- The study of imposition and domination as well as of opposition and resistance: not only the discourses of imperialism and colonialism but also the counterdiscourses of anti-imperialism and anti-colonialism.
- The study of the different phases within imperialism and colonialism, with their resultant subdiscourses: pre-imperialism and pre-colonialism; imperialism and colonialism; neo-imperialism and neo-colonialism.[18]

While postcolonial criticism shares the emancipatory ideals that liberationist hermeneutics embraces, it is deeply suspicious of the liberationist tendency to give the Bible the unquestioned benefit of the doubt, to regard the Bible itself as *the* place where the message of liberation is to be found, and to excuse the Bible from the critical analytical gaze to which other texts (including other readings of the Bible) are subjected. Pablo Richard, for example, maintains that "the problem is not the Bible itself, but the way it has been interpreted. . . . The Bible gives us the testimony of the word of God, it is also the canon or criterion of discernment of the Word of God today."[19] Many postcolonial critics resonate with Black lesbian feminist Audre Lorde's word of caution: "*For the master's tools will never dismantle the master's house.* They may allow us temporarily to beat him at his own game, but they will never enable us to bring about genuine change."[20] Postcolonial critics would urge liberationist hermeneutes to

[17] Sugirtharajah, "Postcolonial Exploration of Collusion and Construction," 93. It is important to note that postcolonialism is not without its discontents. See, for example, Dinesh D'Souza, "Two Cheers for Colonialism," *The Chronicle of Higher Education*, 10 May 2002, pp. B7–9.

[18] Fernando F. Segovia, "Interpreting beyond Borders: Postcolonial Studies and Diasporic Studies in Biblical Criticism," in *Interpreting beyond Borders* (ed. Fernando F. Segovia; The Bible and Colonialism 3; Sheffield, England: Sheffield Academic Press, 2000), 13–14. Also see Fernando F. Segovia, *Decolonizing Biblical Studies: A View from the Margins* (Maryknoll, N.Y.: Orbis Books, 2000), esp. 119–32: "Biblical Criticism and Postcolonial Studies: Toward a Postcolonial Optic," and 133–42: "Notes toward Refining the Postcolonial Optic."

[19] Pablo Richard, "1492: The Violence of God and the Future of Christianity," in *1492–1992: The Voice of the Victims* (ed. Leonardo Boff and Virgil Elizondo; Concilium 6; London: SCM Press; Philadelphia: Trinity Press International, 1990), 66.

[20] Audre Lorde, *Sister Outsider* (Trumansburg, N.Y.: Crossing Press, 1984), 122. Emphasis in the original. On the other hand, there are postcolonial critics who

recall that the Bible arrived in the hands of the colonizers, who saw it as the indispensable means with which the colonized were to be civilized (read "saved").[21] The lingering aftereffects of this European enterprise of ideological colonization are captured vividly in a 1985 letter addressed to Pope John Paul II by a group of Andean Indians:

> We, Indians of the Andes and of America, decided to take advantage of the visit of John Paul II to return to him his Bible, because in five centuries it has given us neither love, peace nor justice. Please take your Bible back again and return it to our oppressors, because they need its moral precepts more than we do. Because ever since the arrival of Christopher Columbus to America the culture, language, religion and European values were imposed by force.
>
> The Bible came to us as part of the imposed colonial change. It was the ideological arm of the colonialist assault. The Spanish sword, that by day attacked and assassinated the body of the Indians, and by night was converted to the cross that attacked the Indian soul.[22]

Conscious of this history and therefore standing at a cautious distance from naive liberationist affirmations of the Bible's inherent emancipatory qualities, the work of postcolonial criticism involves "scrutinizing and exposing colonial domination and power as these are embodied in biblical texts and in interpretations, and . . . searching for alternative hermeneutics while thus overturning and dismantling colonial perspectives."[23] R. S. Sugirtharajah suggests that when its gaze is turned toward biblical texts, postcolonial criticism takes on three tasks:

1. "Scrutiny of biblical documents for their colonial entanglements. . . . In doing this, postcolonial reading practice will reconsider the biblical narratives . . . as emanating from colonial contacts. . . . It will address issues such as nationalism, ethnicity, deterritorialization and identity, which arise in the wake of colonialism."[24]
2. "Reconstructive readings of biblical texts. Postcolonial reading will reread biblical texts from the perspective of postcolonial concerns

---

choose to employ the "master's tools"—including technologies and texts and critical methods imported into the colonial setting—in surprising and remarkably subversive ways.

[21] Postcolonial critic R. S. Sugirtharajah also rightly notes: "In its overzealousness to represent the poor, liberation hermeneutics has ended up as a liberation theology of the poor rather than a theology of liberation by the poor" (*Bible and the Third World*, 242). In so doing, liberationist hermeneutics has unintentionally perpetuated the very patterns of domination and dependency to which liberationist ideals are explicitly opposed.

[22] Cited as quoted in Elsa Tamez, "Quetzalcóatl Challenges the Christian Bible," in *Journal of Hispanic/Latino Theology* 4 (May 1997): 11.

[23] R. S. Sugirtharajah, "Biblical Studies after the Empire: From a Colonial to a Postcolonial Mode of Interpretation," in idem, *Postcolonial Bible*, 16. See the examples of postcolonial biblical criticism in *Semeia* 75 (1996).

[24] Sugirtharajah, *Bible and the Third World*, 251.

such as liberation struggles of the past and present; it will be sensitive to subaltern and feminine elements embedded in the texts; it will interact with and reflect on postcolonial circumstances such as hybridity, fragmentation, deterritorialization, and hyphenated, double or multiple identities."[25]

3. "To interrogate both colonial and metropolitan interpretations . . . to draw attention to the inescapable effects of colonization and colonial ideologies on interpretive works such as commentarial writings."[26]

In the pages that follow, I undertake some first steps toward a postcolonial reading of the Apocalypse of John, following the broad lines of the agenda outlined above. To begin with, in an effort to map the colonial entanglements in which the Apocalypse is enmeshed, I discuss the significance of the imperial cult in the province of Asia. I then engage in a "reconstructive reading" of Rev 13, suggesting that it functions as an anti-imperialistic counterdiscourse. My selection of Rev 13 as a case in point of the counterdiscourse John marshals against the dominant imperial ideology is deliberate on two counts. First, nowhere else in the Apocalypse is John's rhetoric so relentlessly and extensively deployed against the imperial cult. Second, the enormous popularity of this chapter both among those who are preoccupied with deciphering the "number of the beast" (13:18) and among those who attend to "the call for the endurance and faith of the saints" suggests that a fresh look at Rev 13 through the lens of postcolonial criticism may be useful.

Colonial Entanglements: The Imperial Cult in the Province of Asia

Reckoning with Revelation requires us to recognize the depth and the extent of Roman imperial influence on the cities of the seven churches in western Anatolia, a region that first came under Roman control in 133 B.C.E. and which became the Roman province of Asia in 126 B.C.E. The year 89/90 C.E. saw the dedication at Ephesus of the Temple of the Sebastoi, a temple built in honor of the Roman emperors. By that time, imperial temples had already been established elsewhere in the province of Asia (including Pergamum, the first imperial temple in Asia, dated to 29 B.C.E.; Smyrna, 45 C.E.; Philadelphia, 55 C.E.; Sardis, 56 C.E.; Laodicea, 87 C.E.).[27] The cult of the Sebastoi provided the principal symbolic and ritual expression of the relationship between Rome and the province of Asia, between the imperial metropolis and the periphery. Focusing specifically on Ephesus, S. R. F. Price describes the spectacular omnipresence of the Roman emperor and the imperial cult in Ephesian civic space:

---

[25] Ibid., 252–53.

[26] Ibid., 255.

[27] See Adela Yarbro Collins, "Pergamon in Early Christian Literature," in *Pergamon, Citadel of the Gods: Archaeological Record, Literary Description, and Religious Development* (ed. Helmut Koester; Harvard Theological Studies 46; Harrisburg, Pa.: Trinity Press International, 1998), 163–84.

Ephesus was adorned with four imperial temples, a monumental Antonine altar, an imperial portico and four gymnasia associated with the emperor. In addition to these buildings . . . there were also a large number of imperial statues, such as the theatre and the council house, while others stood on the streets. A monumental nymphaeum, or fountain, contained as its center-piece an over life-sized statue of Trajan, and three other similar buildings also featured imperial statues. A building on the lower square was dedicated to the emperor and three monumental gates, in honour of Augustus, Trajan and the Severi, displayed statues of them and their families. . . . The emperor, whose name or image met the eye at every turn, received a striking position in this process of transformation.[28]

The architectural remaking of Ephesus associated with the cult of the emperors represents a significant example of what postcolonial theorists call hybridization, for the Ephesians reshaped their city "not in the image of Rome or Italy, but in accordance with the Greek traditions of western Asia Minor," so that what resulted "was an affirmation of the local Hellenistic heritage and an optimistic assessment of the possibilities for maintaining this heritage in a world ruled by Rome."[29] Architecturally and symbolically, the structures associated with the provincial cult of the Roman emperors constituted a sort of "third space" that was neither fully Roman nor Ephesian, but which mediated each to the other in powerful ways.[30] Because such texts in masonry and stone attested even without words to the impact of the empire on the provincial city of Ephesus, Steven Friesen is correct to conclude that "when John denounced imperial worship, he was not attacking a marginal socioreligious phenomenon." It is clear that "the worship of the emperors played an increasingly important role in society at many levels," and that "municipal identities, regional cohesion and competition, and imperial authority were brought together in this reli-

---

[28] S. R. F. Price, *Rituals and Power: The Roman Imperial Cult in Asia Minor* (Cambridge: Cambridge University Press, 1984), 135–36.

[29] Steven J. Friesen, *Twice Neokoros: Ephesus, Asia, and the Cult of the Flavian Imperial Family* (Religions in the Graeco-Roman World 116; Leiden: E. J. Brill, 1993), 161. On postcolonialism's understanding of hybridity, see Bill Ashcroft, Gareth Griffiths, and Helen Tiffin, eds., *The Postcolonial Studies Reader* (London and New York: Routledge, 1995), 183–84.

[30] On the notion of "third space," see Homi K. Bhabha, "Cultural Diversity and Cultural Differences," in Ashcroft, Griffiths, and Tiffin, *Postcolonial Studies Reader*, 206–9. Friesen emphasizes that the imagery "used to articulate the significance of the Cult of the Sebastoi was not imposed from Rome. The concept of the neokoros city, the design of the temple, the sculptural figures, and the architectural program all originated in the Greek east. The symbolic systems used in the cult show that the institutions were part of the Asian heritage," and the developments associated with the cult of the Roman emperors "were conscious, creative transformations by participants in those traditions who sought to express a new situation using the received symbolic vocabulary" (*Twice Neokoros*, 75).

gious phenomenon. . . . John was combating a serious, and growing, phenomenon."[31]

When we turn to ask about the extent of the influence of the imperial
cult across the various strata of Asian society, it is evident that it enjoyed
a wide base of support. According to Friesen, "When the range of imperial cult phenomena is taken into account . . . including worship, processions, festivals, delegations, sports, governance, inscriptions and coin-
age—the burden of proof lies with those who claim that the majority of
first-century Asians disapproved of such cults," so that John, "in cri-
tiquing imperial worship, did not speak for the masses. He spoke as a minority in his society, and perhaps even as a minority in the churches."[32]
The available evidence suggests that urban elite Asian subjects of the
Roman Empire embraced the advantages and opportunities of their relationship with the imperial metropolis actively and energetically, with
competition among individuals for honorific positions and rivalry among
cities for influence that brought imperial recognition and its attendant
privileges.

Thus, as Friesen suggests, "an appreciation of the municipal and regional dynamics of imperial cults draws one's attention not to Rome but
to the provinces. John's critique was therefore directed more at local enemies than at the distant emperor," and therefore, "Outmoded views of imperial cults that focused on the role of the emperor resulted in a misinter-
pretation of Revelation."[33] The intensity of John's ideological combat has
much to do with the fact that it was fought against overwhelming odds at
such close range. Furthermore, even among Christians in Ephesus and
elsewhere in the seven churches, it is likely that John's partisans were
only one of several groups that responded differently to the challenge of
resistance versus assimilation in the face of the dominant imperial ideology so vividly represented in the province of Asia.[34] Price explains:

> Many societies have the problem of making sense of an otherwise in-
> comprehensible intrusion of authority into their world. The Greeks were
> faced with the rule first of Hellenistic kings and then of Roman emper-
> ors which was not completely alien, but which did not relate to the tra-
> ditions of the self-governing cities. They attempted to evoke an answer

[31] Steven Friesen, "The Cult of the Roman Emperors in Ephesos: Temple Wardens, City Titles, and the Interpretation of the Revelation of John," in *Ephesos Metropolis of Asia: An Interdisciplinary Approach to Its Archaeology, Religion, and Culture*
(ed. Helmut Koester; Harvard Theological Studies 41; Valley Forge, Pa.: Trinity
Press International, 1995), 249. Also see Friesen, *Twice Neokoros*.

[32] Friesen, "Cult of the Roman Emperors in Ephesos," 250.

[33] Ibid.

[34] See Helmut Koester, "GNOMAI DIAPHOROI: The Origin and Nature of Diversification in the History of Early Christianity," in *Trajectories through Early Christianity* (ed. Helmut Koester and James Robinson; Philadelphia: Fortress, 1971),
154–55.

by focussing the problem in ritual. Using their traditional symbolic system they represented the emperor to themselves in the familiar terms of divine power.[35]

While Price maintains that the provincial cult of the Roman emperors "created a relationship of power between subject and ruler,"[36] it would actually be more accurate to say that the cult provided a way for provincial elites to thematize a relationship that was already a sociopolitical given of the empire, and to negotiate that relationship in ways that enhanced civic and individual prestige and power. All of this would have made John's extreme alternative position awfully hard to swallow, for

> In the late first century in Asia, a denunciation of imperial cults constituted a denunciation of city efforts to define themselves, a rejection of proper legal decisions of the *koinon*, and a sarcastic commentary on the public religious activities of the wealthy and of many others. John not only prophesied against imperial power; he also declared illegitimate the presuppositions of the local élite's claim to authority and condemned the general population for their compliance.[37]

Although a provincial assembly (*koinon*) already existed in Asia during the period of the Roman Republic, the interactions between the empire and its Asian province increasingly took concrete shape in ways that were mediated and symbolized by the imperial cult. What was distinctive about Augustus's approval of the temple at Pergamum—a temple that honored him and Rome (personified as Roma)—was that the request for this temple came not from the city of Pergamum but from the provincial assembly of Asia. As Leonard Thompson explains, "The assembly of over a hundred delegates met annually to conduct business, find ways to represent their interests in Rome, and carry out the activities of the imperial cult. . . . At first they met in Pergamum, then at Smyrna (c. 29 C.E.), Ephesus . . . and other cities such as Sardis, Philadelphia and Laodicea," cities that are singled out for attention in John's Apocalypse.[38] Numismatic and inscriptional evidence indicates that at the end of the first century C.E., rivalry for prestige among the Asian provincial cities began to find expression in municipal self-designations that advertised the city's privilege as *neokoros*, "temple warden" of a provincial temple to the emperors. While this began at Ephesus in 89/90 C.E. with the inauguration of the imperial cult there, the practice spread so quickly throughout the Mediterranean world that it became "the primary means by which the larger cities asserted their status in relation to one another."[39] Provincial cities claimed their place on

---

[35] Price, *Rituals and Power*, 247–48.

[36] Ibid., 248.

[37] Friesen, "Cult of the Roman Emperors in Ephesos," 250.

[38] Leonard L. Thompson, *The Book of Revelation: Apocalypse and Empire* (New York: Oxford University Press, 1990), 160.

[39] Friesen, *Twice Neokoros*, 58–59.

the map of influence and power, sorting out their colonial entanglements, as it were, by orienting themselves toward the imperial capital.

Monsters vs. Monuments:
Revelation 13 as Minority Counterdiscourse

While the Asian cult of the Roman emperors, with its temples and games and priesthoods, mapped the majority understanding of the relationship between the imperial center and the provincial periphery, Rev 13 mounts a shrill counteroffensive. Working without the benefit of the formidable resources that the provincial cult of the Roman emperors had amassed to make its convincing case, John called upon other sources to draw a map of the relationship between Rome and Asia that contested the dominant view.[40] In effect, Rev 13 constitutes something of an intricate political cartoon that caricatures the powers-that-be in unflattering and frightening terms as monstrous beasts, one arising from the sea and the other from the land. John's beasts are more than mythological commonplaces: Rev 13 deliberately evokes Dan 7, composed during the years of Jewish persecution under Antiochus Epiphanes (168–164 B.C.E.) as resistance literature for those who opposed the Hellenistic suppression of Jewish religious practices.[41] By importing powerful metaphoric images from a text that was the cultural product of another time and place, and by renaming the imperial powers in terms that recall earlier tensions between resistance and assimilation, the Apocalypse introduces a new hybridity into the complex discourses and counterdiscourses that circulated in the province of Asia.

While the world itself could not contain the books that have already been written about Rev 13 (if I may shamelessly borrow a hyperbole from the last sentence of the Fourth Gospel), the chapter is crucial for understanding how the Apocalypse remaps the relationship between the Roman metropolis and the Asian provincial periphery. I will limit the considerations that follow to two aspects of this alternate map: (1) the beast from the sea and the extent of empire; and (2) the beast from the land and the polemics of praise.

The Beast from the Sea and the Extent of Empire

As Rev 12 closes, the dragon takes its stand "on the sand of the seashore" (12:18). Elisabeth Schüssler Fiorenza notes, "The seashore envisioned here

---

[40] Thompson writes, "In comparison to the public knowledge embodied in the empire, John reveals a deviant knowledge, that is, one that deviates from public knowledge taken for granted in everyday Roman life" (*Book of Revelation*, 193).

[41] See John J. Collins, *Daniel* (ed. Frank Moore Cross; Hermeneia; Minneapolis: Fortress, 1993), 60–65 and 274–324. First Maccabees 41:42 suggests that this suppression of religious differences represented a political strategy of social control: "[T]hen the king wrote to his whole kingdom that all should be one people, and that all should give up their particular customs."

is probably that of the Mediterranean Sea with Rome geographically located on its opposite shore."[42] The beast from the sea has often been taken to stand for the Roman governor of Asia, that is, the proconsul who was the emperor's representative in the province. The governor's arrival from Rome by ship for his annual visit makes it possible to say that he arose from the sea.[43] While on the one hand that visit would have been welcomed by Asian elites as an opportunity to renew their allegiance to Rome and to seek favor for themselves, for their cities, and for the province, for John, on the other hand, only chaos and evil came ashore on the waves of the western sea, and the advent of the emperor's representative spelled trouble.

"In amazement the whole earth followed the beast. They worshiped the dragon, for he had given his authority to the beast, and they worshiped the beast, saying, 'Who is like the beast, and who can fight against it?'" (13:3b–4). Friesen asks: "Which members of the general populace might have objected to the Cult of the Sebastoi? There are few, if any, signs of opposition to Roman rule in Asia by the late first century C.E. By the beginning of Domitian's reign, Rome had controlled the area for over 150 years and the disturbances noted by Roman writers appear to be nothing more than the kinds of local disputes one would expect in a complex urban setting."[44]

The beast's undisputed authority was monstrous in its origins, and wide-reaching in its extent: "[I]t was allowed to make war on the saints and to conquer them. It was given authority over every tribe and people and language and nation" (13:7). Even so, Rev 13 suggests for John's audience that, despite all appearances to the contrary, Roman imperial hegemony was not absolute, for there was a higher and more pervasive power at work than even the Roman Empire and its gods. The passive verb *edothē* ("was given") is used five times times in verses 5–7 to suggest that the authority exercised by the beast is *given* by John's God. Pablo Richard compares this to Paul's statement that "there is no authority except from God" (Rom 13:1), and he proceeds to moralize that "all power comes from God and hence in itself is good. When the empire becomes beast by virtue of its idolatrous and criminal character, the beast transforms this power that comes from God into a power that is perverse. . . . There is no contradiction between Romans 13 and Revelation 13."[45] Looking through a postcolonial lens sharply focused on Revelation's heated anti-imperial counterdiscourse, nothing could be further from the truth. Romans is addressed to an audience in the imperial capital itself, and Paul counsels compliance and submission: "Let every person be subject to the governing authorities; for there is no authority except from God, and

---

[42] Schüssler Fiorenza, *Revelation*, 83.

[43] David E. Aune, *Revelation 6–16* (WBC 52a; Nashville: Thomas Nelson, 1998), 733.

[44] Friesen, *Twice Neokoros*, 164–65.

[45] Richard, *Apocalypse*, 109–10.

those authorities that exist have been instituted by God" (Rom 13:1). John's view from Patmos could hardly have been more different: his partisans are urged to refuse to submit to the beast even when they know that resistance might cost them their lives:

> Let anyone who has an ear listen:
>   If you are to be taken captive, into captivity you go;
>   if you kill with the sword, with the sword you must be killed.
>   Here is a call for the endurance and faith of the saints. (Rev
>   13:9–10)

The Beast from the Land and the Polemics of Praise

Introduced in 13:11, the second beast from the land "functions as the agent of the first beast."[46] While its specific historical referent is debated, its emergence "out of the earth" suggests that this monster is to be identified as a local agent of Roman imperial authority in the province of Asia, directly or indirectly associated with the provincial cult of the emperors.[47] For our purposes it is of particular interest that this second beast functions as the colonial agent plenipotentiary of the first beast, exercising by delegation from the first beast its full authority so as to compel "the earth and its inhabitants to worship the first beast" (13:12).[48]

The wonder-working activity of the second beast has fascinated audiences and present-day commentators alike:

> It performs great signs, even making fire come down from heaven to earth in the sight of all; and by the signs that it is allowed to perform on behalf of the beast, it deceives the inhabitants of earth, telling them to make an image for the beast that had been wounded by the sword and yet lived; and it was allowed to give breath to the image of the beast so that the image of the beast could even speak and cause those who would not worship the image of the beast to be killed. (13:13–15)

Commentators note that the expression in 13:13, "performs signs," occurs only twice in the Apocalypse outside chapter 13. In 16:13, three foul spirits like frogs coming from the mouth of the beast and from the mouth of the false prophet are identified as "demonic spirits, *performing signs*." Revelation 19:20 then tells of the capture and defeat of the beast "and with it the false prophet who had *performed* in its presence the *signs* by

---

[46] Aune, *Revelation 6–16*, 779.

[47] On the identity of the beast from the land, see ibid., 756.

[48] Aune speculates, "'The full authority' of the first beast was in turn based on the authority granted him by the dragon (3:2). The tertiary level of authority exercised by the second beast is thus somewhat problematic and perhaps reflects the author's attempt to connect the narrative in vv 11–18 to that in v 1–10" (ibid., 757). Postcolonial theorists would suggest that the derivative authority of the second beast can be taken to reflect the distance between the imperial center and the provincial periphery.

which he deceived those who had received the mark of the beast and those who had worshiped its image," identifying the second beast of chapter 13 as a false prophet precisely because it performed signs. Deuteronomy 13:1–3 warns, "If prophets or those who divine by dreams appear among you and promise you omens or portents, and the omens or the portents declared by them take place, and they say, 'Let us follow other gods' (whom you have not known) 'and let us serve them,' you must not heed the words of those prophets or those who divine by dreams." This standard for the discernment of true prophecy is quite different from criterion of fulfillment enunciated in Jer 28:9: "As for the prophet who prophesies peace, when the word of that prophet comes true, then it will be known that the Lord has truly sent the prophet." The lines are clearly drawn: John claims that his prophetic words are true (Rev 22:6), while protesting that the counterclaims of the provincial cult of the Roman emperors are false prophecy despite the miraculous signs performed by its agents.[49]

As for the animation of the image of the first beast (Rev 13:15), John sought to expose this as part and parcel of the second beast's strategy of deception.[50] There were numerous images of the Roman emperors in Ephesus and the other cities of the province of Asia, and each of them, animated or not, testified to the extent of Rome's influence.[51] The eloquence by sheer ubiquity of imperial iconography and inscriptions, statues (both animated and otherwise), coins, gymnasia, temples, and other public buildings and monuments would have made made John's claim to the authenticity of his own prophetic words a tough sell. What's worse: John had to convince his readers to accept the economic deprivations to which they would be subjected if they refused to be marked with the sign of the beast: "Also it causes all, both small and great, both rich and poor, both free and slave, to be marked on the right hand or the forehead, so that no one can buy or sell who does not have the mark, that is, the name of the beast or the number of its name" (13:16–17). Just as praise in the province of Asia had everything to do with politics, so too were cult and commerce bound up inseparably.[52] Participation in the provincial cult of the Roman emperors was woven into the fabric of Asian society at almost every level. Uncompromising resistance might well result in marginalization and self-imposed exclusion from public life even if it did not involve martyrdom

[49] See Dieter Georgi, "Who Is the True Prophet?" *HTR* 79 (1986): 123–24.

[50] See Stephen J. Scherrer, "Signs and Wonders in the Imperial Cult: A New Look at a Roman Religious Institution in the Light of Rev 13:13–15," *JBL* 103 (1984): 599–610.

[51] See Price, *Rituals and Power,* 170–206.

[52] See J. Nelson Kraybill, *Imperial Cult and Commerce in John's* Apocalypse (JSNTSup 132; Sheffield, England: Sheffield Academic Press, 1996); and also Jean-Pierre Ruiz, "Praise and Politics in Revelation 19:1–10," in *Studies in the Book of Revelation* (ed. Steve Moyise; Edinburgh and New York: T. & T. Clark, 2001), 69–84.

from organized persecution. Then as now, starvation leads to death more
slowly than the sword, but just as surely and inescapably.

Conclusion: The Apocalypse in the Empire's Embrace

By attending to the complex colonial entanglements of the Apocalypse in
its late-first-century context, postcolonial criticism provides an important
corrective that, in the end, advances the emancipatory ideals held dear by
liberationist biblical interpreters. In addition to the scrutiny of biblical
documents so as to foreground their colonial entanglements, and to the
reconstructive reading of biblical texts so as to bring such postcolonial circumstances as hybridity into account, postcolonial biblical interpretation
has a third task on its agenda, namely, "to interrogate both colonial and
metropolitan interpretations . . . to draw attention to the inescapable effects of colonization and colonial ideologies on interpretive works such as
commentarial writings."[53] As we turn to this task close to two thousand
years after the prophet John committed to writing "the Revelation of
Jesus Christ which God gave him to show his servants what must soon
take place" (Rev 1:1), the monuments of the Roman province of Asia lie in
ruins, while John's book remains, a strange victim of its own success. The
victims became the victors as the voice from Patmos became the voice of
the Christian empire, singing in triumph "Hallelujah! For the Lord our
God the Almighty reigns" (Rev 19:6).

In retrospect, the story of Revelation's story is appealing to many at
least in part because it is the underdog's tale of an imperiled minority that
ultimately wins out. The book and its history encourage a compliant, non-
resistant reading, inviting its audiences to applaud the ultimate winners
at a safe distance of time and space from their initial struggles and hard-
ships.[54] The strife is o'er, the battle done: the story *in* the book and the
story *of* the book both have happy endings. The story *in* the book ends
with the descent of the new Jerusalem (heaven colonizes earth), a heavenly metropolis more monumental than anything money could buy in
first-century Asia. Likewise, the story *of* the book has a happy ending:
mighty Rome has fallen while the Apocalypse has endured, acquiring a
place in the Christian canon as a two-edged sword from the mouths of
many centuries of mounted warriors and empire builders. During the
colonial era, the very same book became the charter for colonizers who
read in its pages the mandate to build the new Jerusalem. But the stories
of Revelation's readers are far from over: the rich are getting richer and
the poor are becoming poorer still. Disenfranchisement and marginalization have not been driven from the scene and speaking the truth to power
still exposes the would-be prophet (whether true or false) to deadly risk.

[53] Sugirtharajah, *Bible and the Third World*, 255.

[54] See the useful distinction among compliant, resistant, sympathic, and engaged reading strategies in Adele Reinhartz, *Befriending the Beloved Disciple: A Jewish Reading of the Gospel of John* (New York: Continuum, 2001).

Postscript

I read and write about the Apocalypse as a Nuyorican by ethnic identification,[55] as a Christian by religious commitment, and as an academic by profession, employed in higher education at a university with a historic commitment to educating immigrants and the children of immigrants. As I take my stand on the sand of the twenty-first-century seashore and read this strange and unsettling book in post–September 11, 2001, New York (a metropolis that is neither Rome nor Ephesus, neither Babylon nor the new Jerusalem), the ancient tensions between resistance and assimilation are freshly complicated by the violent dynamics of globalization. Whose word of prophecy is true, and by what standard? Might it be the optimistic *e pluribus unum* of Diana L. Eck, or the remade world order of Samuel P. Huntington's *Clash of Civilizations,* or are we to look for another?[56] Let anyone who has an ear stay attentive. We might yet be surprised.

[55] My identification as a "Nuyorican" results from having been a New York–born member of the Puerto Rican Diaspora of the 1950s and 1960s that was made both necessary and possible by the neocolonial relationship that is the abiding legacy of the so-called Spanish-American War in 1898. See Yamina Apolinaris and Sandra Mangual-Rodríguez, "Theologizing from a Puerto Rican Context," in *Hispanic/Latino Theology: Challenge and Promise* (ed. Ada María Isasi-Díaz and Fernando F. Segovia; Minneapolis: Fortress, 1996), 218–39. Also see the reflections of Cuban-born cultural critic and biblical scholar Fernando F. Segovia, *Decolonizing Biblical Studies,* esp. 145–56: "My Personal Voice: The Making of a Postcolonial Critic." Also see idem, "Toward a Hermeneutics of the Diaspora: A Hermeneutics of Otherness and Engagement," in Segovia and Tolbert, *Reading from This Place,* 1:57–73.

[56] See Diana L. Eck, *A New Religious America: How a "Christian Country" Has Now Become the World's Most Religiously Diverse Nation* (San Francisco: HarperCollins, 2001); Samuel P. Huntington, *The Clash of Civilizations and the Remaking of World Order* (New York: Simon and Schuster, 1997).

9

Spirit Possession
REVELATION IN RELIGIOUS STUDIES

Leonard L. Thompson

Among the many explanations for spirit possession, spirits are taboo. Spirit possession may be explained as the product of schizophrenia or hysteria or physiological malfunction. It may be a means of compensating for social deprivation or of protesting by groups that have been marginalized socially or of gaining power and authority by those outside established structures of power. But to mention spirits as real powers is a transgression, for it erodes our notion that a body is a fixed and stable entity, separated spatially from other discrete bounded objects in the world. It is acceptable to discuss energy fields that move mysteriously or light that shifts from particle to wave, but it is not acceptable to reckon with spirits. They are never to be mentioned as a cause of spirit possession.[1]

Nonetheless, people from virtually every area of our planet, both past and present, claim that they, or certain persons in their community, have been possessed by spirits. "Others" take possession of their consciousness, either partially or totally.[2] The Book of Revelation is a record of one of those persons. In it, the writer John tells what he saw and heard when spirit possessed. I take his account at face value: He was spirit possessed. Consider the following essay a case study or an ethnography of spirit pos-

---

[1] For some interesting, diverse reading in that area, see Ioan P. Culianu, *Out of This World: Otherworldly Journeys from Gilgamesh to Albert Einstein* (Boston: Shambhala, 1991); Felicitas D. Goodman, *Where the Spirits Ride the Wind* (Bloomington: Indiana University Press, 1990); and David Bohm, *Wholeness and the Implicate Order* (London: Ark, 1980).

[2] For recent reviews of literature on spirit possession, see Frederick M. Smith, "The Current State of Possession Studies as a Cross-Disciplinary Project," *Religious Studies Review* 27, no. 3 (2001): 203–12, and Shail Mayaram, "Recent Anthropological Works on Spirit Possession," *Religious Studies Review* 27, no. 3 (July 2001): 213–22.

session in that tribe called Christian during the grand years of the Roman Empire, with special attention to Revelation.

John: A Spirit-Possessed Prophet

John was a Christian who wrote Revelation sometime in the latter part of the first or the beginning of the second Christian century in the eastern end of the Roman Empire.[3] Among Christians of his time, spirit possession was an accepted phenomenon. So Paul, a Christian leader who wrote letters to churches several years before John wrote Revelation, devoted three chapters of one letter to the proper understanding of spiritual gifts (1 Cor 12–14). Paul urges those at Corinth to "pursue love and strive for the spiritual gifts, and especially that you may prophesy" (1 Cor 14:1).

Four times in Revelation, John refers to being spirit possessed. In introducing his first vision, he explains to his readers, "I was possessed by the spirit on the Lord's day" (Rev 1:10).[4] In the same state, John ascended into heaven, at the beginning of his second vision (Rev 4:1–2). Then toward the end of the book, an angel took John, spirit possessed, on a ride, first in a desert to see the judgment of the great whore (17:3) and, later, on a mountain to see the holy city of Jerusalem coming down from God in heaven (21:10; cf. Ezek 37:1).

While under the influence of the spirit, John saw visions which he recorded in Revelation as prophetic words.[5] He promised a blessing to the one who read aloud (to the congregation) and to those who listened to his words of prophecy (Rev 1:3). Later in the book, when he swallowed a scroll bitter to his stomach, godly beings said to him, "You must prophesy again . . ." (Rev 10:11). And at the end of the book, John gave a warning not to add or take away anything "from the words of the book of this prophecy" (Rev 22:19).

The Spirit World

The spirit world of those Christians was populated by a variety of suprahuman beings. Here are some of John's names for them. A god, who was

---

[3] See chapter 2 above, "Ordinary Lives: John and His First Readers." Parts of this chapter will make more sense if "Ordinary Lives" is read first.

[4] The Greek phrase is *en pneumati.* The prepositional phrase indicates that John is under the influence of or under the control of a spirit or some kind of spirit. The verb *ginomai* ("was") with *en* indicates here a state of being, "under a spirit's influence" (cf. BDAG 198), in other words, spirit possession or possession by a spirit or by spirits (Rev 22:6). Whether John went to the spirit (ecstasy) or the spirit entered into John (enthusiasm) is not a critical issue.

[5] Eusebius, a Christian historian of the fourth century, also makes a clear connection between spirit possession and prophecy: Moses possessed the divine spirit "and so he was called a prophet" (*Praep. ev.* 8.10.4). See also Eph 3:5, in which a prophet receives divine revelation "by the spirit [*en pneumati*]," the same phrase that is found in Rev 1:10.

also called Father, Lord God, and the Almighty, created the world and was superior to all other spiritual forces. Jesus, or Christ or Son of God or Messiah or Lamb, was superior to all spiritual beings except the God. He had been a human being, but the God raised him from the dead and he ascended into heaven. Finally there were various good spirits and holy angels who spoke and performed acts in John's visions. For example, each of the messages to the seven congregations (Rev 2–3) ends with an exhortation to listen to the spirit (Rev 2:7, 11, 17, 29; 3:6, 13, 22). Twice in Revelation a divine spirit speaks, once in response to a voice from heaven (Rev 14:13) and once in an antiphonal litany with Jesus, an angel, and the bride of Christ (22:9–20).[6] Angels appear frequently in John's visions, singing in heaven, taking messages to earthlings, and performing acts on behalf of God (Rev 5:11; 22:16; 7:1).[7] All of those spiritual forces operated on the same channel and spoke the same language.[8] John could be guided by any one of them.

Evil powers also inhabited that spirit world, though they were finally not as powerful as the God. In Revelation, they include three major forces: an evil dragon or Satan (Rev 12:9), the beast from the sea (to whom the dragon gave authority, 13:2), and the beast from the earth (who had the sea beast's authority, 13:12). Each of those powers had their own spirits. So, when the sixth angel poured out his bowl, John saw three foul, immoral spirits come from the mouths of those three evil powers. Those spirits were able to perform miracles (*sēmeia, signs*) and to mislead "the kings of the whole world" (Rev 16:13–14). Those foul, immoral spirits, along with demons and unclean beasts, also haunted the fallen city of Babylon (Rev 18:2).

That spirit world was sometimes set in a three-story universe, with the good spirits above and the evil spirits below the human plane (Rev 4:1; 9:2), but the spirit-other was fluid, able to circulate in and around humans and their affairs.[9] In their multidimensional space, all things came together, if not here then there. Perhaps they operated in space like holographic photography in which every part contains the whole. In any case, spirits eliminated spatial boundaries. They could be in more than one place at the same time. Seven spirits existed before the throne of God as

---

[6] Christian literature from about the same period refers to the spirit of God (1 Cor 2:14), of the Lord (Acts 5:9), of Christ (1 Pet 1:11), or the Holy Spirit (Matt 12:32).

[7] The term "angel" appears sixty-seven times in Revelation. In the rest of the New Testament the term occurs 108 times.

[8] Paul summarizes succinctly at 1 Cor 12:4–6: "Now there are varieties of gifts, but the same Spirit; and there are varieties of services, but the same Lord; and there are varieties of activities, but it is the same God who activates all of them in everyone."

[9] *Pneuma*, the Greek word for spirit, also means "air movement," such as breath or wind (see BDAG).

seven flaming torches (Rev 1:4; 3:1; 4:5), but they were also seven eyes of the Lamb, and they circulated throughout all the earth (Rev 5:6; cf. Zech 4:10; *1 Enoch* 20; Tob 12:15).

According to Christians (and other religious sects in the Roman Empire), humans also had spirit, though it was not as mobile as the suprahuman spirits. The human spirit, along with the soul and the mind, stayed more or less framed in and contained by a visible, outer body so long as it lived. The soul (*psychē*) was the life force (Rev 8:9; 12:11; 16:3; 18:13) that could continue to exist in its individuated state after death, at least in humans (6:9; 20:4).[10] At Rev 18:14 it is referred to as the seat of desire for luxurious items. Mind (*nous*) was the faculty that made possible thinking and acquiring wisdom. In Revelation, mind had to be used to understand obscure sayings (Rev 13:18; 17:9). The body (*sōma*) referred to the visible part of an animal (including humans), either dead or alive. It could also refer to a person who was viewed as only a body to be put in service (Rev 18:13).[11]

Spirits of the Prophets

Spirit was the only aspect of the human personality that was also present in the suprahuman world. Spirit joined with spirit to make possible spirit-possessed prophets. We may imagine John's experience to be something like that of the one ascending in the "Mithras Liturgy." That person's spirit ascended, running ahead, and drew spirit from the divine into itself (*PGM* 4.625–630).[12] "Spirits of the prophets," a phrase Paul uses at the end of his discussion of spirit possession (1 Cor 14:32), included both the human and the suprahuman dimensions of spirit. The God was Lord over the spirits, but Paul reminded the Corinthians that "the spirits of prophets are subject to the prophets" (1 Cor 14:32).[13] The "prophetic spirit" had, thus, a dual position: It was that which God sent, and it was part of the human makeup of a prophet. Being at home in both the divine and the human, the spirit made a natural link between the two.

When John became spirit possessed, he did not lose awareness of his place in the human world. To paraphrase Paul, he prophesied with his mind as well as his spirit, and with mind (*nous*) he retained his own thoughts, reflections, and awarenesses while participating in an expanded view of things (cf. 1 Cor 14:14–15). He punctuated his visions with "I saw" or "I heard," he conversed with others in the spirit world

---

[10] The notions of soul and spirit are sometimes interchangeable (cf. Rev 11:11 in reference to "the spirit of life" and Rev 13:15).

[11] For combined use of those terms, see 1 Thess 5:23; Heb 4:12; and Phil 1:27.

[12] See Hans Dieter Betz, ed., *The Greek Magical Papyri in Translation* (Chicago: University of Chicago Press, 1986), 50.

[13] For God as the Lord over spirits, see also *Jub.* 10.3; Rev 22:6; Heb 12:9; frequently in *1 Enoch*.

(Rev 10), and he remembered what he saw and heard.[14] His awareness, however, was expanded or extended so that he could see aspects of the world, and objects and events in the world, that were not evident in his more normal, restricted vision. He gained a god's-eye view of Asian life. In broader terms, John was more shaman than medium, "an active agent and never merely a vehicle. . . . his ecstasy, far from annulling the self, frees it to realize to the fullest powers normally beyond its reach."[15]

That mixture of subjective and objective experience in Christian prophecy, or of individual personality and otherness, is a familiar one in the history of inspiration. Homer and Virgil named the Muse as the source of their words, but their idiom of epic was distinctive. Einstein dreamed parts of his theories and felt that his ideas came from outside him, but they came out in a scientific idiom recognized by other scientists of his era. Dizzy Gillespie said, "All the music is out there in the first place, all of it. From the beginning of time, the music was there. All you have to do is try to get a little piece of it. I don't care how great you are, you only get a little piece of it." But the music "out there" filtered through his intelligence and technical abilities before it came out the bell end of his trumpet.[16]

The Setting of Spirit Possession

John says little about the conditions in which he became spirit possessed. In the opening chapter of Revelation he says that he was on the isle of Patmos and that he became spirit possessed on the Lord's Day (1:9–10). That was the day when Christians came together in celebration of the resurrec-

---

[14] Compare the experience of Mokichi Okada, founder of Johrei: "At about midnight one night in 1926, the most peculiar sensation came over me, a feeling I had never experienced before. It was an overwhelming urge that I simply cannot describe. . . . There was no way to suppress the power that was using my voice. So I gave in. . . . a torrent was let loose" (quoted in Roger Schmidt, *Exploring Religion* [Belmont, Calif.: Wadsworth, 1988], 161–62). Contrast Perpetua's spirit possession, described as a "kind of sleep," an ecstasy, or a trance. She remembered nothing of it when she awoke (see *Martyrdom of Perpetua and Felicitas* 20 in Herbert Musurillo, *Acts of the Christian Martyrs* [Oxford: Clarendon Press, 1972], 129). Ephesians 5:18 may imply that spirit possession was analogous to drunkenness. See also Plato, *Complete Works* (edited and compiled by John M. Cooper; Indianapolis: Hackett, 1997), 942: "As long as a human being has his intellect in his possession he will always lack the power to make poetry or sing prophecy" (*Ion* 534.B; cf. *Timaeus* 71.E).

[15] Robert M. Torrance, *The Spiritual Quest: Transcendence in Myth, Religion, and Science* (Berkeley: University of California Press, 1994), 137. So also Hultkratz: "[T]he shaman remains aware and in partial control of the situation, while the medium is understood by her or his community to have relinquished all control to the spirit" (quoted in Smith, "Possession Studies," 206).

[16] See James and Michael Ventura Hillman, *We've Had a Hundred Years of Psychotherapy—And the World's Getting Worse* (New York: Harper Collins, 1992), 59.

tion of Jesus (their cult hero) and participated in a religious meal after confessing their sins.[17] Paul assumed that prophecy occurred in worship, probably on the Lord's Day, when Christians at Corinth came together. In their worship, the Corinthians should "let two or three prophets speak, and let the others weigh what is said" (1 Cor 14:29). Hermas also referred to such a gathering when he stated that true prophets prophesied in an assembly of righteous men (Christians). There the angel of the prophet (or the prophetic spirit) "resting on that person fills the person" (*Mand.* 11.9). We may, therefore, assume that John was in a Christian congregation on Patmos "on the Lord's Day."[18]

In that communal gathering, certain activities could apparently be done to help bring on spirit possession and prophecy. In *The Shepherd of Hermas,* when a true prophet comes into an assembly of righteous men who believe in the divine spirit, they pray for the spirit to fill the prophet so that he can prophesy (*Mand.* 11.9).[19] After they pray, " the angel of the prophetic spirit that rests upon that person fills the person, who, being filled with the holy spirit, speaks to the whole crowd as the Lord wishes" (*Mand.* 11.9).

Were other techniques employed to bring on spirit possession? John does not mention any. Perhaps he did not want to suggest that humans had a role in initiating it. Perhaps such techniques were not relevant for his purposes. Or, perhaps, it was so commonplace that description was unnecessary.[20] John's silence should not lead us to conclude that techniques were not employed.[21] At the same time, evidence for techniques can only be indirect.

---

[17] See *Did.* 14; *Barn.* 15; Ignatius, *Magn.* 9.

[18] For prophesying in a gathering of worship, see also Ignatius, *Philad.* 7.1–2; *Did.* 11.7; 1 Thess 5:19–21. See Christopher Forbes, *Prophecy and Inspired Speech in Early Christianity and Its Hellenistic Environment* (Peabody, Mass.: Hendrickson, 1997), 246: "[T]hat the setting of early Christian prophecy was the assembled community appears to be incontrovertible." For a discussion of John on Patmos, see chapter 2 above, "Ordinary Lives: John and His First Readers," section "Item Three," pp. 32–34.

[19] Carolyn Osiek, *Shepherd of Hermas: A Commentary* (Hermeneia; Minneapolis: Fortress, 1999), 145: "[T]rue prophecy is exercised only in the context of the community and only when the holy spirit wills." A false prophet avoids an assembly of righteous men, but if he enters such a meeting and prayer is offered, that prophet is rendered speechless (*Mand.* 11.14).

[20] Suppose fish could learn about human behavior. They would be puzzled about the phenomenon of breathing and surprised that humans never described how it occurred, even when they referred to "heavy breathing" or being "short of breath."

[21] David E. Aune, "The Apocalypse of John and the Problem of Genre," *Semeia* (Decatur, Ga.: Scholars Press) 36 (1986): 82; this edition of *Semeia* was edited by Adela Yarbro Collins, on the theme "Early Christian Apocalypticism: Genre and Setting." There were prophetic schools, but we know nothing about how they op-

Singing and music were the most likely stimulants for John and other prophets to become spirit possessed. The writer of Ephesians exhorted the church at Ephesus: "Do not get drunk with wine, for that is debauchery; but be filled with the Spirit by sounding forth among yourselves psalms and hymns and spiritual songs, singing and making melody to the Lord in your hearts" (Eph 5:18–19).[22] When hymns were sung in the context of worship, they were human acts of praise directed to the deity, and they were also a means by which the spirit became present among the worshipers. The author of the *Odes of Solomon,* a late-first-century hymnbook from Syria or Palestine, expressed that duality, writing, "So speaks in my members the Spirit of the Lord / And I speak by his love" (6.1), or, "Teach me the odes of thy truth / That through thee I may bear fruit / Open to me the harp of thy holy Spirit / That with all its notes I may praise thee" (14.7). Tertullian stated the two-way street of hymnody succinctly: Regarding the psalmist David, the singer "sings to us of Christ and through his voice Christ indeed also sang concerning himself."[23] Spirit joined with spirit in singing, as in prophesying, so that what was sung or spoken had a dual source, involving the human and the divine.

In other religious groups culturally proximate to John, singing also evoked spirit possession. Philo, a Jew who lived in the first Christian century, knew of the Therapeutae, a Jewish sect that existed in the first Christian century in Egypt and "in many places in the inhabited world." Eusebius goes into great detail to claim that they were Christians (*Hist. Eccl.* 2.16–17), but that is unlikely. According to Philo, the Therapeutae held a sacred vigil after supper, in which "they sing hymns to God composed of many measures and set to many melodies, sometimes singing together, sometimes in antiphonal harmonies, as they move their hands and dance and prophesy" (*Contempl.* 84).[24] For them, singing in different ways and manners was a means to induce inspiration. Philo compares their drunkenness to that of the Bacchic rites, but they are drunk on "the strong wine of God's love" (cf. Eph 5:18–19).

---

erated, for example, whether a person could receive training to become spirit possessed.

[22] The relationship between singing and spirit possession is somewhat ambiguous, for the participle "sounding forth" could express cause, manner, means, purpose, or condition of being filled with the spirit. I translate it as means. Christians at Corinth, who (over)valued spirit possession, sang in the spirit, but Paul exhorted them to sing also with the mind (1 Cor 14:15). See also Col 3:16.

[23] Tertullian, *On the Flesh of Christ* 20. Compare Michael Taussig's comment on singing in the Putumayo shamanism in southwest Colombia: "[T]he shaman's singing is both his way of reaching out to and connecting with powerful spirits, just as it is those very same spirits that are singing through him, by means of the vehicle that is his body" (Michael Taussig, "Transgression," in *Critical Terms for Religious Studies* [ed. Mark C. Taylor; Chicago: University of Chicago Press, 1998], 358).

[24] The Greek term for inspired or prophesying is *epitheiazontes.*

Among the Dead Sea Scrolls is a series of texts called "Angelic Liturgy" or "Songs of the Sabbath Sacrifice" (second pre-Christian century). Carol Newsom describes their function "as the praxis of a communal mysticism." By reciting those songs, the community was led through a progressive experience that culminated in the worshipers experiencing "the holiness of the *merkābāh*." That is, those worshiping had their awareness expanded to include a vision of God's heavenly throne in the form of a chariot (Hebrew, *merkābāh*), and they joined harmony with the angels who sang around that heavenly chariot-throne.[25]

In vision texts similar to Revelation, singing is also mentioned in connection with ascending to and seeing the throne of God in a vision (cf. Rev 4). In the *Ascension of Isaiah* (probably written by 150 of the Christian era), before Isaiah entered the seventh heaven "where the one who is not named dwells" (i.e., the God), Isaiah sang praises with the angels, "naming the primal Father and his Beloved, Christ, and the Holy Spirit, all with one voice.[26] So, also, in the *Apocalypse of Abraham*, a revelation written sometime between 70 and 150 of the Christian era, Abraham is taken up by an angel after he made sacrifice (Gen 15:17). Abraham sees a frightful sight, his spirit weakens, but he and the angel worship. Then Abraham recites the song that the angel taught him. The angel tells him to recite it without ceasing. The words of the song are given. Then as Abraham was still reciting the song, he sees the great throne of God (*Ap. Ab.* 17–18).

On the basis of that evidence, several historians of religion have concluded that singing songs with the angels in heaven was a technique for becoming spirit possessed. Christopher Rowland, following Gershom Scholem, writes: "As he [Scholem] points out, hymns . . . played an important part in the preparation of the mystic to behold the glories of the *merkabah*, as well as being part of the songs which were sung in honour of God by the heavenly host."[27] Ithamar Gruenwald makes a grand connection among the later *hekaloth* hymns, the "Angelic Liturgy" of the Dead Sea Scrolls, along with hymns and doxologies in apocalyptic literature including the Book of Revelation: "What originally were the hymns of the angels have become theurgical incantations which help the mystic to achieve his goal. . . . He can use the angelological hymns for his own theurgic purposes [i.e., to establish contact with the divine spirits]."[28]

[25] James H. Charlesworth and Carol A. Newsom, ed. and trans., *The Dead Sea Scrolls: Volume 4B* (Tübingen: Mohr Siebeck, 1999), 4. There is actually a plurality of chariot-thrones referred to, as occurs in later Merkabah literature. See 4Q403.2. 15 and comments by Newsom in Carol Newsom, *Songs of the Sabbath Sacrifice: A Critical Edition* (Atlanta: Scholars Press, 1985), 237.

[26] *Ascen. Isa.* 8.16–18, translation by M. A. Knibb in *OTP* 2.169.

[27] Christopher Rowland, "The Visions of God in Apocalyptic Literature," *Journal for the Study of Judaism* 10, no. 2 (1979): 152.

[28] Ithamar Gruenwald, *Apocalyptic and Merkavah Mysticism* (Leiden: E. J. Brill, 1980), 152. Contrast Martha Himmelfarb, "The Practice of Ascent in the Ancient

Other stimuli were sometimes employed for becoming spirit possessed. Martha Himmelfarb points out that weeping may have been a common preparatory technique.[29] John wept bitterly "because no one was found worthy to open the scroll or to look into it" (Rev 5:4). Immediately afterward, he had a vision of the throne and the Lamb (Rev 5:6). Preparation for prophesying could also include fasting, praying, pronouncing the divine name, and flagellation.[30]

The Role of the Spirit and Spirit-Language

Spirit possession is, thus, a complex phenomenon. When John became spirit possessed, he did not turn into a puppet whose mouth and voice were controlled by a spirit-ventriloquist. As with the Delphic priestesses at Delphi, the spirit-other did not compose the words. Rather, John joined with the spirit-other in shaping the prophecy that he spoke. That spirit set the prophetic process in motion in John, inciting him to see and to hear in new ways, and then the process continued in accordance with John's natural disposition.[31] Other prophets saw and heard other things according to their natural disposition. (Dizzy Gillespie and Keith Jarrett were both inspired by the music "out there," but when it flowed through each of them, the music took on a distinctive shape.) Some other factors also entered into the process. John's personal preparation, perhaps fasting and praying, affected his physical state, which in turn affected his receptivity to the spirit-other. Since early Christian prophecy occurred in a communal setting, aspects of that setting helped to shape prophecy: the prayers of the righteous, the rhythm and lyrics of the hymns and psalms sung, and the particular concerns, issues, and spiritual maturity of those present.

That sketch of the process raises several questions. What does the spirit do when it incites the prophet? How does the prophet's natural disposition shape the prophecy? If the words and visions are not given to the

---

Mediterranean World," in *Death, Ecstasy, and Other Worldly Journeys* (ed. John J. Collins and Michael Fishbane; Albany: State University of New York Press, 1995), 123–37. In the history of spirit possession, music and dancing are frequently used as techniques for entering a possessed state. In Israelite prophecy, see 1 Sam 10:10; 1 Kgs 18:26. Aelius Aristides refers to dancing by priests of Cybele (P. Aelius Aristides, *The Complete Works: Vol II, Orations XVII–LIII* [ed. Charles A. Behr; Leiden: E. J. Brill, 1981], 130). See also Mayaram, "Recent Anthropological Works," 217–19, and Torrance, *Spiritual Quest*, 145–46.

[29] See Himmelfarb, "Practice of Ascent," 130–32. Enoch experienced great distress and wept with his eyes while he was asleep (2 *En.* 1.2). Baruch was weeping over the destruction of Zion when "suddenly a strong spirit lifted me and carried me above the wall of Jerusalem. And I saw, and behold, there were standing four angels . . ." (2 *Bar.* 6.2–4, translated by A. F. J. Klijn in *OTP* 1:622).

[30] See Aune, "Problem of Genre," 82–83, and Gruenwald, *Apocalyptic*, 52. Compare *Apoc. Ab.* 9–10; Dan 9:3. Flagellation is referred to in 1 Kgs 18:28.

[31] See Plutarch, *Moralia* 397.B.

prophet, then does the prophet simply project his or her views and de-
sires onto the prophetic screen so that they are given divine sanction?
What does the spirit contribute to the process?

The last question seems to be the critical one. It is easy to imagine the
prophet's role, more difficult to understand the spirit's. First, it is clear
that the spirit does not send down from above specific messages to be
channeled through the prophet. Rather than sending down messages
from the divine world above, the spirit opens up the human world below.
From the start, the situation in Asia was a part of John's prophecy.

The spirit worked with what was available in that social and cultural
situation of John and those Asian Christians. So the visions in Revelation
consist of images, symbols, and narratives from John's religious traditions, primarily in Judaism and Christianity. John saw many of the same
things in his visions that were described in *1 Enoch*, the *Apocalypse of Abraham*, or the *Ascension of Isaiah*. He did not see what visionaries among the
Australian Aranda or the Polynesian Maori saw. Ascension into heaven
occurred on a cloud (Rev 11:12), not a crane as among Chinese Taoists.
John saw angels, not ancestors; Jesus the slain lamb, not an enlightened
Buddha; the Lord God on a heavenly throne, not the Mother of a Cari-
bou. In short, the spirit operated within a culturally specific context.[32]

The spirit also had to work with the natural disposition of prophets,
which included their views and experiences of the Roman Empire and
the place of Christians in it. From what we can reconstruct, John did not
have a very positive attitude toward the empire. He portrays it as an evil
force in league with Behemoth and Leviathan—primordial mythic, evil
beasts in Jewish tradition.[33] Christians who participated in the society and
economy of the empire by buying and selling carried "the mark of the
beast" (Rev 13:17). On the other hand, at Pergamum and Thyatira there
were prophets who prophesied just the opposite view (Rev 2:12–29).
Their natural disposition included views and experiences that were positive toward the Roman Empire. They, or those who shared their views
and experiences, were craftsmen or traders who enjoyed and appreciated
the peace and prosperity of the empire. They said that Christians could
participate in Roman society, even in public gatherings, guild meetings,
or private homes where they ate meat that had been offered to local
deities.[34]

Did the same spirit work in both John and those other prophets? Or
did John or the other prophets prophesy by the help of the evil spirits that
inhabited the spirit world? That was possible, for there were false

---

[32] Those unfamiliar with the symbols and narratives of that religious tradition—for example, a convert at Sardis from the Phrygian Cybele or a twenty-first-
century Christian—could easily misunderstand Revelation.

[33] Rev 13; cf. 2 *Esd.* 6.49–52; *1 En.* 60.8; *2 Bar.* 29.4.

[34] See chapter 2 in this volume, "Ordinary Lives: John and His First Readers,"
under the heading "Consequences: John's Opposition to Settled Householders."

prophets from the beginning of the Christian movement who performed marvelous signs and proclaimed prophetic words by means of those evil spirits (Matt 24:24; Rev 19:20).[35] It is clear that John thought that the Balaamites and Jezebel misled Christians, but they no doubt thought that John was misleading. I doubt, however, that either would have called the other a false prophet inspired by demonic spirits. John's strongest statement against Jezebel simply states that she "calls herself a prophet" (Rev 2:20). Let us assume that both John and Jezebel would have passed the test of being true prophets. How did the difference in messages then arise? Did the spirit-other send the same message to both John and Jezebel, and then each one added to it his and her own views and experiences? If so, what did the spirit contribute to the prophetic process? Did the spirit talk out of both sides of its mouth?

At least this much can be said about spirit-language: It was not univocal; it did not fix on one strict meaning or reference. Plutarch reminded his readers that, as Heracleitus said, the Delphic oracle "neither tells nor conceals, but indicates [sēmainō]" (Mor. 404.E). It neither fully disclosed nor completely concealed: It always indicated or pointed to something more than what was apparent. At the beginning of Revelation, John used the same word. The King James Version, following the Latin Vulgate, translates as follows: "The Revelation of Jesus Christ, which God gave unto him . . . and he sent and signified [sēmainō; Latin, sīgnificō] it by his angel unto his servant John" (Rev 1:1). The spirits sent their message in language that contained something more than what appeared in the plain words.

There seems to be a tension between spirit-language and the natural disposition of prophets, as well as those who read or listen to prophets. The natural inclination of humans who search out visions, interpret dreams, or consult oracles is to find unambiguous information. Even at the present time, readers of Revelation want to know to whom precisely the number 666 refers or in what time frame the "forty-two months" are to be calculated (Rev 13:5) or when and where Armageddon will occur. Very specific answers to those questions are updated regularly, as time goes on. Spirit-language, on the other hand, is not univocal. The spirit made prophetic speech ambiguous and multivocal, by using metaphors, similes, and symbols. John saw a woman clothed with the sun, with the

---

[35] According to the pagan Lucian, sometime in the second century a prophetic figure by the name of Peregrinus bilked Christians of "not a little revenue" (Peregr. 13). The Didache warns of itinerant false prophets who, when spirit possessed, cry out "give me money" or order a meal to eat (11.8, 12). Tests had to be devised to identify those false prophets. The most effective test was to watch how a prophet lived, for "you will know them by their fruits" (Matt 7:15–16); cf. Matt 24:11; 1 Thess 5:19–22; 1 Cor 12:3; Hermas, Mand. 11. For more details, see David E. Aune, Prophecy in Early Christianity and the Ancient Mediterranean World (Grand Rapids: Eerdmans, 1983), 222–29.

moon under her feet, and on her head a crown of twelve stars (12:1). The one seated on the throne looked *"like* jasper and carnelian" (Rev 4:3). And the seven angels with seven plagues were a great sign that John saw in heaven, a symbol signifying manifold meanings (15:1). Humans want language that signifies less than the spirits intend.

The spirits apparently did not unequivocally condemn Rome as an evil empire warring against the true God. For example, an angel carried John into a wilderness to see a vision of the judgment of a great whore seated on a scarlet beast, filled with blasphemous names, with seven heads and ten horns. She held a cup of abominations in her hand. On her forehead was a secret, mysterious name. She was drunk from the blood of the saints and from the blood of those witnessing to Jesus (Rev 17). She was obviously a symbol of evil, opposed to those who followed Jesus. The mysterious name on her forehead identified her as Babylon the great mother of whores. But who exactly was she?

An angel explained the vision, but even that explanation was not univocal.[36] "This calls for a mind that has wisdom: the seven heads are seven mountains on which the woman is seated. And the seven heads are seven kings: five have fallen, one is ruling, and the other has not yet come" (17:9–10). John may have intended the vision to point unambiguously to the Roman Empire and its emperors, but the vision remains multivocal. The "seven mountains" could indicate the seven hills upon which Rome was built, but the symbolism of seven mountains was in the religious tradition known to John. For example, the writer of *1 Enoch* also saw seven mountains, "all different one from the other . . . all resembled the seat of a throne" (24.1–4). Identification of the seven kings is even more uncertain. If the seven kings represented seven Roman emperors, it was not clear which seven were intended in the vision.[37] Even with the interpretations of the angel, the vision of the whore did not univocally refer to the Roman Empire and Roman emperors.[38]

The task of spirit-language was to open up the human world which John (and others), by his natural disposition, sought to limit in precise, defined ways. Through the spirit-language of symbol and metaphor, the spirits transformed the social, economic, and political situation of Asia

---

[36] For angels or other divine figures who interpret visions, see Dan 7; 2 Esd 12.

[37] See David Aune's chart in *The HarperCollins Study Bible* (New York: HarperCollins, 1993), 2330.

[38] In general, the visions are less univocal than the dialogues or pronouncements in Revelation. For example, the war in heaven is explained by a loud voice (Rev 12:7–12); the loud voices in heaven explain the meaning of the horrendous events at the blowing of the seven trumpets (11:15–19); the significance of the great crowd in heaven is given by one of the elders (7:9–17). Chapters 2 and 3 of the first vision are lengthy pronouncements and the most univocal of all the visions in the book. Should one assume that the prophet took a more active role in the dialogues and pronouncements than in the visions?

into a religious situation. They disclosed dimensions to that life and expanded the human awareness of those dimensions so that Asian life and the Roman Empire opened onto something more abundant—and complex—than unmitigated evil or unalloyed good.[39] That is, through the spirit, everyday life spilled over with an "overflow," a "surplus," and "abundance" of what William James called something More.[40] The spirits contested the social order in this sense: It was contingent upon something More. Emperors, imperial edicts, celebrations of Roman culture, as well as bishops, house churches, and economic necessities were but the ephemeral surface of a deep ocean of reality. That contingency was expressed in Revelation by visions of heavenly scenes and by descriptions of a new heaven and a new earth that would supersede the present world.

Conclusion

In the last analysis, spirit-language in Revelation indicates or signifies *not a specific content, but an activity,* the very activity of spirit possession. Those who listened to it in worship were drawn to a "kindred other—call it futurity, potentiality, or spirit—through which the individual self is expanded."[41] The metaphoric and symbolic form of spirit-language made its lure more enticing. The setting of worship intensified the power of the words. Just as hymns and liturgical songs (so prominent in Revelation) that were sung in the context of worship functioned as both human acts of praise and a means by which the spirit became present, so also reading aloud and listening to the Book of Revelation were both human acts and the means by which the spirit came upon the worshipers, enlarging and transforming their lives.[42] Thus spirit possession, spirit-language, and reading or hearing that language all opened up ordinary human life to the world of the spirits, to the world of the something More.[43] All three ac-

[39] For "abundance," see chapter 2 above, "Ordinary Lives: John and His First Readers," pp. 25–26.

[40] Cf. William James, *The Varieties of Religious Experience* (New York: New American Library, 1902), 384–85: "Is such a 'more' merely our own notion, or does it really exist? If so, in what shape does it exist? . . . [V]arious theologies . . . all agree that the 'more' really exists; though some of them hold it to exist in the shape of a personal god or gods, while others are satisfied to conceive it as a stream of ideal tendency embedded in the eternal structure of the world." John and early Christians obviously conceived of it as a personal God.

[41] Torrance, *Spiritual Quest,* 284–85.

[42] David Aune was on the right track when he proposed that "apocalypses mediate a new actualization of the original revelatory experience" (Aune, "Problem of Genre," 89).

[43] I deliberately name that abundance in the world by the more generic "More" rather than by the name of a personal deity, the idiom that John uses, in order to allow for a broader understanding of spirit possession that could include entities such as energy fields or undivided wholeness. See the bibliography at n. 1.

tivities offered new ways of seeing and being in the world, ways that en-
compassed, but transcended, the planning and projecting of human endeavor.

10

The Lion/Lamb King

Reading the Apocalypse from Popular Culture

Jon Paulien

It was called Judgment Day. On that day and with one blow the entire human race was brought to the verge of extinction. To make matters worse, the remnants of human life were continuously threatened by monstrous parodies of human intelligence.

The only hope of saving the world lay in the hands of a woman and her unborn child. Without warning, a monstrous being was sent on a mission to destroy that mother so that her child would never be born. Failing in that mission, the forces that were trying to destroy the human race turned their relentless fury against her son. After a harrowing escape, the son directs a great war to rescue the human race from annihilation. Ultimately, humanity is delivered from fiery destruction by two actions: (1) the willing self-sacrifice of one whose death makes life possible for all of humanity, and (2) the destruction of evil in a huge cauldron of molten metal and fire.

Devotees of action/adventure movies in general and Arnold Schwarzenegger movies in particular will immediately recognize in the above scenario the basic theme of *Terminator* and *Terminator 2*, a violent pair of cinematic action thrillers that set new standards for suspense and special effects.[1] The continuing evocative power of the two *Terminator* movies lies in the emotional chords that they touch in today's world.[2] The human

[1] *Terminator 2*, by itself, cost an unheard-of (at the time) ninety-four million dollars to make. See Stuart Klawans, "Terminator 2: Judgment Day," *The Nation*, 9 September 1991, 278; "Hasta la Vista, Babies," *The Economist*, 13 July 1991, 68; Richard Corliss, "Terminator 2: Judgment Day," *Time*, 8 July 1991, 56; David Ansen, "Terminator 2: Judgment Day," *Newsweek*, 8 July 1991, 57. Synopses and other information about these and most other motion pictures can be found on the Internet Movie Database at http://us.imdb.com/.

[2] Michael Hirschorn declared the original *Terminator* movie the most important film of the 1980s in *Esquire*, 3 September 1990, 116–17. The great popularity of

race does indeed feel itself at peril, and the concept of runaway computers and intelligent but malevolent robots is at least plausible.

What may slip by most action-movie buffs is the fact that the above scenario is not a new one. Nearly two thousand years ago an isolated man on a distant island penned his dream of great and imminent peril to the human race, of horrific and relentless beasts that sought to destroy a woman and her child, of a salvation of the human race that was achieved through death, and of the final destruction of evil in a lake of fire. That dream was recorded in a book called the Apocalypse, and that book (also called the Book of Revelation) found its way (in spite of protest) into the Christian Bible, which still influences society today.[3]

An Influential Book

I have been unable to determine whether the authors of the *Terminator* concept themselves intended allusions to the Apocalypse in the two movies.[4] The director of the pair of films (James Cameron), however, has shown considerable interest in biblical scholarship and may well have intended to build on the themes of the Apocalypse. In any case, the Apocalypse is far more influential in current popular culture than most people realize.

The very term "Apocalypse" has become a synonym for "Doomsday," a reference to the end of the world, whether by violence, economic catastrophe, or natural disaster. For a movie dramatizing the "horror" of war and what it did to those Americans who fought in Vietnam, Francis Coppola chose the title *Apocalypse Now*. A speech on the fiscal irresponsibility of American policy by noted New York City economist Felix Rohatyn was reported in the *New York Daily News* of May 29, 1987, under the headline "Rohatyn: Apocalypse Soon!" The term "apocalypse" has been used even more recently with regard to global warming,[5] the health effects of proximity to electric power lines,[6] urban population growth,[7] increased traffic on the Internet,[8] welfare reform,[9] and alpine snowboards![10] The term was

---

Terminator 2 is evidenced by its 204 million dollars in theater receipts in North America alone.

[3] An excellent summary of the interaction of the *Terminator* movies with the Apocalypse is found in Roland Boer, "Christological Slippage and Ideological Structures in Schwarzenegger's *Terminator*," *Semeia* 69/70 (1995): 173–74.

[4] For summaries of the spiritual nature of the film series, and its allusions to Mary and Jesus, among other biblical characters, see Klawans, "Terminator 2," 278, and Corliss, "Terminator 2," 55–56.

[5] Michael D. Lemonick, "Heading for Apocalypse?" *Time*, 2 October 1995, 54; cf. review of *Earth First! Environmental Apocalypse* by S. Hollenhorst in *Choice*, July–August 1996, 1816.

[6] Jon Palfreman, "Apocalypse Not," *Technology Review*, 3 April 1996, 24.

[7] Fred Pearce, "Urban Apocalypse Postponed?" *New Scientist*, 1 June 1996, 4.

[8] Richard Overton, "Internet Apocalypse," *PC World*, July 1996, 45.

[9] Jill Nelson, "Apocalypse Now," *The Nation*, 26 August 1996, 10.

[10] Dana White, "Rip Rides," *Skiing*, February 1992, 91.

also used as a title for recent novels,[11] for a musical recording by a Moroccan folk band,[12] and with reference to court congestion and delays,[13] the demise of the sun,[14] overpopulation,[15] AIDS,[16] and the unfortunate events in Waco, Texas, in 1993.[17]

Speeches by President Reagan called attention to the battle of Armageddon. Also drawn from the Apocalypse, the battle of Armageddon is the name given to the final battle involving all the nations of the earth resulting in the end of history as we know it. Note also the pleading of General Douglas MacArthur at the close of the Second World War:

> A new era is upon us. . . . The utter destruction of the war potential, through progressive advances in scientific discovery, has in fact now reached a point which revises the traditional concept of war.
>
> Men since the beginning of time have sought peace. . . . military alliances, balances of power, leagues of nations all in turn failed, leaving the only path to be by way of the crucible of war.
>
> We have had our last chance. If we do not now devise some greater and more equitable system, Armageddon will be at our door.[18]

More recently, *Armageddon* was adopted as the title of a science-fiction movie about a runaway asteroid that threatens earth.

The rock star formerly known as Prince was raised in a Seventh-day Adventist home in which the beasts of Revelation were often daily fare in reaction to the latest news from Dan Rather or CNN.[19] Along with voracious sexuality,[20] the themes of his music are often laced with images from the Apocalypse. The lyrics from his hit song "7," for example, allude to an

[11] *The Apocalypse Watch*, by Robert Ludlum; and *Night of the Apocalypse*, by Daniel Easterman. In the book *Writing the Apocalypse: Historical Vision in Contemporary U.S. and Latin American Fiction* (Cambridge: Cambridge University Press, 1993), Lois Parkinson Zamora surveys more than a dozen recent "apocalyptic" novels. See the review by John Mowat in *Journal of American Studies* 28 (2 August 1994): 301–2.

[12] See the review of "Apocalypse across the Sky," a CD recording by the Master Musicians of Jajouka, in *The New York Times*, 12 July 1992, sec. 2, p. H23.

[13] "Apocalypse When?" *The National Law Journal*, 9 January 1995, A20.

[14] Malcolm W. Browne, "New Look at Apocalypse: Dying Sun Will Boil Seas and Leave Orbiting Cinder," *The New York Times*, 20 September 1994, C1, C11.

[15] "Apocalypse Soon," *The Economist*, 23 July 1994, A25.

[16] "African Apocalypse," *Time*, 6 July 1992, 21.

[17] Richard Woodbury, "After the Apocalypse," *Time*, 17 January 1994, 17; "Children of the Apocalypse," *Newsweek*, 3 May 1993, 30.

[18] Douglas MacArthur, *Reminiscences: General of the Army, Douglas MacArthur* (New York: McGraw Hill, 1964), 276.

[19] Steve Turner, *Hungry for Heaven* (Downer's Grove, Ill.: InterVarsity Press, 1995), 193.

[20] Ibid., 193–94. While Prince has felt that the closest one can come to a feeling of transcendence lies in promiscuous sexuality, his religious beliefs seem fairly typical of evangelical Christianity on the whole.

"angel" coming down with a "key," an army's marching feet, a "plague and a river of blood," and end with the promise of "a new city with streets of gold." Still, this is not a song about religion in the traditional sense; rather, it is about human love and the obstacles that stand in its path.

Further images that have their source in the Apocalypse include the concept of antichrist (a terrifying end-time tyrant based on the descriptions of the beast of chapter 13), the falling star Wormwood (a demonic figure in *The Screwtape Letters*, by C. S. Lewis), the four apocalyptic horsemen (applied tongue-in-cheek to a highly successful backfield on the Notre Dame football team),[21] the end-time millennium (a Latin term for the thousand-year period that comes at the close of earth's history in the Apocalypse), and the horrifying nothingness of the Abyss (a bottomless pit which is both the source and the destiny of all evil in the world). Additional images that have influenced one element or another of contemporary society include the idea of a mystic Babylon,[22] a new Jerusalem, the Alpha and the Omega, the Mark of the Beast,[23] and the cryptic number of the antichrist, 666.

Due to the tremendous influence of the Apocalypse in today's world, there has also been a resurgence of scholarly interest in the book at major centers of learning such as Harvard, Notre Dame, and the University of Chicago, and in scholarly societies such as the Society of Biblical Literature and the Chicago Society for Biblical Research. The book you hold in your hand is a product of this interest.

A Believable Scenario

But the scholarly interest in Revelation is not dry and dusty; it has raised many issues that are relevant today. As a way of thinking about the world, apocalyptic seeks to understand the successive human ages and their culmination in a catastrophic struggle between the forces of good and evil. Apocalyptic seems to help people make sense of the universe and where they stand in it.[24] This is a major reason why we have seen such a resurgence of interest in apocalyptic in the last half-century.[25]

Like John, the author of the Apocalypse, people today think of themselves as living, at least potentially, in the last generation of earth's history. It was more than two decades ago that a group of scientists known as the Club of Rome predicted that, within thirty years, civilization would collapse under the weight of increasing population and the lack of food.

[21] See online: http://und.ocsn.com/trads/horse.html.

[22] Pat Frank, *Alas, Babylon* (Toronto: Bantam Books, 1970). This novel explores a scenario of nuclear war and the nature of the life after.

[23] Tim LaHaye's Left Behind series is notable here (Wheaton, Ill.: Tyndale House).

[24] Stephen D. O'Leary, *Arguing the Apocalypse: A Theory of Millennial Rhetoric* (New York: Oxford University Press, 1994), 5.

[25] Ibid., 7.

Since that time a multitude of problems that threaten survival have come to our attention. In 1973–74 and 1979, major energy shortages raised world consciousness to the limits on natural resources. The greenhouse effect (a gradual warming of the earth due to the effects of pollution) threatens to melt the polar ice caps and inundate coastal areas. The destruction of the world's last sizable rain forest in Brazil raises questions about the earth's ability to maintain the necessary supply of oxygen in its atmosphere to sustain animal and human life. The movie *Independence Day* raised the specter of hostile alien invasion. Alien objects, such as giant meteorites, comets, and asteroids, are also considered threats to the continuation of life.[26] The threat of germ and chemical warfare, toxic-waste dumps, the destruction of the earth's ozone layer, terrorist attacks, and new health threats such as AIDS and Ebola have made everyone aware of human mortality.[27]

As I write, the awesome horror of nuclear war between nations has taken a temporary back seat to the suicidal madness of a handful of terrorists. While the *Bulletin of the Atomic Scientists* has maintained a constant warning of the end with its famous "minutes to midnight" clock, the threat posed by that clock has been scaled back in the last decade because of developments in the former Soviet Union.[28] But while optimism regarding the prospects of nuclear war may now reign in some quarters, the nuclear arsenals in the former Soviet Union remain largely intact, while the systems controlling them have become increasingly unstable. The chances of former Soviet weapons getting into terrorist hands, or of some "pariah" nation developing its own arsenal, seem less a matter of "if" than of "when." There is even the *Terminator*-like specter of a programming malfunction on the part of one or more computers that run the world's nuclear arsenals. So the apocalyptic threat that still poses the most terror for modern civilization is the power embedded in the nucleus of the atom.

The threat of "terrorist nukes" has led President George W. Bush to call for the scrapping of the ABM (anti-ballistic missile) Treaty of 1972. He feels that the nuclear threat from terrorists or rogue nations is far greater than the threat from China or the Soviet Union ever was. He and others

[26] See the cover story in *Newsweek*, 23 November 1992. Toward the close of the 1990s, the movies *Armageddon* and *Deep Impact* focused on the danger to earth of large celestial objects.

[27] The anthrax scares in the wake of the attacks on the World Trade Center and the Pentagon (11 September 2001) brought the specter of biological warfare firmly into public consciousness. Anthrax, fortunately, is treatable and non-communicable. If terrorists were to find a way to reintroduce smallpox, on the other hand, the consequences could be catastrophic.

[28] This nuclear optimism was reversed in 1998 by the addition of India and Pakistan to the list of nuclear powers. See Bill Joy, "Why the Future Doesn't Need Us," *Wired*, April 2000, 254.

believe that the ability to counter an isolated missile threat (carrying nuclear warheads, of course) is one of the top priorities for civilized nations at the turn of the millennium. So nuclear apocalypse will likely remain a recurring theme in both the sciences and the arts.

Not long ago, it was the awareness of the nuclear threat that caused children in many places to question whether they would ever reach adulthood, and to make life decisions on that basis. Note the poem of a thirteen-year-old Russian student:

> The entire Earth will become
> a wasteland. All buildings
> will be destroyed . . .
> All living things will perish—
> no grass, no trees, no greenery.[29]

That the survival of humanity is now in question is amply illustrated in the arts. Robert Morris, a New York City artist, has become famous for sculptures that illustrate piles of human body parts, as if torn apart by a nuclear holocaust. Alexander Melamid and Vitaly Komar stunned the art world with their painting "Scenes from the Future—The Guggenheim." This painting depicts a broken-down Guggenheim Museum in New York surrounded by a nuclear desert.[30] Movies such as *The Day After* and *The Road Warrior* not only depict the horror of nuclear destruction but also explore the nature of life afterward, or at least what can be imagined of such a time. Thus a recent philosophical trend is "post-apocalypticism," which all but considers nuclear destruction inevitable and seeks to understand what kind of future humanity has in the light of that impending reality.

As the Apocalypse makes clear, this generation is not the first to perceive that it could be the last. The difference is, this is the first generation that has perceived that the end could come without reference to God.[31] Somehow the idea that God could bring about the end allows for the possibility that God could save as well. But the secular apocalypse faced by this generation could be the result of an accident of history, even the random madness of a terrorist with a "Doomsday Machine." Thus we face the end as potentially an "abyss of meaninglessness." Perhaps the human condition was best expressed in the words of the Terminator itself, a computer-generated being, part human and part machine, "It's in your nature to destroy yourselves."

At the eve of the new millennium, the Terminator thesis got a big boost from an unexpected source.[32] A warning about the dangers of technology came from none other than Bill Joy, chief scientist at Sun Microsys-

---

[29] Douglas Davis, "Nuclear Visions," *Vogue*, November 1984, 202.

[30] Ibid., 197–99.

[31] Bernard Brandon Scott, *Hollywood Dreams and Biblical Stories* (Minneapolis: Fortress Press, 1994), 199.

[32] Joy, "Why the Future Doesn't Need Us," 238–62.

tems and the creator of Java, a software application that helped make the Internet what it is today. While Joy is certainly no Luddite, he argues the perils of technology on the grounds of "unintended consequences." Just as the widespread use of antibiotics and DDT have had unforeseen and potentially disastrous consequences, Joy argues that Murphy's Law is an inevitable part of technological advances in computing as well.[33]

Building on the work of Ray Kurzweil and Dan Moravec, Joy notes that computer systems are very complex, involving interaction among and feedback between many parts. Any changes to such a system will cascade in ways that are difficult to predict. If Moore's Law of hardware advancement (doubling computer performance every eighteen months at no increase in cost) continues to operate, by 2030 we could be able to build machines that rival human beings in intelligence. When such "robots" exceed human intelligence and become able to self-replicate, the extinction of the human race becomes conceivable, perhaps as early as 2050.[34]

Joy sees the danger in genetics, nanotechnology, and robotics (GNR) as even greater than the dangers of nuclear, chemical, and biological warfare. The reason is that the latter are military weapons that remain under human control. The dangers of GNR, on the other hand, are grounded in their commercial and economic benefits. They will, therefore, be promoted and developed by the marketplace, with unintended consequences that will be outside governmental control. He concludes, "This is the first moment in the history of our planet when any species, by its own voluntary actions, has become a danger to itself—as well as to vast numbers of others."[35]

A distinguished list of readers supported and/or interacted with Joy's thesis,[36] providing legitimization for even greater eschatological anxiety than before. A counterthesis finally appeared a few months later.[37] Jaron Lanier, a specialist in virtual-reality systems, argued that Joy and his supporters have confused "ideal" computers with real computers. While we can conceptualize ideal computers, we only know how to build dysfunc-

---

[33] Ibid., 239.

[34] Ibid., 240, 243. Joy sees the possibility of "enhanced evolution" through the interchangeability of human and machine, but he is obviously not optimistic about the outcome of such evolution.

[35] Ibid., 248. Joy cites the philosopher John Leslie as estimating the risk of human extinction at 30 percent. Joy believes that the only solution to this danger is to consciously limit the development of potentially dangerous technologies, "by limiting our pursuit of certain kinds of knowledge" (254). He cites Thoreau as saying that we will be "rich in proportion to the number of things which we can afford to let alone" (258).

[36] See the "Rants and Raves" section of the July 2000 issue of Wired magazine (61–80). That the article triggered scores of responses from some of the world's top thinkers shows that Joy hit a raw nerve in current human consciousness.

[37] Jaron Lanier, "One-Half of a Manifesto: Why Stupid Software Will Save the Future from Neo-Darwinian Machines," Wired, December 2000, 158–79.

tional ones. Real computers break for reasons that are often less than clear, and they seem to resist our efforts to improve them, often due to legacy and lock-in problems.[38] While Moore's Law continues to work for hardware systems, software seems to be getting worse and worse as systems become more complex.

While in theory, therefore, the hardware could become sophisticated enough to exceed human intelligence, Lanier notes that human beings themselves do not seem able to write software that would make such a superior machine possible. If anything, Moore's Law seems to reverse when it comes to software. As processors become faster and memory becomes cheaper, software becomes correspondingly slower and more bloated, using up all available resources.[39] So Lanier conceives Joy's eschatological nightmare to end as follows: "Just as some newborn race of superintelligent robots are about to consume all humanity, our dear old species will likely be saved by a Windows crash. The poor robots will linger pathetically, begging us to reboot them, even though they'll know it would do no good."[40] Thus the human race will be saved from extinction by "stupid software."

Regardless of the outcome of this debate, it is clear that John's Apocalypse speaks to fears and possibilities that are just as real in today's world as they were in John's.

Parallels with Contemporary Genre

A further reason our generation finds the Apocalypse both weird and attractive is that apocalyptic as a genre is very much alive and well in popular culture today. At first glance, for example, the cartoon movie *The Lion King* seems to be a simple animal story. Why then did more than seventy million people go to theaters (and millions more buy or rent the video) to see a cartoon? Because *The Lion King* is not really about animals. It is about people and groups of people and how they interact with each other; it is about taking risks, developing relationships, avoiding conflict, and confronting issues that make a difference in everyday life.

But *The Lion King* is even more than a sociological treatise in disguise. It is based on an African version of apocalyptic. It involves the ruin and restoration of a paradise wherein all have a place and all function in happiness and prosperity. It is about the destruction of the environment because of evil that arises out of the animal kingdom from a dark place at

---

[38] Ibid., 162.

[39] Ibid., 170–74.

[40] Ibid., 172. A helpful analogy: Trips on Manhattan streets were faster a hundred years ago than they are today. While cars are faster than horses (hardware advances) the bottlenecks caused by the utility of the advance (software issues) has slowed traffic to a crawl. Result: in Manhattan horses are faster than cars (ibid., 174). Today most gigahertz computers seem slower than the twenty-megahertz "giants" of a decade ago!

the edge of paradise. It is about the hope for the future that can arise when a redeemer seizes his destiny with courage. And sales figures indicate that *The Lion King* struck a chord in the American consciousness that few movies have.

That is what makes the Apocalypse so powerful. Although it reads like an animal story (Rev 11:7; 12:1–17; 13:1–18; 17:1–18), it is not really about animals. It is a cartoon fantasy about people and their relationships, about interactions among groups of people, both good and evil, about the relationship between God and the human race, and how human history is going to turn out. In other words, it is a cartoon about the same kinds of issues we all wrestle with from day to day.

Movies tend to be successful when they intersect with the basic struggles, conflicts, and tensions within a society.[41] They function as a reality check and intersect with that society's popular myths and fears. Movies like *The Lion King, Independence Day, Blade Runner, The Matrix,* and *Terminator 2* show that apocalyptic genre is as popular today as it was when the Book of Revelation was written.[42] The credibility of apocalyptic movies depends on whether the way they portray present trends playing out into the future is believable. The same was true of ancient apocalypses.[43]

Apocalyptic's value in today's world, therefore, lies not primarily in its predictive power, but in its diagnostic ability.[44] Apocalyptic helps us to understand ourselves, both as individuals and as part of humankind as a whole. It mirrors reality in a way that bypasses our psychological and emotional defense mechanisms, and strikes home with powerful force where we least expect it. Since genuine self-understanding is an essential prerequisite of productive change, this role of apocalyptic, both ancient and contemporary, continues to make a difference in the world as we know it.

When reading the Apocalypse in conjunction with contemporary images like the *Terminator* movies, one increasingly comes to the conclusion that both strands of apocalyptic agree on the trends in their respective societies. They agree that society is headed toward catastrophe and chaos unless some extraordinary intervention should occur. They also agree on the diagnosis: the inhumanity of human beings toward one another. In enslaving or abusing other human beings, we set ourselves up as false gods acting out our own distorted version of reality.[45] Apocalyptic helps us see the self-deception that lurks within.

Why Bother?

Does it make sense to study the Apocalypse in the age of information, when there are so many choices to make? The above realities argue for

---

[41] Scott, *Hollywood Dreams*, 11.
[42] Ibid., 193.
[43] Ibid., 198–99.
[44] Ibid., 213.
[45] Ibid., 201, 213.

the importance of such study. The book has been highly influential in today's world; you will miss the meaning of many popular allusions if you are unfamiliar with its content. The scenario of the Apocalypse is increasingly believable in a nuclear age. And the apocalyptic genre is an important window into how people think and feel about the future.

But there are other reasons why a book like the Apocalypse is deserving of study. For one thing it comes at the end of the Christian Bible, which for millions of people functions as a source of authority for their life and worldview. For many it is even a source of vital information that affects political, moral, and ethical decisions. Whether or not one buys into such a reading of the book, it wields an influence in today's world far out of proportion to its level of recognition within contemporary society.

But such authoritarian readings have a dark side. It has been said that the Apocalypse "either finds a man mad or leaves him mad." Most of us have, at one time or another, encountered somebody who, referring to the Apocalypse, drew up some incredible scheme about when the world would end, or how the Middle East peace process would work itself out. And although we may not have known what to do with the scheme, we sensed that there was something far-fetched about it.

There is nothing new about this kind of reading of the Apocalypse. It has been used in the past to support many movements of dubious character. In the Middle Ages, many groups in Western Europe, particularly in France, saw in the concept of the millennium a prediction that the end of the world would come around the year 1000.[46] This excitement was relatively small compared to that caused when the Franciscan followers of Joachim of Floris interpreted the repeated references in Revelation to a period of 1,260 days or forty-two months as a prediction that the end of the world would come around 1260 C.E. Considerably more bizarre was the movement in Muenster, Germany, in 1534 that declared that the city of Muenster was the new Jerusalem of the Apocalypse. The leaders of the movement sought to establish this earthly utopia by force of arms.

Other more or less bizarre interpretations of Revelation have continued to abound to the present day. Antichrist has been identified as various emperors and popes of the Middle Ages, Napoleon III of France, Hitler, Mussolini and even President Reagan (after all there are six letters in each of his three names—Ronald Wilson Reagan). Armageddon has been associated with World Wars I and II as well as the infamous World

---

[46] Although the excitement surrounding 1000 C.E. was not as great or as widespread as is generally held in the popular consciousness, it is now recognized to have taken place in parts of Europe at least, contrary to earlier scholarly opinion expressed in Jacques Barzun and Henry F. Graaf, *The Modern Researcher* (New York: Harcourt, Brace, 1957), 104–6. See Henri Focillon, *The Year 1000* (New York: Unger, 1970); Richard Erdoes, *A.D. 1000: Living on the Brink of Apocalypse* (San Francisco: Harper and Row, 1988); Jon Paulien, "The Millennium Is Here Again: Is It Panic Time?" *AUSS*, no. 2 (1999): 167–78.

War III. Babylon the Great has been equated with the common market, the Roman Catholic Church, and the communist system. The mark of the beast has been associated with the bar-coding system used in supermarkets and credit cards utilizing the number 666.

More frightening yet were the developments in Waco, Texas, in 1993. Misapplication of the Apocalypse by David Koresh resulted in the deaths of scores of innocent people, including four federal agents. These words and their interpretation can be dangerous; in the wrong hands the Apocalypse can be as dangerous as a terrorist's bomb. Sober and careful exegesis of the Apocalypse is not just a game; it can be a life-and-death matter. If the people deceived by David Koresh had been schooled in the kind of sober approach to the Apocalypse that you find in this book, they would have rejected his demagoguery and many of them would be alive today.

There is one final reason to study the Apocalypse. Mysteries and puzzles are fun. People enjoy hunting for clues and wrestling with problems. The Apocalypse is like a Nintendo game in which you keep getting stuck at a certain spot until you figure out a secret clue or solve a problem that permits you to continue. It feels great every time a new piece of your understanding of Revelation falls into place. It is exciting to discover new mysteries that need to be investigated and solved.

Conclusion

In light of the powerful influence of the Apocalypse, it is imperative that we understand the true nature of its influence. This book is dedicated to helping students wrestle with the fertile variety of meanings available in the Apocalypse without making the kind of blunders that led to Muenster and Waco. There is much to be lost, both from ignoring the book and from reading it in speculative and unhealthy ways.

At the conclusion of *Terminator 2,* there is hope, an optimistic view of the end. The maternal savior figure offers a voiceover, "For the first time I face the future with a sense of hope; if a machine, a Terminator, can learn the value of human life, maybe we can too."

No one knows if a movie series like the *Terminator* will become a classic, a turning point in the evolution of human thought. But in the Apocalypse we have a guaranteed classic, a book that has stood the test of time. Facing the same basic issues that the human race faces today, the Apocalypse offers both a warning of doom and a promise of hope. It sees in the human race an infinite value worth the sacrifice of an infinite God. Perhaps we can learn from an author who, like us, faced the prospect of an imminent end, yet faced it with a confidence that many of us have lost.

Conclusion

CHOOSING BETWEEN READINGS: QUESTIONS AND CRITERIA

David L. Barr

A volume such as this raises central questions of how we ought to read a book like Revelation and how we should deal with competing, even conflicting, readings. Are all readings valid? Are some better than others? Why do different readers give different interpretations? How do we use multiple interpretations? How do we choose between conflicting interpretations? These are significant issues and, now that we have experienced the various interpretations given in these essays, it is time to address them.

To begin, we must admit that there is no agreement on such questions; they are as debated as the interpretation of Revelation itself. The various contributors to this volume would likely each answer them differently. But for purposes of analysis, let's imagine two poles on a continuum. On the one side we imagine people who believe there is only one right interpretation: what the author intended. The task of the interpreter is to utilize whatever tools necessary (linguistic, historical, literary, social) to rediscover that meaning, which resides entirely within the text. In this view the text completely controls meaning, and the validity of an interpretation is determined by its faithfulness to the text.[1]

At the other pole we imagine people who believe all interpretations are valid, or at least partially valid and partially faulty. No text is "self-interpreting," and every interpreter brings a unique perspective that colors his or her interpretation. And while history may be of some use, we must remember that history itself is a reconstruction based on the values, perceptions, and goals of the historian. The goal of an objective interpretation based solely on the text is an illusion; there are as many readings of a text as there are readers. In this view the reader completely controls the meaning of a text, and the validity of a reading corresponds to its usefulness in a particular social, political, and historical context.[2]

---

[1] A good representative of this approach in general literary criticism is E. D. Hirsch, *Validity in Interpretation* (New Haven: Yale University Press, 1967).

[2] A good representative of this approach in general literary criticism is Stanley E. Fish, *Is There a Text in This Class?* (Cambridge: Harvard University Press, 1980).

Each of these polar views has its points to make, but few readers live at the poles. Much more common, and certainly the view I find most persuasive, is a mediating position that finds meaning only in the continual interaction between the text and the reader. Both text and reader constrain readings, but neither by itself compels a certain understanding. The reader must always make a choice of readings based on factors outside the text, but the text itself provides the evidence for the validation of such choices.[3] In my view there are a great many and differing valid readings of a text like Revelation, but there are also misreadings, weak readings, and false readings. The best way to explain this is to consider a particular case.

Near the middle of John's story is a scene of a dragon who, frustrated by his inability to destroy a heavenly woman, turns to make war on her children (12:17). This war will be carried out with the assistance of two monsters, one conjured from the earth the other from the sea. The earth monster is described thus:

> Then I saw another beast that rose out of the earth; it had two horns like a lamb and it spoke like a dragon. It exercises all the authority of the first beast on its behalf, and it makes the earth and its inhabitants worship the first beast, whose mortal wound had been healed. It performs great signs, even making fire come down from heaven to earth in the sight of all; and by the signs that it is allowed to perform on behalf of the beast, it deceives the inhabitants of earth, telling them to make an image for the beast that had been wounded by the sword and yet lived; and it was allowed to give breath to the image of the beast so that the image of the beast could even speak and cause those who would not worship the image of the beast to be killed. Also it causes all, both small and great, both rich and poor, both free and slave, to be marked on the right hand or the forehead, so that no one can buy or sell who does not have the mark, that is, the name of the beast or the number of its name. This calls for wisdom: let anyone with understanding calculate the number of the beast, for it is the number of a person. Its number is six hundred sixty-six. (13:11–18)

This beast has fascinated interpreters of Revelation from earliest times, and there are literally hundreds of interpretations offered. Let me begin with an interpretation that is clearly wrong. During the U.S. presidential elections in 1984, a pamphlet circulated claiming that Ronald Wilson Reagan was the beast, because he is the only president to have six letters in each of his three names: 6-6-6.

Now without debating whether some of Reagan's social policies were

---

[3] A good representative of this approach in general literary criticism is Paul B. Armstrong, *Conflicting Readings: Variety and Validity in Interpretation* (Chapel Hill and London: University of North Carolina Press, 1990). Armstrong suggests three tests for a valid interpretation: inclusiveness, intersubjectivity, and utility (13–16), which I discuss later.

beastly, we can say clearly that this is an erroneous interpretation, for it shows complete ignorance of the way ancient peoples used numbers. They would not have counted the letters in a name, but added up the values of those letters. Both the Hebrews and the Greeks made the letters of their alphabets do double duty as numbers, so each letter had a numeric value corresponding to its position in the alphabet. (The Romans, of course, were the first to invent a separate way of writing numbers: the dreaded Roman numbers.)[4] My point, simply, is that this is an erroneous interpretation. Some interpretations are wrong.

But how do we decide? What distinguishes a valid from an erroneous interpretation? A better from a worse? A weak from a strong reading? Again there is no agreement, but given the nature of the disagreement we should look for factors both in the text and in the reader. In regard to the text, Paul Armstrong[5] argues that better readings are marked by their inclusiveness: a reading

> becomes more secure as it demonstrates its ability to account for parts without encountering anomaly and to undergo refinements and extensions without being abandoned. (13)

Or stated negatively, when a reading fails to make sense of all the parts of a work, or when the sense made of one part conflicts with the sense of another, or when it leads to absurdities when it is logically extended, then that is an erroneous (Armstrong's word is "illegitimate") reading. Thus an interpretation of the meaning of the beast and of 666 in chapter 13 must work when applied to the beast (and to the use of numbers) in other parts of Revelation.

In regard to the reader, Armstrong argues that better readings are marked by intersubjectivity, that is, the ability to appeal to multiple subjectivities. What an earlier generation of scholars pursued as an "objective interpretation" has proven to be an oxymoron. Interpretation is by definition a subjective enterprise. Better readings are those that many different readers find convincing. Again, to state the reverse, when a reading fails to convince a significant number of other readers of its worth it is at least a weak, and probably a wrong, reading.

To this logical pair, Armstrong adds a third test: efficacy, that is, the evaluation of a reading on pragmatic grounds to see whether or not it has the power to lead to new discoveries and a continued comprehension.[6]

Better readings lead us further into a text, open up new insights, suggest avenues for further exploration. I later argue that this same criterion can be applied to the reader side of the text/reader dialectic: better read-

---

[4] For an overview see Karl Menninger, *Number Words and Number Symbols: A Cultural History of Numbers* (Cambridge, Mass.: MIT Press, 1969).

[5] See his *Conflicting Readings*, 1–19. This is the best introductory treatment of these issues that I have seen.

[6] Ibid., 15.

ings are those that have the potential to open up new insights about ourselves as readers.

The application of these principles to the interpretation of Revelation
suggests that there are multiple valid interpretations. Even conflicting interpretations can be valid. But this does not suggest that all readings are
equally valid; rather, it suggests criteria by which we can judge some
readings to be illegitimate, or simply wrong. Before returning to the specific readings offered in this book, let me develop these ideas a bit further
by considering three very general and very different approaches to the
interpretation of Revelation: prophetic (viewing the book as about the future), historical (viewing it as about the past), and symbolic (viewing it as
about the present). We can think of these as three initial guesses to what
the book is about. How does each of these approaches interpret the beast
of Rev 13?

Some interpreters make the initial guess that Revelation is really
about the future. This has been and continues to be the most common approach. Many have thought that everything in the work is predictive, including the seven churches, which have often been viewed as "church
ages" or epochs stretching from John's time to the contemporary period.
More common is the view that everything after 4:1 (when John ascends
to heaven) is predictive of some future event. Thus the beast whose number is 666 represents some future human ruler. Most commonly today, interpreters who take a predictive approach identify the beast with some
Middle Eastern ruler,[7] often Saddam Hussein or Mu'ammar al-Qadhafi.

Some interpreters make the initial guess that Revelation is really
about the past. This, after all, is what we assume about every other book
written in the past. Thus the seven churches are real assemblies of Christians located in the named cities. And the beast whose number is 666 is
some historical figure from John's time. Of the several possibilities, the
most commonly cited is Nero, whose Greek title (Caesar Nero) written in
Hebrew letters adds up precisely to 666.[8]

Some interpreters make the initial guess that Revelation is really
about timeless truths that are as true today as they were in John's day.
Thus the book can be read as explaining present realities. In this view the
beast whose number is 666 takes its identity from the meaning of the symbolic number 6, which the text calls "a human number." Since humans
were created on the sixth day, according to the first creation story (Gen 1),
this is an appropriate symbol. And since the week was often a symbol for

---

[7] John F. Walvoord calls this ruler a "new strong man of the Middle East," *Armageddon, Oil, and the Middle East Crisis* (Grand Rapids: Zondervan, 1990), 156.

[8] G. B. Caird, *A Commentary on the Revelation of St. John the Divine* (New York:
Harper & Row, 1966); for a recent review of the theory and a clear explanation of
how the ancients used numbers see Richard J. Bauckham, "Nero and the Beast,"
in *The Climax of Prophecy: Studies on the Book of Revelation* (Edinburgh: T. & T. Clark,
1993), 384–452.

the present age, wherein the seventh day represents God's rightful rule, humanity is ever short of the Sabbath rest. In the same way, the eighth day represents the beginning of the new week and the new age; the name Jesus in Greek adds up to 888. This view takes these symbolic references as the real meaning of the work.[9]

This abbreviated explanation of these three views is enough to see how radically they differ. They come to three contradictory conclusions about the meaning of the beast, and, in principle, they disagree on the meaning of every element in the book. All three stand up well to the criteria listed above: inclusiveness (each can be applied to every detail of the work); intersubjectivity (each has a significant community of adherents); and utility (each opens up new aspects of the Apocalypse and promises new insights).[10] None can be proven false.[11] But there are degrees and differences, and we must make a choice of how we will read. What cannot be done is to avoid the choice, to claim that we simply take Revelation for what it says, for what it says is determined by the initial choice we make.

In this volume various authors have made differing initial choices and have thereby produced differing readings of Revelation. Friesen in chapter 3 has chosen to start his reading by examining the phenomenon of emperor worship, something far removed from modern experience. He wants to explore the specific social dynamics of John's world. Paulien in chapter 10 has chosen to start his reading of Revelation by looking at elements of contemporary popular culture, showing modern imaginations of how the end might come. This leads him to the further conclusion that the value of such writings is not whether the future they imagine actually comes to pass; their value lies in the light they shed on our current situation. The degree to which such writings help us understand ourselves, our culture, and our place in history is the true measure of their worth. So which is the better reading?

As I have thought about the issues that guide my own selection of interpretations, I find them closely related to the principles from Armstrong discussed above: inclusiveness, intersubjectivity, and utility. So let me recast these principles as questions, expand them in a couple of ways, and add one further principle.

---

[9] Austin Farrer, *A Rebirth of Images: The Making of St. John's Apocalypse* (Gloucester, Mass.: Peter Smith, 1970).

[10] This is less true of the prophetic view, for it is more concerned with understanding secret meanings in the world outside the text, that is, who actually is the beast. But this is a different sort of utility, and many people are willing to pay good money on the chance they will learn this secret.

[11] Again this is less true of the prophetic view, for when it has made specific predictions based on the Apocalypse, it has always been wrong. Thus, Hal Lindsey originally predicted the world would end in 1988—forty years after the founding of the state of Israel (Hal Lindsey with C. C. Carlson, *The Late Great Planet Earth* [New York: Bantam Books, 1970], 43).

What can we learn from this reading? This is derived from the principle of intersubjectivity—a rather nice word for the idea that people sometimes agree. Actually the word comes from an old debate about whether knowledge is objective or subjective ("If a tree falls in the forest and there is no one there to hear it, does it make any sound?"). This third view denies that knowledge can ever be wholly objective or subjective. There are trees that fall, and there are people who hear them. Now these people may describe the sound differently, may even experience different sorts of sound depending on where they are standing. But our best hope of knowing the sound of a tree falling is to understand the mutual subjective perceptions: intersubjectivity. This means that I can compare my reading with others and can compare the various readings of others. The corollary of intersubjectivity is dialogue. Thus encountering both Paulien's reading and Friesen's reading, side by side in the same book, gives us a different understanding than simply reading either of them alone. It presents us with the possibility of overhearing their dialogue and of entering into dialogue with them.

Intersubjectivity does not mean that every reading is right, but it does suggest that we can probably learn something from any reading. And since it frankly admits to the subjectivity of interpretation it raises the further possibility of asking why certain interpretations appeal to certain people. What is the relation of an interpretation to a person's social location and political agenda? To what other interpreters does a given reader appeal for support? How broadly accepted is a given view? Choosing an interpretation is never simply a matter of following the majority, but when a reading becomes idiosyncratic and cuts itself off from other readings, the likelihood of it being a sound reading diminishes. And since the ultimate goal is dialogue, the question becomes not simply is this a sound reading, but rather: what can I learn from this reading to advance my own interpretation?

How consistent is the interpretation? This is the principle of inclusiveness, and it can be applied on several levels. The primary consideration is how well a given reading handles all the diverse elements of a text. Does it make sense of the actions, the characters, the settings, and all the other elements of a story? Every interpretation highlights some elements of a text and downplays others; what about the elements downplayed? Conversely, does the interpretation of individual elements add up to a convincing whole?

In addition to these elements of internal consistency, I would suggest another: for a reading to be a strong reading it has to fit with whatever is known about the actual audience and author of a work. Thus the very common reading of Revelation as calling for faithfulness in a time of persecution has been severely undermined by recent studies that find no evidence of Roman persecution of Christians in John's time and place.[12]

---

[12] See chapter 2 of this book.

Interpretations strive for comprehensiveness, and those interpretations that achieve a broad view while remaining true to the details of the text and the details of the context are the stronger readings. But reading is never done in a vacuum; they are not just academic exercises, so it is necessary to ask a further question.

What are the consequences of following this interpretation? Readings have consequences. Paulien, for example, describes the fatal consequence connected with David Koresh's reading of the Apocalypse as it played out in Waco, Texas. We could also point to readers today who believe so strongly that the world is going to end soon that they see no need to be concerned with ecology. There would be no need to preserve the earth for future generations, for there would be no future generations.[13] The consequences of such a reading are irresponsible behavior, I judge; and thus I judge the reading faulty even if it might be defensible as a valid reading on other grounds. Hence my third and most subjective criterion: one must choose between alternative valid readings on the basis of their ethical implications. This is a difficult concept, for it can be objected that I am demanding that all interpretations be moral. Is no literature immoral? If we are interpreting an immoral story, can the interpretation admit that immorality?

Of course there is immoral literature. There is literature that is racist, sexist, even genocidal. It is widely recognized, for example, that the poetry of T. S. Eliot is pervaded with anti-Semitic sentiments.[14] This does not mean that Eliot's poetry is no longer valuable, but it does mean that the responsible interpreter must account for this anti-Semitism. But the issue I want to reflect on is not how to deal with immoral literature but rather how to choose between interpretations. When two valid interpretations are available, one element in judging them is their moral consequences. Perhaps a particular case will be helpful.

The story in Revelation makes extensive use of violence, and in the end we find a very disturbing scene:

> Then I saw the beast and the kings of the earth with their armies gathered to make war against the rider on the horse and against his army. And the beast was captured, and with it the false prophet who had performed in its presence the signs by which he deceived those who had received the mark of the beast and those who worshiped its image. These two were thrown alive into the lake of fire that burns with sulfur. And the rest were killed by the sword of the rider on the horse, the sword that came from his mouth; and all the birds were gorged with their flesh. (19:19–21)

[13] See Jim Castelli, "The Environmental Gospel according to James Watt," *Chicago Tribune,* 25 October 1981, B2.

[14] See Anthony Julius, *T. S. Eliot, Anti-Semitism, and Literary Form* (Cambridge: Cambridge University Press, 1995).

What does this scene mean? And how does this criterion of ethical concern enter the discussion? First of all this criterion causes us to recognize the problem. Because interpreters have to be accountable for the implications of their interpretations, we become sensitive to moral issues. In this case, the execution of all members of the opposing army (seemingly *after* the battle is won) will now be viewed in moral terms. And while morality is a culturally conditioned judgment, here is an action condemned by international law. The responsible interpreter must account for the ethics of the text and, in this case, either condemn such action or suggest an interpretation that changes the moral equation.[15]

I choose the latter strategy, arguing for the importance of the fact that it is not a sword in the rider's hand (power) that slays the enemy but a sword in his mouth (persuasion, testimony).[16] Now I say that I choose this strategy, but I choose it because I think it is a correct interpretation. In terms of Armstrong's definition of a valid interpretation discussed above: it is inclusive (thus I aim to show that every seeming exercise of power in John's story turns out on close examination to contain some such reversal); it is intersubjective (numerous interpreters have adopted this view); and it is useful (it leads to new insights about the nature of John's story). And here I want to extend the concept of usefulness: it is also useful in the actual world within which we interpret these texts. Interpreting this symbol of the sword as the power to persuade rather than the power to coerce encourages our better human instincts. It is an interpretation that turns us away from the desire to annihilate our enemies toward the need to enter into dialogue with, and faithful testimony to, them. This is a more pragmatic concern, but important. One final pragmatic issue rounds out my approach.

What is my purpose in reading? Not only does what you find depend on what you are looking for, but the way you pursue the looking determines the sorts of things you can find. If you are looking for a needle in a haystack, a magnet is by far the preferred instrument. But if you are aiming to count the hayseeds, the magnet will be useless. Different methods applied to the same phenomenon give different answers. The great achievement of modern intellectual life is the development of discipline-based knowledge. Science tells us about the physical world, with testable and empirical methods. But biology can never tell us whether the family is a good institution or which form of family organization is the best. So-

---

[15] For further exploration of these issues, see Richard G. Bowman and Richard W. Swanson, "Samson and the Son of God or Dead Heroes and Dead Goats: Ethical Reading of Narrative Violence in Judges and Matthew," *Semeia* 77 (1997): 59–73.

[16] David L. Barr, *Tales of the End: A Narrative Commentary on the Book of Revelation* (Santa Rosa, Calif.: Polebridge Press, 1998), 137, 145–47. See also chapter 7, "Undercurrents and Paradoxes."

ciology and anthropology can address such questions. The method we choose to apply determines in part the kinds of answers we are likely to arrive at. Thus when Paulien begins with the modern world his method predisposes him to find the relevance of the Apocalypse; and when Friesen begins with history his method predisposes him to find the Apocalypse vital for the first century, but its relevance for today would have to be imagined. Whether you follow Paulien or Friesen depends in part on what you are looking for. When you know your goal, choosing the path to the goal is considerably easier.

It is no small thing, then, to choose a valid reading. It involves judgments of inclusiveness, intersubjectivity, and usefulness. Further, choosing between valid readings is a complex and ambiguous enterprise. My own strategy adopts and extends these three criteria. First, better readings are the ones that relate best to the multiple subjective readings of the text. Readings that are idiosyncratic, to the point of neglecting other readings, are probably wrong. However, the real point of intersubjectivity is not to pronounce one reading right or wrong, but to enter into dialogue with other readings. We must each build our own interpretation, but such building will succeed best when we interact with other readers. Second, a strong reading is an inclusive reading, accounting for the rich diversity of any literary text. In addition, the better reading is the one most in accordance with what is known about the author and audience addressed. Third, the better reading is the most useful one, with a baseline of usefulness being a clear moral compass. Fourth and finally, the better reading depends most of all on the goal pursued; some readings are better for some goals and weaker for other goals.

If I wanted to know how hot a certain room was, I would choose a thermometer as my instrument. If I wanted to know how dry the air was in the room, a humidistat is the right tool. If I wanted to know how bright it was, I would need a light meter. But suppose I wanted to know how well it would function as a classroom? Each of these measurements would provide useful information and, combined, would begin to suggest how comfortable the room might be. But I would also want to talk to other people who had used the room. They would not all agree, but their multiple subjectivities would be useful to me. Finally, of course, I would visit the room myself and make my own judgment.

It has not been our goal in this book to teach you how to read Revelation. Nor has it been a goal to convince you that our reading(s) is the correct one(s). Of course, each of us thinks he or she is reading Revelation correctly. Our goal has been to share these multiple readings (intersubjectivity) so that you can read Revelation for yourself, testing whether you can extend our readings to include the rest of Revelation's story (inclusiveness) and whether they allow you to open up further insights into this fascinating work (utility). We also hope that we have shown that different approaches result in novel insights and that we have encouraged you to take multiple readings with different methods (comprehensiveness).

The authors of these essays agree on many points; they also disagree on many points. But by choosing to publish our essays together we are making the claim that each of our insights can be refined in conversation with others. We believe that the meaning of a work of literature is not like the meaning of a mathematical problem. In math, there is usually one correct answer, everyone should get the same answer, and once the answer is known the problem is no longer interesting. Not so in literature. Not so with the Apocalypse of John.

The meaning of the Apocalypse is not something separable from the experience of reading it. It does not give you an answer (to history, to life, to religion) that, once known, makes the story moot (or mute for that matter). Meaning emerges from the experience of the story. Of course, what you experience will depend on how well prepared you are to reflect on the literary structures and devices, the historical contexts and conflicts, the social settings and institutions that provide the backdrop on which John paints his scenes—as well as the settings within which we read it today. It is our common conviction and hope that these essays will assist in that endeavor. If our book enables you to be a more discerning reader, it will have been worth the labor of its making.

Bibliography

The Ante-Nicene Fathers: Translations of the Writings of the Fathers Down to A.D. 325. Edited by A. Roberts and J. Donaldson. 1885. Reprint, Grand Rapids: Eerdmans, 1981. [Abbreviated as *ANF.*]

Armstrong, Paul B. *Conflicting Readings: Variety and Validity in Interpretation.* Chapel Hill and London: University of North Carolina Press, 1990.

Augustine. *The City of God.* New York: Modern Library, 2000.

Aune, Davie E. "The Apocalypse of John and the Problem of Genre." *Semeia* (Decatur, Ga.: Scholars Press) 36 (1986): 65–96. [Issue edited by Adela Yarbro Collins, with the theme "Early Christian Apocalypticism: Genre and Social Setting."]

———. *Prophecy in Early Christianity and the Ancient Mediterranean World.* Grand Rapids: Eerdmans, 1983.

———. "Revelation." Pp. 1300–19 in *HarperCollins Bible Commentary.* Edited by James L. Mays. San Francisco: Harper & Row, 1988.

———. *Revelation: Word Biblical Commentary.* 3 vols. Nashville: Thomas Nelson, 1997–98.

———. "The Social Matrix of the Apocalypse of John." *BR* 26 (1981): 16–32.

Balsdon, J. P. V. D. *Romans and Aliens.* Chapel Hill: University of North Carolina Press, 1979.

Barnes, Timothy D. *Constantine and Eusebius.* Cambridge: Harvard University Press, 1981.

Barr, David L. "The Apocalypse as a Symbolic Transformation of the World: A Literary Analysis." *Interpretation* 38 (1984): 39–50.

———. "The Apocalypse of John as Oral Enactment." *Interpretation* 40 (1986): 243–56.

———. *Tales of the End: A Narrative Commentary on the Book of Revelation.* The Storytellers Bible 1. Santa Rosa, Calif.: Polebridge Press, 1998.

———. "Towards an Ethical Reading of the Apocalypse: Reflections on John's Use of Power, Violence, and Misogyny." Pp. 358–73 in *Society of Biblical Literature Seminar Papers.* Atlanta: Scholars Press, 1997.

———. "Using Plot to Discern Structure in John's Apocalypse." *Proceedings of the Eastern Great Lakes and Midwest Biblical Societies* 15 (1995): 23–33.

Barzun, Jacques, and Henry F. Graff. *The Modern Researcher.* New York: Harcourt, Brace & World, 1957.

Bauckham, Richard J. *The Climax of Prophecy: Studies on the Book of Revelation.* Edinburgh: T. & T. Clark, 1993.

Bauer, Walter, F. W. Danker, W. F. Arndt, and F. W. Gingrich, eds. *A Greek-English Lexicon of the New Testament and Other Early Christian Literature*. 3d ed. Chicago: University of Chicago Press, 1999. [Abbreviated as BDAG.]

Beasley-Murray, G. R. *The Book of Revelation*. Rev. ed. London: Oliphants, 1978.

Beckwith, I. T. *The Apocalypse of John: Studies in Introduction*. New York: Macmillan, 1919.

Bell, Albert A. "Date of John's Apocalypse: The Evidence of Some Roman Historians Reconsidered." *NTS* 25 (October 1978): 93–102.

Betz, Hans Dieter. *The Greek Magical Papyri in Translation, Including the Demotic Spells*. Vol. 1. Chicago: University of Chicago Press, 1986.

Boatwright, Mary T. "Plancia Magna of Perge: Women's Roles and Status in Roman Asia Minor." Pp. 249–72 in *Women's History and Ancient History*. Chapel Hill: University of North Carolina Press, 1991.

Boer, Roland. "Christological Slippage and Ideological Structures in Schwarzenegger's Terminator." *Semeia* 69/70 (1995): 165–93.

Bohm, David. *Wholeness and the Implicate Order*. London: Ark, 1980.

Boring, M. Eugene. *Revelation*. Interpretation: A Bible Commentary for Teaching and Preaching. Atlanta: John Knox, 1989.

Bousset, Wilhelm. *Die Offenbarung Johannis*. 6th ed. Göttingen: Vandenhoeck & Ruprecht, 1906.

Bovon, François. *Révélations et écritures Nouveau Testament et littérature apocryphe Chrétienne: Recueil d'articles*. Monde de la Bible. Geneva: Labor et Fides, 1993.

Bowman, Richard G., and Richard W. Swanson. "Samson and the Son of God or Dead Heroes and Dead Goats: Ethical Reading of Narrative Violence in Judges and Matthew." *Semeia* 77 (1997): 59–73.

Bremen, Riet van. "Women and Wealth." Pp. 223–42 in *Images of Women in Antiquity*. Detroit: Wayne State University Press, 1983.

Broughton, T. R. S. *Roman Asia*. Edited by Tenney Frank. 6 vols. An Economic Survey of Ancient Rome 4. Baltimore: Johns Hopkins University Press, 1938. Reprint, New York: Octagon Books, 1975.

Caird, G. B. *A Commentary on the Revelation of St. John the Divine*. Harper's New Testament Commentaries. New York: Harper & Row, 1966.

Castelli, Jim. "The Environmental Gospel according to James Watt." *Chicago Tribune*, 25 October 1981, B2.

Cerfaux, Lucien. *L'Apocalypse de Saint Jean lue aux Chretiens*. Lectio divina. Paris: Cerf, 1955.

Charles, R. H. *A Critical and Exegetical Commentary on the Revelation of St. John*. Edinburgh: T. & T. Clark, 1920.

Charlesworth, James H., and Carol A. Newsom, ed and trans. *The Dead Sea Scrolls: Volume 4B*. Tübingen: Mohr Siebeck, 1999.

Chatman, Seymour. *Story and Discourse: Narrative Structure in Fiction and Film*. Ithaca, N.Y.: Cornell University Press, 1978.

Collins, Adela Yarbro. *The Combat Myth in the Book of Revelation*. Chico, Calif.: Scholars Press, 1976.

———. *Crisis and Catharsis: The Power of the Apocalypse*. Philadelphia: Westminster Press, 1984.

———. "Feminine Symbolism in the Book of Revelation." *Biblical Interpretation* 1 (1993): 20–33.

———. "'What the Spirit Says to the Churches': Preaching the Apocalypse." *Quarterly Review* 4 (1984): 69–84.

Collins, John J., ed. *Semeia* (Chico, Calif.: Scholars Press) 14 (1979). [The issue theme was "Apocalypse: The Morphology of a Genre."]

Colwell, Ernest Cadman. "Popular Reactions against Christianity in the Roman Empire." Pp. 53–71 in *Environmental Factors in Christian History*. Edited by John Thomas McNeill et al. Chicago: University of Chicago Press, 1939.

Crook, J. A. *Law and Life of Rome, 90 B.C.–A.D. 212*. Aspects of Greek and Roman Life. Ithaca, N.Y.: Cornell University Press, 1985.

Culianu, Ioan P. *Out of This World: Otherworldly Journeys from Gilgamesh to Albert Einstein*. Boston: Shambhala, 1991.

Day, John. *God's Conflict with the Dragon and the Sea in the Old Testament*. Cambridge: Cambridge University Press, 1985.

Deininger, Jürgen. *Die Provinziallandtage der römischen Kaiserzeit von Augustus bis zum Ende des dritten Jahrhunderts N. Chr.* Vestigia: Beiträge zur alten Geschichte. Munich: C. H. Beck, 1965.

Douglas, Mary. *Natural Symbols: Explorations in Cosmology*. New York: Penguin, 1973.

Duff, Paul Brooks. *Who Rides the Beast? Prophetic Rivalry and the Rhetoric of Crisis in the Churches of the Apocalypse*. Oxford: Oxford University Press, 2001.

Erdoes, Richard. *A.D. 1000: Living on the Brink of Apocalypse*. San Francisco: Harper & Row, 1988.

Farmer, Ron. *Beyond the Impasse: The Promise of a Process Hermeneutic*. Macon, Ga.: Mercer University Press, 1997.

———. *The Revelation to John: A Commentary for Today*. St. Louis: Chalice Press, forthcoming.

Farrer, Austin. *A Rebirth of Images: The Making of St. John's Apocalypse*. 1949. Reprint, Gloucester, Mass.: Peter Smith, 1970.

———. *The Revelation of St. John the Divine*. Oxford: Oxford University Press, 1964.

Feyerabend, Paul. *Conquest of Abundance*. Chicago: University of Chicago Press, 1999.

Fish, Stanley E. *Is There a Text in This Class?* Cambridge: Harvard University Press, 1980.

Forbes, Christopher. *Prophecy and Inspired Speech in Early Christianity and Its Hellenistic Environment*. Peabody, Mass.: Hendrickson, 1997.

Friesen, Steven J. "Cult of the Roman Emperors in Ephesos: Temple Wardens, City Titles, and the Interpretation of the Revelation of John." Pp. 229–50 in *Ephesos: Metropolis of Asia*. Edited by Helmut Koester. Valley Forge, Pa.: Trinity Press International, 1995.

———. *Twice Neokoros: Ephesus, Asia, and the Cult of the Flavian Emperors*. Religions of the Greco-Roman World. Leiden: E. J. Brill, 1993.

Frilingos, Chris. "Making Males in an Unmade World: A Manly Paradise in the Book of Revelation." Paper presented at the annual meeting of the Society of Biblical Literature, Nashville, 2000. [To be published in revised form as "Sexing the Lamb," in *Semeia*.]

Geertz, Clifford. *Negara the Theatre State in Nineteenth-Century Bali*. Princeton, N.J.: Princeton University Press, 1980.

Glasson, T. F. *Revelation of John*. Cambridge: Cambridge University Press, 1987.

Goodman, Felicitas D. *Where the Spirits Ride the Wind: Trance Journeys and Other Ecstatic Experiences*. Bloomington: Indiana University Press, 1990.

Grant, Frederick C. *Hellenistic Religions: The Age of Syncretism*. Indianapolis: Liberal Arts Press, Bobbs-Merrill, 1953.

Grant, Robert M. *Eusebius as Church Historian*. Oxford: Clarendon Press, 1980.

———. *Greek Apologists of the Second Century*. Philadelphia: Westminster, 1988.

———. "The Social Setting of Second-Century Christianity." Pp. 16–29 in *Jewish and Christian Self-Definition*. Edited by E. P. Sanders. Philadelphia: Fortress Press, 1980.

Gruenwald, Ithamar. *Apocalyptic and Merkavah Mysticism*. Leiden: E. J. Brill, 1980.

Hemer, Colin. *Letters to the Seven Churches of Asia in Their Local Setting*. Edited by David Hill. Journal for the Study of the New Testament Supplemental Series 11. Sheffield, England: JSOT/Sheffield Academic Press, 1986.

Hillman, James, and Michael Ventura. *We've Had a Hundred Years of Psychotherapy and the World's Getting Worse*. New York: Harper Collins, 1992.

Himmelfarb, Martha. "The Practice of Ascent in the Ancient Mediterranean World." Pp. 123–37 in *Death, Ecstasy, and Other Worldly Journeys*. Edited by John J. Collins and Michael Fishbane. Albany: State University of New York Press, 1995.

Hirsch, E. D. *Validity in Interpretation*. New Haven: Yale University Press, 1967.

Holmberg, Bengt. *Sociology and the New Testament: An Appraisal*. Minneapolis: Fortress Press, 1990.

Humphrey, Edith M. *The Ladies and the Cities: Transformation and Apocalyptic Identity in Joseph and Aseneth, 4 Ezra, The Apocalypse, and the Shepherd of Hermas*. Sheffield, England: Sheffield Academic Press, 1995.

Die Inschriften von Ephesos. Edited by Helmut Engelmann et al. Bonn: Habelt, 1979–84. [Abbreviated as *IvE*.]

Inscriptiones graecae ad res romanas pertinentes. Edited by René Cagnat et al. 4 vols. Paris: Ernest Leroux, 1901–27. [Abbreviated as *IGR*.]

James, William. *The Varieties of Religious Experience*. New York: New American Library, 1902.

Julius, Anthony. *T. S. Eliot, Anti-Semitism, and Literary Form*. Cambridge: Cambridge University Press, 1995.

Kearsley, Rosalinde. "Some Asiarchs from Ephesos." Pp. 53–54 in *New Documents Illustrating Early Christianity*. Edited by G. H. R. Horsley. North Ryde, Australia: Ancient History Documentary Research Centre, Macquarie University Press, 1987.

Kiddle, Martin. *The Revelation of St. John*. London: Hodder & Stoughton, 1940.

Kraft, Heinrich. *Die Offenbarung des Johannes*. HNT 16a. Tübingen: Mohr [Siebeck], 1974.

Kraybill, J. Nelson. *Imperial Cult and Commerce in John's Apocalypse*. Sheffield, England: Sheffield Academic Press, 1996.

Krodel, Gerhard A. *Revelation*. Augsburg Commentary on the New Testament. Minneapolis: Augsburg, 1989.

Lakoff, George. "Metaphor, Morality, and Politics: Or, Why Conservatives Have Left Liberals in the Dust." Pp. 139–56 in *The Workings of Language: From Prescriptions to Perspectives*. Edited by Rebecca S. Wheeler. Westport, Conn.: Praeger, 1999.

Lambrecht, Jan. "A Structuration of Revelation 4:1–22:5." Pp. 77–104 in *L'Apocalypse*

Johannique et l'apocalyptique dans le Nouveau Testament. Louvain: Louvain University Press, 1980.

Lawrence, D. H. *Apocalypse.* 1931. Reprint, New York: Viking Press, 1982.

LeHaye, Tim. *Revelation Illustrated and Made Plain.* Grand Rapids: Zondervan, 1976.

Lenski, R. C. H. *The Interpretation of St. John's Revelation.* Minneapolis: Augsburg, 1963.

Lewis, C. S. *The Screwtape Letters.* New York: Macmillan, 1943.

Lindsey, Hal, with C. C. Carlson. *The Late Great Planet Earth.* New York: Bantam Books, 1970.

Lohmeyer, E. *Die Offenbarung des Johannes.* 2d ed. Tübingen: J. C. B. Mohr, 1953.

Lohse, Eduard. *Die Offenbarung des Johannes Übersetzt und Erklärt.* 8th ed. Neue Testament Deutsch. Göttingen: Vandenhoeck & Ruprecht, 1960.

Louw, Johannes P., and Eugene A. Nida, eds. *Greek-English Lexicon of the New Testament Based on Semantic Domains.* 2d ed. New York: United Bible Societies, 1989.

Lund, Nils Wilhelm. *Studies in the Book of Revelation.* [Chicago]: Covenant Press, 1955.

Malherbe, Abraham J. *Social Aspects of Early Christianity.* 2d ed. Philadelphia: Fortress Press, 1983.

Mayaram, Shail. "Recent Anthropological Works on Spirit Possession." *Religious Studies Review* 27 (July 2001): 213–22.

Menninger, Karl. *Number Words and Number Symbols: A Cultural History of Numbers.* Edited by Paul Broneer. Cambridge, Mass.: MIT Press, 1969.

Michaels, J. Ramsey. *Interpreting the Book of Revelation.* Grand Rapids: Baker Book House, 1992.

———. *Revelation.* IVP New Testament Commentary Series. Downers Grove, Ill.: InterVarsity Press, 1997.

Moore, Stephen D. "Revolting Revelations." Pp. 183–200 in *The Personal Voice in Biblical Interpretation.* Edited by Ingrid Rosa. London: Routledge, 1999.

Mounce, Robert H. *The Book of Revelation.* New International Commentary. Grand Rapids: Eerdmans, 1977.

Moyise, Steve. "Does the Lion Lie Down with the Lamb?" Pp. 181–94 in *Studies in the Book of Revelation.* Edited by Steve Moyise. Edinburgh: T. & T. Clark, 2001.

Musurillo, Herbert. *Acts of the Christian Martyrs.* Oxford: Clarendon Press, 1972.

The Nag Hammadi Library in English. Edited by James M. Robinson. San Francisco: Harper & Row, 1977. [Abbreviated as *NHL.*]

Newsom, Carol. *Songs of the Sabbath Sacrifice: A Critical Edition.* Atlanta: Scholars Press, 1985.

Nicholas, Barry. *An Introduction to Roman Law.* Oxford: Clarendon Press, 1962.

The Old Testament Pseudepigrapha. Edited by James H. Charlesworth. 2 vols. Garden City, N.Y.: Doubleday, 1983–85. [Abbreviated as *OTP.*]

O'Leary, Stephen D. *Arguing the Apocalypse: A Theory of Millennial Rhetoric.* Oxford: Oxford University Press, 1994.

Olupona, Jacob Obafemi Kehinde. *Kingship, Religion, and Rituals in a Nigerian Community: A Phenomenological Study of Ondo Yoruba Festivals.* Acta Universitatis Stockholmiensis. Stockholm: Almqvist & Wiksell International, 1991.

Osiek, Carolyn. "House Churches and the Demographics of Diversity." *Religious Studies Review* 27 (July 2001): 228–31.

———. *Shepherd of Hermas: A Commentary*. Minneapolis: Fortress Press, 1999.

Papyri graecae magicae: Die griechischen Zauberpapyri, unter Mitarbeit von A. Abt [et al.]. Edited by Karl Lebrecht Preisendanz. Leipzig: B. G. Teubner, 1928. [Abbreviated as *PGM*.]

Pippin, Tina. *Apocalyptic Bodies: The Biblical End of the World in Text and Image*. London: Routledge, 1999.

———. *Death and Desire: The Rhetoric of Gender in the Apocalypse of John*. Louisville: Westminster John Knox, 1992.

Plato. *Complete Works*. Edited and compiled by John M. Cooper. Indianapolis: Hackett, 1997.

Pliny. *The Letters of Pliny the Younger*. Hammondsworth, England: Penguin, 1969.

Price, S. R. F. *Rituals and Power: The Roman Imperial Cult in Asia Minor*. Cambridge: Cambridge University Press, 1984.

Prigent, Pierre. *L'Apocalypse de Saint Jean*. Commentaire du Nouveau Testament. Lausanne, Switzerland: Delachaux & Niestlé, 1981.

Ramsay, William M. *The Letters to the Seven Churches of Asia and Their Place in the Plan of the Apocalypse*. New York: Hodder and Stoughton, 1906.

Reddish, Mitchell. *Revelation*. Macon, Ga.: Smyth & Helwyns, 2001.

Robinson, John A. T. *Redating the New Testament*. Philadelphia: Westminster, 1976.

Roloff, Jürgen. *The Revelation of John: A Continental Commentary*. Translated by John E. Alsup. Minneapolis: Fortress Press, 1993.

Rowland, Christopher. "The Visions of God in Apocalyptic Literature." *Journal for the Study of Judaism* 10, no. 2 (1979): 137–54.

Saffrey, H. D. "Relire L'Apocalypse a Patmos." *Revue biblique* 82 (1975): 385–417.

Schmidt, Roger. *Exploring Religion*. Belmont, Calif.: Wadsworth, 1988.

Scholem, Gershom G. *Major Trends in Jewish Mysticism*. 1961. Reprint, New York: Schocken Books, 1995.

Schüssler Fiorenza, Elisabeth. "Apokalypsis and Propheteia: The Book of Revelation in the Context of Early Christian Prophecy." Pp. 133–56 in *The Book of Revelation: Justice and Judgment*. Philadelphia: Fortress Press, 1985.

———. *The Book of Revelation: Justice and Judgment*. 2d ed. Minneapolis: Fortress Press, 1998.

———. *Invitation to the Book of Revelation*. Garden City, N.Y.: Image Doubleday, 1981.

———. *Revelation: Vision of a Just World*. Minneapolis: Fortress Press, 1991.

Scott, Bernard Brandon. *Hollywood Dreams and Biblical Stories*. Minneapolis: Fortress Press, 1994.

Smallwood, E. Mary. *The Jews under Roman Rule, from Pompey to Diocletian: A Study in Political Relations*. Leiden: E. J. Brill, 1976.

Smith, Frederick M. "The Current State of Possession Studies as a Cross-Disciplinary Project." *Religious Studies Review* 27, no. 3 (2001): 203–12.

Sweet, J. P. M. *Revelation*. Philadelphia: Westminster Press, 1979. Reprint, Trinity Press International, 1990.

Swete, Henry B. *The Apocalypse of St. John*. 3d ed. London: Macmillan, 1909.

Taussig, Michael. "Transgression." Pp. 349–64 in *Critical Terms for Religious Studies*. Edited by Mark C. Taylor. Chicago: University of Chicago Press, 1998.

Theissen, Gerd. *Sociology of Early Palestinian Christianity*. Translated by John Bowden. Philadelphia: Fortress Press, 1978.

Thomas, Robert L. *Revelation 1–7: An Exegetical Commentary.* Chicago: Moody Press, 1992.

Thompson, Leonard L. *The Book of Revelation: Apocalypse and Empire.* Oxford: Oxford University Press, 1990.

———. *Revelation.* Nashville: Abingdon Press, 1998.

———. "A Sociological Analysis of Tribulation in the Apocalypse of John." *Semeia* 36 (1986): 147–74.

Torrance, Robert M. *The Spiritual Quest: Transcendence in Myth, Religion, and Science.* Berkeley: University of California Press, 1994.

Valeri, Valerio. *Kingship and Sacrifice Ritual and Society in Ancient Hawaii.* Chicago: University of Chicago Press, 1985.

Verner, David C. *The Household of God: The Social World of the Pastoral Epistles.* Chico, Calif.: Scholars Press, 1983.

Wainwright, Arthur. *Mysterious Apocalypse: Interpreting the Book of Revelation.* Nashville: Abingdon Press, 1993.

Walvoord, John F. *Armageddon, Oil, and the Middle East Crisis.* Revised ed. 1974. Reprint, Grand Rapids: Zondervan, 1990.

———. *The Revelation of Jesus Christ: A Commentary.* James T. Jeremiah Collection. Chicago: Moody Press, 1966.

Watson, Alan, ed. and trans. *The Digest of Justinian.* Philadelphia: University of Pennsylvania Press, 1998.

Weiss, Johannes. *Die Offenbarung des Johannes: Ein Beitrag zur Literatur- und Religionsgeschichte.* Göttingen: Vandenhoeck & Ruprecht, 1904.

Whitehead, Alfred North. *Adventures of Ideas.* New York: Free Press, 1967.

———. *Symbolism: Its Meaning and Effect.* 1927. Reprint, New York: Fordham University Press, 1985.

Whitehead, Alfred North, David Ray Griffin, and Donald W. Sherburne. *Process and Reality: An Essay in Cosmology.* Edited by David Ray Griffin and Donald W. Sherburne. Corrected ed. Gifford Lectures. 1929. Reprint, New York: Free Press, 1978.

Wilken, Robert L. *The Christians as the Romans Saw Them.* New Haven: Yale University Press, 1984.

Wilson, J. Christian. "The Problem of the Domitianic Date of Revelation." *NTS* 39 (1993): 586–605.

Zamora, Lois Parkinson. *Writing the Apocalypse: Historical Vision in Contemporary U.S. and Latin American Fiction.* Cambridge and New York: Cambridge University Press, 1989.

Zorn, Carl M. *Die Offenbarung St Johannis.* Zwickau, Germany: Johannes Hermann, 1910.

Contributors

David L. Barr
Professor of Religion
Wright State University

Paul Duff
Associate Professor of Religion
The George Washington University

Ronald L. Farmer
Dean of the Wallace All Faiths Chapel and
    Associate Professor of Religious Studies
Chapman University

Steve Friesen
Associate Professor and Chair
Department of Religious Studies
University of Missouri

Edith M. Humphrey
Associate Professor of New Testament
Pittsburgh Theological Seminary

Jon Paulien
Professor of New Testament Interpretation
Andrews University

Jean-Pierre Ruiz
Associate Professor
Department of Theology and Religious Studies
St. John's University

Leonard L. Thompson
Emeritus Professor
Lawrence University

Index of Ancient Sources

Hebrew Bible and Apocrypha

Genesis
1	166
3:16–17	92
15:17	144

Exodus
19:4	87

Leviticus
17:7	44

Numbers
24	84
25:1–2	44
31:16	44

Deuteronomy
13:1–3	133
31:16	44
32:1ff.	87
32:11	87
34	92

1 Samuel
10:10	144

1 Kings
16	84
18:28	145

2 Kings
9:22	44

Psalms
2:8	73
73:16–17	91

Isaiah
6	16
11	115
47:1–15	84

Jeremiah
2	44
28:9	133

Ezekiel
1–3	16
1:28	92
28:2	84
37:1	138

Daniel
7	130, 148
7:9	94
9:3	145

Amos
7:1–9	102

Zechariah
3:8–4:10	115
4:10	140

1 Maccabees
41:42	130

Tobit
12:15	140

Second Testament

Matthew
7:15–16	147
7:15–20	43
10:41	42
12:32	139
24:9	32
24:11	147
24:24	147
26:6	33

Mark
6:6–13	42
9:33	33

Luke
10:1–12	42
24:11, 24	43

John
16:21	32

Acts
5:9	139
6:5	44
7:38	33
11:19	32
11:27	34
13:1	34
16:14, 40	41
21:9–12	34

Romans
13:1	131
14:13–23	112

1 Corinthians
2:14	139
8–10	67, 79, 112
8:8	79
12–14	138
12:3	147
12:4–6	139
12:28	43
12:28–31	42
14:1	138
14:14–15	140
14:15	143

Ephesians
14:26–32	34
14:29	142
14:32	140

Ephesians
2:20	42
3:5	42
4:11	42
5:18–19	143

Philippians
1:27	140
2:15	46

Colossians
3:11	39
3:16	143
4:15	40

1 Thessalonians
5:19–21	142
5:19–22	147
5:23	140

Philemon
2	40

Hebrews
4:12	140
12:9	140
13:14	45

James
1:27	32

1 Peter
1:1	39
1:11	139
3:15–16	46

2 Peter
2:1	43

1 John
4:1	43

Revelation

1	14	2:23	76
1:1	147	3:1	140
1:1–2	15	3:2	132
1:1–6	121	3:4b	83
1–3	115	3:6, 13, 22	139
1:2	33	3:9	43
1:3	42, 66, 106, 138	3:10	43, 106
1:4	15, 26, 115, 140	3:10–11, 16	46
1:5	112, 116	3:11–12	85
1:6	112	3:12	83
1:8	112	3:18	44
1:9	105, 106, 122	3:21	83
1:9–10	15, 32, 141	4–5	44, 45, 115
1:9–11	26	4:1–22:5	115, 116
1:10	135	4:1	15, 82, 85, 114,
1:10–11	15		138, 139, 166
1:12–20	83	4:1–2	15
1:12, 20	115	4:2	148
1:13ff.	22	4:2ff.	22
1:16	115	4:5	140
1:20	22	4:6	116
2	73	5	91
2–3	40, 65, 83, 88,	5:1–14	116
	106, 118, 139, 148	5:2	114
2:2	42	5:3–4	114
2:2–3	106	5:4	145
2:4	43	5:5	114
2:5, 16, 21–23	46	5:5–6	100
2:6	66	5:6	114, 115, 140, 145
2:7, 11, 17, 29	139	5:11	139
2:7b	83	6	112, 144
2:9–10	32	6–20	112, 115
2:10	66	6:9	33
2:12, 16	115	6:9–11	28, 117
2:12–17	67	6:9ff.	21
2:12–29	146	6:10	100, 107
2:14	66	6:11	100, 102, 106
2:14–15	44	6:12	20
2:14, 20	44	6:16–17	111
2:15	66	7:1	136
2:16	102	7:1ff.	20
2:17b	83	7:1–17	22
2:18–29	66, 67, 69, 69, 71, 73, 75	7:2–3	102
2:19	106	7:5ff.	22
2:20	66, 74, 76, 78, 84, 147	7:9–17	28, 148
2:20–23	72	7:14	45
2:21	68	8–9	113
2:22	32, 73, 76	8:3ff.	21

Revelation (cont'd)

8:3–5	116	13:1	89
8:5	20	13:1–2	15
8:9	140	13:1–4	22, 43
9:2	139	13:1–10	61
9:4	102	13:1–18	159
9:21	98	13:3b–4	131
10	141	13:5	144
10–14	88	13:5–7	131
10:11	42, 85, 138	13:7	131
11:2	87	13:8	19
11:2, 3, 11	87	13:9–10	132
11:3ff.	22	13:10	99, 106, 107
11:3–6	42	13:11	115, 132
11:7	20, 102, 159	13:11–18	49, 164
11:11	140	13:12	132, 139
11:12	81, 146	13:12–15	62
11:13	20	13:13–15	132
11:15	18, 85, 105, 112	13:15	102, 103, 133, 140
11:15–19	148	13:16–17	133
11:16–19	85	13:17	28, 43, 146
11:19	20, 21, 85	13:18	15, 30, 126, 140
12	49, 69, 70, 72, 73, 74,	14	19
	75, 83, 89, 91, 95, 101	14:4	74
12:1ff.	22	14:8	88
12:1–2	15	14:9–11	103
12:1–6	85	14:12	106
12:1–17	159	14:13	28, 139
12:3	89	14:14–19	88
12:4	78	14:15	103
12:4, 13–14	74	14:19–20	113
12:6	87	14:20	98, 103
12:7ff.	22	15–16	88
12:7–8	101	15:1	148
12:7–9	69	15:2	107
12:7–12	105, 117, 148	15:3	19, 112
12:9	139	15:5	21
12:10–12	86, 88, 89	16	113
12:10–13	69	16:2	102
12:11	19, 101, 117, 140	16:3	140
12:12	91	16:6	101
12:13–17	87	16:9, 11	98
12:14	87	16:13–14	139
12:14–16	69	16:16	21
12:15	95	16:18	20
12:17	87, 164	17	69, 70, 72, 73,
12:18	130		75, 91, 104, 148
13	56, 121, 126,	17–18	89, 113, 121, 122
	130, 146, 154, 166	17:1–2	15

Revelation (cont'd)

17:1–5	76	19:16	112
17:1–18	159	19:17–18, 21	113
17:2–6	76	19:19	21
17:3	89, 90, 92, 138	19:19–21	103, 169
17:3ff.	22	19:20	113, 132, 147
17:4–6	70, 78	19:21	19, 98
17:5	90	20–21	121, 122
17:6	78	20:4	33, 94
17:7–14	70	20:4, 6	117
17:8, 11	27	20:8ff.	21
17:9	28, 140	20:10	103
17:9–10	148	20:10, 14–15	113
17:9–11	28	20:11	94
17:11	27	20:14	98
17:14	19, 100, 112	20:15	103
17:15–17	70	21–22	83
17:16	20, 74, 96, 102	21:1	116
17:17	104	21:1–5	92
17:18	70, 104, 105	21:1–22:5	44, 115
18	89, 91	21:1–22:6	69
18–19	104	21:4	94
18:2	139	21:8	113
18:2ff.	21	21:10	92, 138
18:2, 9, 16, 19	89	21:14	14, 19
18:4	41, 90, 91	21:22–23	19
18:7	89	21:23–27	116
18:10	90	22:1–3	94, 116
18:10ff.	91	22:2	78
18:13	140	22:3	101
18:14	94, 140	22:6	133, 138, 140
18:20	42, 90, 91	22:6–21	115, 116
18:21ff.	21	22:7	20
18:23	75, 94	22:7, 12, 20	81
18:24	29, 91, 92	22:8	15, 21
19–20	92	22:9	42, 94
19–21	22	22:9–20	139
19:1–8	92	22:12–14	45
19:1–10	133	22:16	139
19:3	92	22:18	66
19:6	92, 134	22:19	66, 138
19:7	101	22:21	15
19:8	92		
19:10	21, 94		
19:12	94		
19:12–16	20		
19:14–15	44		
19:15	98, 112, 113, 115		

Other Ancient Sources

1 Enoch

20	140
24.1–4	148
60.8	146

2 Baruch
6.2–4 145
29.40 146

2 Enoch
1.2 145

2 Esdras
6.49–52 146
12 148

Aelius Aristides
Orations
17–53 144
26 46

Apocalypse of Abraham
9–10 145
17–18 144

Ascension of Isaiah
8.16–18 144

Augustine
City of God
20 13

Barnabas
15 142

Cassius Dio
67.14.2 30

Clement of Alexandria
Salvation of the Rich
42 32

Dead Sea Scrolls
1QS 1.4 43
4Q4 3.2.15 144

Didache
11–12 42
11.3–6 43
11.7 142
11.7–12 43
11.8.2 147
13.1–4 43
14 27, 142

Epistle to Diognetus
5 41

Eusebius
Ecclesiastical History
2.16–17 143
2.25.5 34
3.1 42
3.1–2 34
3.17–18 30
3.18 30
3.18.1 42
3.19–20 32
3.20.7 32
3.23 32
3.39.11–13 1
4.18 27
4.26 31
4.26.2 12
4.26.9 31
7.24.7 42
Preparation for the Gospel
8.10.4 138

Gospel of Peter
12.50 26

Hermas
Mandate
11 147
11.9 142
11.14 142
Similitude
1.1 40

Ignatius
Magnesians
9 142
Philadelphians
7.1–2 142
Romans
4.1–2 41

IGR
4.100 59
4.257 59
4.353 57
4.464 56
4.1156a 55

IGR (cont'd)
4.1238	55
4.1238–39	55
4.1241	55, 56
4.1242	56
4.1323	54
4.1325	54

Irenaeus
Against Heresies
1.26.3	44
4.20.11	42

IvE
2.232	56
2.233	57
2.234	57
2.235	56
2.237	57
2.238	56
2.239	57
2.240	57
2.241	57
2.429	53
3.728	54
4.1016	53
4.1017	53
5.1492	56
6.2048	57

Josephus
Antiquities of the Jews
4.137	44

Jubilees
10.6	140

Justin Martyr
1 Apology
31	27
Dialogue with Trypho
1	27
81	27, 42
81.15	12

Lucian
Peregrinus
13	147

Odes of Solomon
6.1	143
14.7	143

PGM
4.625–630	140

Philo
On the Contemplative Life
84	143

Plato
Ion
534.B	141
Timaeus
71.E	141

Pliny
Epistle
1	31
1.6	30
6.31	55
10.96	46
10.96.1	36
97.10	36

Pliny the Elder
Natural History
4.70	33

Plutarch
De Pythiae Oraculis
4.70	34
Moralia
397.B	145
404.E	147
Sibylline Oracles
3.63–70	27
4.119–20, 130–39	27
12.125–132	30

Suetonius
Nero
16	34
16.2	46
57	27

Tacitus

Agricola

45   31

Annals

4.30   33

15.44   34, 35, 46

History

2.8   35

2.8–9   27

Tertullian

Apology

2   41

2.8   37

5   31

On the Flesh of Christ

20   143

Prescription against Heretics

36   34

Index of Modern Authors

Altenbaumer, James E., 22
Alter, Robert, 21
Ansen, David, 151
Apolinaris, Yamina, 135
Aquino, María Pilar, 120
Armstrong, Paul, 164, 165, 170
Aune, David E., 11, 16, 27, 34, 60, 68,
    131, 132, 142, 145, 147, 148,
    149

Balsdon, P. V. D., 33
Barnes, Timothy D., 29
Barr, David L., 11, 17, 18, 19, 61, 64, 78,
    97, 101, 115, 170
Barzun, Jacques, 160
Bauckham, Richard J., 166
Beasley-Murray, G. R., 61, 62
Beckwith, Isbon T., 59
Bell, Albert A., Jr., 35
Betz, Hans Dieter, 140
Bhabha, Homi K., 123, 127
Boatwright, Mary Taliaferro, 58
Boesak, Allan A., 122
Bohm, David, 137
Boring, M. Eugene, 12, 61
Bousset, Wilhelm, 59
Bovon, François, 60
Bremen, Riet van, 58
Broughton, T. R. S., 38, 39
Browne, Malcolm W., 153

Caird, G. B., 60, 166
Cambier, Jules, 61
Cardenal, Ernesto, 120
Castelli, Jim, 169
Cerfaux, Lucien, 61
Charles, R. H., 42, 59
Charlesworth, James H., 144

Chatman, Seymour, 13, 106
Collins, Adela Yarbro, 11, 16, 22, 62,
    64, 93, 107, 111, 126, 142
Collins, John J., 15, 81, 130, 144
Colwell, Ernest, 46
Cone, James, 120
Corliss, Richard, 151, 152
Court, John M., 22
Crook, John A., 33
Culianu, Ioan P., 137

Davis, Douglas, 156
Day, John, 22, 116
Deininger, Jürgen, 51
deSilva, David, 60, 64
Douglas, Mary, 77
D'Souza, Dinesh, 124
Duff, Paul B., 44, 78
Dussel, Enrique, 19, 122

Easterman, Daniel, 153
Eck, Diana L., 135
Engineer, Ali Ashgar, 120
Erdoes, Richard, 160

Fabella, Virginia, 120, 123
Farmer, Ronald L., 110, 111
Farrer, Austin, 11, 61, 167
Feyerabend, Paul, 25
Fish, Stanley, 163
Fishbane, Michael, 144
Focillon, Henri, 160
Forbes, Christopher, 142
Foster, E. M., 12
Frank, Pat, 154
Friesen, Steven J., 22, 52, 53, 55, 127,
    128, 129, 131, 167
Frilingos, Chris, 103

Geertz, Clifford, 50
Genette, Gerard, 20
Georgi, Dieter, 133
Goodman, Felicitas D., 137
Gorgulho, Gilberto da Silva, 121
Gottwald, Norman K., 120
Graaf, Henry F., 160
Grant, Frederick C., 40
Grant, Robert M., 29, 37, 41
Gruenwald, Ithamar, 16, 144, 145
Gutiérrez, Gustavo, 120

Hanson, Paul D., 22
Harris, Michael A., 107
Himmelfarb, Martha, 144, 145
Hirsch, E. D., 163
Hirschorn, Michael, 151
Hollenhorst, S., 152
Holmberg, Bengt, 42
Humphrey, Edith M., 11, 82, 83
Huntington, Samuel P., 135

Iser, Wolfgang, 13

James, William, 149
Joy, Bill, 155, 156, 157
Julius, Anthony, 169

Kearsley, Rosalinde, 53, 55
Kiddle, Martin, 95
Klawans, Stuart, 151, 152
Koester, Helmut, 39, 55, 126, 128
Kraft, Heinrich, 61
Kraybill, J. Nelson, 39, 40, 133
Krodel, Gerhard, 61
Kurzweil, Ray, 157

Ladd, George Eldon, 49
LaHaye, Tim, 49, 154
Lakoff, George, 23
Lambrecht, Jan, 12
Lanier, Jaron, 157
Lawrence, D. H., 109
Leitch, Thomas M., 18
Lemonick, Michael D., 152
Lenski, R. C. H., 50
Lévi-Strauss, Claude, 16
Lewis, C. S., 154
Lindsey, Hal, 14, 49

Lohmeyer, Ernst, 49
Lohse, Eduard, 59
Lorde, Audre, 124
Louw, Johannes P., 105
Ludlum, Robert, 153
Lund, Nils Wilhelm, 12

MacArthur, Douglas, 153
Malherbe, Abraham J., 40
Mangual-Rodríguez, Sandra, 135
Mayaram, Shail, 137, 144
Menninger, Karl, 165
Mesters, Carlos, 120
Michaels, J. Ramsey, 11, 12
Moore, Stephen D., 99, 157
Moravec, Dan, 157
Mosala, Itumeleng, 120
Mounce, Robert H, 60
Mowat, John, 153
Moyise, Steve, 98, 133
Musurillo, Herbert, 141

Nanko, Carmen, 119
Nelson, Jill, 152
Newsom, Carol, 144
Nicholas, Barry, 37
Nida, Eugene A., 105

Oduyoye, Mercy Amba, 120
O'Leary, Stephen D., 154
Olupona, Jacob, 50
Osiek, Carolyn, 39, 142
Overton, Richard, 152

Palfreman, Jon, 152
Paulien, Jon, 160, 167
Pearce, Fred, 152
Pieris, Gustavo, 120
Pippin, Tina, 93, 103, 104
Price, Simon, 50, 51, 52, 58, 126, 127,
    128, 129, 133
Prigent, Pierre, 61

Radice, Betty, 31
Ramsay, William, 60, 63
Reddish, Mitchell, 11
Richard, Pablo, 120, 121, 124, 131
Robinson, J. A. T., 29, 39, 128
Roloff, Jürgen, 15, 61

Rowland, Christopher, 144
Ruiz, Jean-Pierre, 121, 133

Saffrey, H. D., 33
Said, Edward, 123
Scherrer, Stephen J., 133
Schmidt, Roger, 141
Scholem, Gershom, 144
Schüssler Fiorenza, Elisabeth, 12, 42,
  59, 64, 82, 93, 99, 112, 121, 130, 131
Scott, Bernard Brandon, 156, 159
Segovia, Fernando F., 119, 120, 124,
  135
Smallwood, E. M., 30
Smith, Frederick M., 137, 141
Spivak, Gayatri Chakravorty, 123
Sugirtharajah, R. S., 120, 123, 124, 125,
  126, 134
Sweet, J. P. M., 15, 18, 115, 116
Swete, Henry Barclay, 59

Taussig, Michael, 143
Theissen, Gerd, 42
Thomas, Robert L., 49, 131
Thompson, Leonard L., 28, 31, 34, 39,
  44, 61, 64, 90, 111, 129, 130

Tolbert, Mary Ann, 120
Torrance, Robert M., 141, 144
Trivedi, Harish, 123
Turner, Steve, 153

Ulfgard, Haken, 22

Valeri, Valerio, 50
Ventura Hillman, James, 141
Ventura Hillman, Michael, 141

Wainwright, Arthur, 1, 16, 97
Wall, Robert W., 15
Walvoord, John F., 49, 166
Watson, Alan, 33
Weiss, Johannes, 60
West, Gerald, 120
White, Dana, 152
Whitehead, Alfred North, 110
Wilken, Robert L., 35
Wilson, J. Christian, 34
Wilson, Mark W., 60
Woodbury, Richard, 153

Zamora, Lois Parkinson, 153
Zorn, Carl M., 50

Subject Index

4 *Ezra*, 91
"666," 154, 161, 164, 165: historical, prophetic, and symbolist views compared, 166
"7" (song), 156
"888," 167

Aelius Aristides, 144
Amos, 102
angelic liturgy, 144
angels: in Revelation, 139; worship of, 21, 94
antichrist, 13, 29, 49, 154, 160
Antiochus Epiphanes, 130
Antipas, 28, 41
apocalypse: apocalyptic way of thinking, 77, 154; dangers of, 160; genre, 14, 81; of John (*see* Revelation, Book of); meaning today, 152; modern genre parallels, 158; purpose of, 106; traits, 15; value today, 159
Apocalypse of Abraham, 144, 146
Apocalypse Now (film), 152
Armageddon. *See* Harmagedon
Armageddon (film), 153
Ascension of Isaiah, 144, 146
Asia: as backdrop for Revelation, 16; cities of, 38; economy, 38; founding of province, 126; government, 51; imperial cults in, 50–52; location of, 26; loyalty to Rome, 131; and Rome, 39. *See also* economic issues
associations: guilds, 40, 44, 111, 146; religious, 40
Augustine, 12, 13

Babylon, 18, 69–71, 76, 88–91, 104, 139; active woman, 75; children of,

94; compared with Jezebel, 74, 75, 79; compared with woman clothed with the sun, 89; contrasted with Jerusalem, 94; destruction of, 98, 104; identity of, 148; interpretations of, 161; as symbol for exploitation, 122; symbolic of Rome, 17, 28
Balaam, 44, 66, 67, 68, 107, 147: counterpart to Jezebel, 84
bar-coding system, 161
Bar Kokhba War, 27
basal lures, 110
basileia: meaning of, 106
Beast from the Land, 132–34: identity of, 59–63
Beast from the Sea, 130–32
Bible: and colonization, 125; and emancipation, 125; as historical document, 14; influence today, 152; interpretation of, 119
Blade Runner (film), 156
boundaries, 45
Bride of the Lamb, 91–96
Buddha, 146

characterization, 13, 65
characters: contrasting, 65, 79; female, 69–70; as narrators, 106; of Revelation, 19
churches, 65–68: factions in, 77, 128; as historical epochs, 166; house, 40; as narratee, 106
cities of Asia Minor, 38, 51: ethnic diversity, 39; government of, 51. *See also* individual cities
coercion: as ethical problem, 98–99, 110–17

Colossae, 40
culture: conflict with, 44, 63, 111, 131; integrated, 58; and spirit possession, 146
Cybele, 144, 146

Day After, The (film), 156
Dead Sea Scrolls, 144
delay, 101: problem of, 99–100
Delphi: oracle, 145, 147
Domitian, 31, 32, 34, 37, 52, 54, 57, 111, 131: according to Eusebius, 29, 30, 31, 32; and Nero, 35; in Roman histories, 31
dragon, 17, 69, 86, 88: actor of third story, 15; creates monsters, 164; defeated, 92; fall of, 89; leads astray, 73; Satan, 86; victory over, 88; warrior, 17, 69, 86, 101; woman's enemy, 87; worshiped, 131
dualism, 77

earthquakes, 20
ecological crisis, 101, 169
economic issues, 28, 38, 39, 40, 41, 42, 44, 46, 111, 121, 129, 133, 146
Eden, 17, 94, 95, 158. *See also* Eve
Eliot, T. S., 169
emperor worship. *See* imperial cults
endurance, 46: meaning of, 99, 106
Enoch, 145, 146, 148
Ephesus, 12, 16, 27, 38, 39, 40, 43, 52, 53, 54, 90, 128, 129: architecture, 127; factions, 65; Roman influence, 133; temple at, 54, 56, 126; visibility of imperial cult, 127
ethics: of Apocalypse, 100–102; and interpretation, 169. *See also* moral judgments; Revelation, ethical stance
Eucharist, 27, 78, 79
Eusebius, 26, 29, 30, 31, 32, 34, 35, 42, 143: on persecution, 34
Eve, 18, 23, 94
Ezekiel, 16, 92, 95

factions, 44, 65, 66, 76–79, 128
fall of Babylon: repeated, 21

final battle: repeated, 21. *See also* Harmagedon
Flavia Domitilla, 30
Flavius Clemens, 30
food: Paul's view, 67; sacrificial, 67, 78–79, 84, 111; significance of, 44, 76
fornication, 76: meaning of, 44, 66, 68

Genesis, 78, 95
genre, 15, 158
Gillespie, Dizzy, 141
greenhouse effect, 155
guilds. *See* associations
Gulf War, 22, 29

Harmagedon, 113, 147, 153
Hegesippus, 32
Heracleitus, 147
Hermas, 39, 142
hermeneutics: liberationist, 119; meaning of, 109; process, 109–10. *See also* interpretation
historical context, 26–36, 105–8. *See also* persecution
historical criticism, 14
Hosea, 67
house churches, 40, 45, 149
householders, 43–45
hupomonē: meaning of, 106
hybridization, 126, 130, 134: meaning of, 127

Ignatius of Antioch, 37, 41, 77
imperial cults: and city identity, 129; as colonialization, 126–30; and economics, 133; festivals, 56, 57; high priesthoods, 53; influence of, 128; integrated with culture, 58, 62; local, 55; local versus provincial, 52; and other religious institutions, 56; overview, 50–52, 126–30; participation in, 52–59, 111; visibility of, 127
Independence Day (film), 155
interpretation: ethics of, 169–70; evaluation of, 165–67; fundamentalist, 14; futurist, 13, 49, 166; historical, 166; history of, 1; liberationist,

interpretation (cont'd)
119–23; literal or symbolic, 118;
material versus symbolic, 1; postcolonial, 123–26; postcolonial and
liberationist, 123, 124; problem of,
163; process, 117–18; summary,
171; symbolic, 166; three ages, 13
interpretations: questions for, 167–71
intersubjectivity, 14, 167, 168, 171:
defined, 165
Irenaeus, 12, 30, 32, 34
Isaiah, 95

Jerusalem, 13, 18, 17, 38, 44, 71, 76,
134: as bride, 91–96; contrasted
with woman clothed with the sun,
95; destroyed by Babylon, 75;
destroyed by Titus, 42; as female
character, 78; as symbol, 122
Jesus: as pattern, 46; characterizations
of, 16, 19; death of, 101, 114, 116;
point of view, 44; Revelation as
story of, 18; suffering of, 100, 107;
symbolic number of name, 167;
worship of, 142
Jezebel, 44–46, 67–69, 71, 73, 75–79, 84,
85, 88, 90, 93, 95, 96, 106, 107, 111,
117, 147: address to all, 84; associated with promiscuity, 76; children
of, 72, 84; compared with Babylon,
74; compared with woman of chapter 12, 72; fate sealed, 84; historical,
44; John's description of, 66, 71; as
leading astray, 75; as mother, 89;
queen, 86; reason for John's opposition to, 77; rival prophet, 66, 68;
significance of, 84; symbolic name,
17; teaching of, 66; traits of, 72, 75
Joachim of Flora, 13, 160
John, 14: attitude toward empire, 146;
banishment, 32-34; dualism of, 77;
identity of, 14, 42, 82; opponents,
43, 128; previous history, 41–42; on
Patmos, 33; spirit-possessed, 138;
traditions about, 30
Justin Martyr, 12, 27

koinon, 51
Koresh, David, 161

Lamb, 100: as character, 19; imitated,
49; suffering of, 100; symbolic
meaning, 19
lament, 89
language: as action, 149; A-utopian,
121; code and symbol, 61; as ethical issue, 102–5; function of, 110;
repetition, 20–21; sexual, 67; of the
Spirit, 145–49; symbolic, 1, 147;
violence of, 102
Laodicea, 16, 39, 40, 44, 85, 126, 129:
proud and blind, 90
Lawrence, D. H., 112
Left Behind series, 49, 154
Leto, 23
liberationist readings, 119–23
Lindsey, Hal, 14, 167
Lion King, The (film), 158
Lord's Day, 26, 33, 141
Lucian, 147
Luther, Martin, 29

MacArthur, General Douglas, 153
Marcion, 40
Marcus Aurelius, 31
Matrix, The (film), 159
Melito of Sardis, 12, 31
merkābāh, 144
methods of interpretation, 1: choosing, 170
Michael, 86: as warrior, 69, 101
millennium, 13, 154, 156, 160
"Mithras Liturgy," 140
morality. See ethics
moral judgments: coercion, 98–99;
delay, 99; in reading, 25, 47, 97,
169, 170
Moses, 87, 92, 138
mysticism: ascent to heaven, 16;
merkābāh, 144
myth, 11–23: beasts in, 130, 146; holy
war, 101; power of, 232; in
Revelation, 22, 28

narratee, 106
Nero, 27, 35: dates of reign, 27; legends of return, 27; number of
name, 166; persecution of, 34; rep-
utation of, 31; suicide, 35

Nicolaitans, 44, 111
numbers, 15, 87, 165, 166: Roman, 165

O. Henry, 17
Origen of Alexandria, 12
outline. *See* Revelation, structure of

Papias, 1
Parthians, 113
partnership: meaning of, 105
Patmos: John on, 32–34, 43, 141;
    John's banishment, 32; location of
    author, 26; setting of first story, 17
Paul, 34, 39: in Asia Minor, 39; on
    authority, 131; on food, 67, 79, 112;
    letter form, 15; on prophecy in
    worship, 142; on spirit possession,
    138, 140
Pergamum, 28, 38, 41, 53, 58, 65, 66,
    84, 90, 102: competing prophets,
    146; factions, 44; food issues, 67;
    local imperial cult, 56; temple at,
    52, 126, 129
Perpetua, 141
persecution, 28–36, 105, 111, 121, 130,
    168: summary, 35
Peter, 34, 39
Philadelphia, 28, 38, 40, 83, 85, 129:
    faithful, 85; poverty of, 43; temple
    at, 126
Philo, 143
Phoebe, 39
Pliny: letter regarding Christians, 36;
    view of Domitian, 30
plot: chart of, 16; defined, 12–14; of
    Revelation, 14–19; of Revelation
    interpreted, 19. *See also* Revelation,
    structure of
Plutarch, 146, 147
point of view, 44, 107
Polycarp, 38
porneia, 74, 76: meaning of, 66, 67
postcolonial interpretation, 123–26:
    summary, 134
postcolonialism: field of study, 124;
    meaning of, 123, 124; tasks of, 125
power: divine, 110–17, 112; images of,
    112; persuasive, 114–17
predictions, 97, 160

priesthoods: status of, 51, 54; terms of,
    55; for women, 54
priests: in Christ, 116; in imperial
    cults, 53
Prince: singer's background, 153
process philosophy, 110
prophets, 66: itinerant, 42; rival, 84;
    settled, 43; Spirit-inspired, 140–41;
    symbolic language, 147; true ver-
    sus false, 133

readers: as male, 93
Reagan, Ronald, 153, 164
refugee queen. *See* woman clothed
    with the sun
repetition, 20–21
Revelation, Book of: as counterdis-
    course, 130: ethical stance,
    100–102, 117–18, 122; implied audi-
    ence, 68; as moral dilemma, 104,
    109; narratees, 106; narrative lev-
    els, 106; opening and closing, 14;
    plot, 14–19; plot interpreted,
    11–23; point of view, 44, 107; pur-
    pose of, 107, 117–18; rhetoric, 130;
    setting, 26–36, 105–8 (*see also* perse-
    cution); social conflict, 44, 45; story
    of, 11–12, 134; structure of, 11, 82,
    115; as three stories of Jesus, 18;
    use in times of crisis, 29; where
    written, 26; why study? 160;
    women in, 21, 69–76, 104
Road Warrior, The (film), 156
Rome, 28, 64, 70, 103, 105, 126, 130,
    148: policy on Christianity, 36–45;
    symbolism of, 45; view of
    Christians, 46; worship of, 52

Saddam Hussein, 23, 166
Satan, 13, 28: conquest of, 86, 105;
    force behind John's opponents, 78;
    power behind ruling elite, 64;
    rules Rome, 41, 45
seven bowls, 20, 102, 113
seven seals, 100, 112
seven trumpets, 17, 20, 102, 113, 148
shamanism, 143
Shepherd of Hermas, The, 142
signs: of Beast, 132; miracles, 139

singing: and prophecy, 143
Smyrna, 12, 16, 28, 38, 53, 129: poverty of, 43; temple at, 52, 126
spirit: human, 140; and language, 145–49; with mind and soul, 140
spirit possession, 138, 140–41: and culture, 146; meaning of Greek, 138; techniques, 141–45
spirit world, 138–40
structure. See Revelation, structure of
Suetonius, 30, 31, 34, 36
suffering, 41: of Jesus, 107; means to victory, 46, 100, 115
surface lures, 110
symbolic reversals, 101

Tacitus, 30, 31, 35
Terminator (film), 151
Terminator 2 (film), 159, 161
Tertullian, 31, 34, 37, 143
theophany: defined, 16
Therapeutae, 143
Thlipsis, 32, 105–6
three-story universe, 139
Thyatira, 39, 41, 45, 55, 56, 66, 71, 73, 84, 85, 90: competing prophets, 146; factions, 44, 65; food issues, 67
time: distortions of, 20; ritual, 27
torture, 98, 103, 105
Trajan: letter regarding Christians, 36
tribulation, 32, 105. See also Thlipsis
Two Witnesses, 90, 102

undercurrent, 110

Victorinus, 12
violence, 23: context for protest literature, 122; ethical evaluation, 169; language of, 102; rejection of, 99; in Revelation, 98–99, 110–17; surplus of, 102, 103; symbolic reversal, 101, 114; types of, 102–5

Waco, Texas, 153, 161, 169
war: against opponents, 102; by beast and dragon, 112; cosmic, 107; final, 17; Gulf War, 22; in heaven, 69, 86, 101, 105; holy-war myth, 23, 101; human role in, 116–17; nuclear, 155; theme of Revelation, 102, 109
Watt, James, 169
Whitehead, Alfred North, 110
whore of Babylon, 69–71; traits of, 70, 75. See also under Babylon
wilderness, 22, 69, 71, 74, 78, 87, 89, 90, 95, 148
woman clothed with the sun, 69–71: children of, 69, 87; compared with Babylon, 89; traits of, 70, 72
women: characters in Revelation, 65, 94; chart of female characters, 70; city as metaphor, 82–85; offices, 58; portrayed as good or evil, 93; in trades, 39. See also Revelation, women in
World Trade Center, 97, 155
worship: of angels, 21, 94; of emperor (see imperial cults); of Jesus, 142; and prophecy, 142; significance of, 132

Printed in the United States
15620LVS00004B/275-302